WOMEN, POLICY AND POLITICS

WOMEN, POLICY AND POLITICS

The Construction of Policy Problems

Carol Lee Bacchi

SAGE Publications
London • Thousand Oaks • New Delhi

SAGE Publications Ltd
6 Bonhill Street
London EC2A 4PU

SAGE Publications Inc.
2455 Teller Road
Thousand Oaks, California 91320

SAGE Publications India Pvt Ltd
32, M-Block Market
Greater Kailash – I
New Delhi 110 048

British Library Cataloguing in Publication data

A catalogue record for this book is available
from the British Library

ISBN 0 7619 5674 3
ISBN 0 7619 5675 1 (pbk)

Library of Congress catalog record available

Typeset by Mayhew Typesetting, Rhayader, Powys
Printed in Great Britain by The Cromwell Press Ltd,
Trowbridge, Wiltshire

to Stephen

CONTENTS

Acknowledgements   ix

Introduction: Taking Problems Apart   1

Part One: What's the Problem? An Approach to Policy   15

Preamble   15

  1   Policy Studies: Traditional Approaches   17

  2   Rethinking Policy Studies   32

  3   Rethinking 'Social Problems'   50

Part Two: The Problem of Women's Inequality   65

Preamble   65

  4   Pay Equity: On Whose Terms?   72

  5   Discrimination: Who Is Responsible?   93

  6   Education Policy: Access or Transformation?   112

  7   Child Care Policy: Who Gains?   130

  8   Abortion: Whose Right?   148

  9   Domestic Violence: Battered Women or Violent Men?   164

 10   Sexual Harassment: What is Sexual About It?   181

Conclusion: The Politics of Policy Studies   199

Bibliography   208

Index   237

ACKNOWLEDGEMENTS

The approach to policy developed in this book – a What's the Problem? approach – was fine-honed over several years of teaching undergraduate Policy courses in the Politics Department, University of Adelaide. The students' enthusiasm for the approach and the critical insights it generated convinced me to put it into print. My colleagues in the Department, in particular Doug McEachern, Chris Beasley, Carol Johnson, Greg McCarthy, Clem Macintyre, Marion Maddox and Peter Mayer, offered valuable insights and enthusiastic encouragement. The Office of the Status of Women, South Australia, headed by Carmel O'Loughlin, and the South Australian Health Commission, through Cara Ellickson, provided the opportunity to test the usefulness of the approach amongst those involved in policy making.

I was based at the McGill Centre for Research and Teaching on Women, in Montreal, between March and June 1997. The congenial atmosphere generated by Shree Mulay, Blossom Shaffer and Monica Hotter enabled me to conduct important research. A Faculty Research Award from the Canadian High Commission made this stay feasible. While in Canada I had the opportunity to test out my ideas on a number of people. I received important critical feedback from Susan Phillips, Pat Armstrong, Rianne Mahon and Marion Palley from the University of Delaware. Back in Australia, Trish Harris from Murdoch University read and commented upon Part One of the book. Her very positive evaluation gave me a much needed boost at a difficult time in the writing. As I mention in Chapter 5, Wendy Bastalich deserves acknowledgement for her insights into the regulatory effects of skills discourse. Two University of Adelaide Research Grants provided some much-needed time for research and writing up.

I would also like to thank Kate Leeson for her always prompt and efficient research assistance, Jayne Taylor for her unsolicited role as purveyor of key documents, my nieces Kristina and Michelle for help with research and child minding, and Chris McElhinney and Tina Esca for assistance with the final preparation of the manuscript.

The editorial staff at Sage, especially Karen Phillips, have been most helpful during the production of this volume. The readers provided by Sage, notably Jeanne Gregory, offered encouragement and useful critical insights. Any remaining lapses are, of course, my own.

And to my dear son, Stephen, eternal gratitude for enriching my life and sharpening my conviction that who we are is not solely a matter of what we get paid to do.

By clarifying that which we oppose, we set the groundwork for creating a vision of that for which we long.

Marcia Westkott (1983) 'Women's Studies as a Strategy for Change: Between Criticism and Vision' in G. Bowles and R. D. Klein (eds) *Theories of Women's Studies*. London: Routledge and Kegan Paul. p. 212

With the loss of simple answers the questions too have become infinitely more difficult.

André Brink (1991) *An Act of Terror*. London: Martin Secker & Warburg. p. 612

TAKING PROBLEMS APART

Have you ever read a newspaper article about a controversial topic and thought that you would have approached the issue from a completely different angle? Have you ever compared the two perspectives, yours and that of the columnist or reported speaker, and noted that the contrast in views had all sorts of consequences, including how to deal with the issue? If so, you have already been applying the approach which I will outline in this book, an approach I call 'What's the Problem?' – a shorthand for 'what's the problem represented to be?' At its most basic, the insight is commonsensical – how we perceive or think about something will affect what we think ought to be done about it. In the words of the psychologists Don Bannister and Fay Fransella (1977: 57), '[T]he way we look at things determines what we do about measuring or changing those things; be it the problem child at school, racial prejudice, disturbed behaviour in the individual . . .'. The flip-side of this, and the guiding premise of a What's the Problem? approach, is that every policy proposal contains within it an explicit or implicit diagnosis of the 'problem', which I call its problem representation. A necessary part of policy analysis hence includes identification and assessment of problem representations, the ways in which 'problems' get represented in policy proposals.

While this might appear commonsensical, it is not the way we are taught or encouraged to think about political issues. These are often talked about or written about as if there were only one possible interpretation of the issue at stake. I do not mean that we are not offered competing opinions on particular issues; this of course is the stuff of party political banter. But we are not encouraged to reflect upon the ways in which issues take shape within these discussions. This is illustrated most clearly in policy studies, where students are often asked to study the policy process *as if* policies were attempts, more or less successful, to 'deal with' a range of issues or 'problems'. Even when students are warned that indeed those affecting and initiating policy have assumptions and values, the investigation seldom reaches into the effects these will have on the way the people concerned describe or *give shape to* a particular political issue.

In contrast, the approach developed in this book takes as its starting point that it makes no sense to consider the 'objects' or targets of policy as existing independently of the way they are spoken about or represented, either in political debate or in policy proposals. Any description of an issue or a 'problem' is an interpretation, and interpretations involve judgement and choices. Crucially, we also need to realize that interpretations are interventions since they have programmatic outcomes; that is, the interpretation offered will line up with particular policy recommendations (see Fraser, 1989: 166–75). More directly, policy proposals of necessity contain interpretations and hence representations of 'problems'. Therefore, we need to shift our analysis from policies as attempted 'solutions' to 'problems', to policies as constituting competing interpretations or representations of political issues.

I use the phrase 'What's the Problem?' as a way of achieving this refocusing. The phrase is intended to provoke an analysis which begins with asking of any particular policy proposal or policy the questions what is the 'problem' represented to be; what presuppositions are implied or taken for granted in the problem representation which is offered; and what effects are connected to this representation of the 'problem'? Important follow-up questions would probe what is left unproblematic in particular representations, and how 'responses' would differ if the 'problem' were represented differently. The focus on interpretations or representations means a focus on discourse, defined here as the language, concepts and categories employed to frame an issue. In Ness Goodwin's (1996: 67) words, the approach 'frames policy not as a response to existing conditions and problems, but more as a discourse in which both problems and solutions are created'. This means that the objects of study are no longer 'problems' but problematizations – 'all those discursive practices that introduce something into the play of true and false and constitute it as an object for moral reflection, scientific knowledge or political analysis' (Foucault, 1984: 257, 265, cited in Reekie, 1994: 464). The focus on effects means that in this analysis discourse refers not just to ideas or to ways of talking, but to practices with material consequences. This understanding of discourse will be elaborated in Chapter 2.

This book applies a What's the Problem? approach to a number of issues directly affecting the lives of many women, issues frequently taken as the focus in courses on women and policy. In doing this, I am not endorsing the common reference to 'women's issues', a notion I intend to challenge. Every issue affects the lives of women and a What's the Problem? approach could be applied to any policy area. In addition, a What's the Problem? approach offers a way to think beyond single issues, and questions the kind of separation implied by a listing of discrete policy areas. In contrast to many studies of policy, a What's the Problem? approach encourages us to think about the interconnections between policy areas, and to reflect upon which issues remain unaddressed or undiscussed because of the ways certain 'problems' are represented.

One of the main limitations of current approaches to policy studies is the way in which they take as given the 'material' for analysis.

This becomes the pieces of legislation, or the directives, or the laws which have been passed. Policy in some accounts equals 'what governments do'. Other policy analysts (see Pal, 1992, cited in Burt, 1995; Theodoulou and Cahn, 1995: 2) have been willing to accede that it is also important to examine what governments refuse to do, that inaction can be as important as action. But in these accounts we are still encouraged to reflect upon only that which is addressed in political debate. In other words, it has to be *deliberate* refusal to act which we consider. A What's the Problem? approach encourages deeper reflection on the contours of a particular policy discussion, the shape assigned a particular 'problem'. In many cases, it is not a matter of deliberately refusing to act but of talking about a 'problem' as if 'acting' is simply inappropriate or not an issue. Frances Olsen (1985) has noted the ways in which labelling items on a political agenda 'public' or 'private' serves to achieve this effect. So, the 'private' domestic sphere or 'private' enterprise are by this labelling located outside of 'public' accountability (see also Plumwood, 1995). Olsen also emphasizes that decisions by governments affect the circumstances which provide the background to decisions we make about how we live our lives; hence, governments are 'intervening' all the time, even when they are not 'acting' in the traditional sense – not providing publicly funded child care or free-standing abortion clinics, for example. Importantly, for the point being made here, these issues might never come up for discussion, and hence it would be impossible to identify and talk about *deliberate* inaction. In this way, a What's the Problem? approach is markedly different from analyses that ask why and how some issues *make it* to the political agenda, while others do not (see, for example, Bachrach and Baratz, 1963; Cobb and Elder, 1983; Kingdom, 1995). Its starting point is a close analysis of items that *do* make the political agenda to see how the construction or representation of those issues limits what is talked about as possible or desirable, or as impossible or undesirable.

Rob Watts (1993/4: 116) elaborates how a conventional view of policy assumes a model of state intervention which needs to be contested. In this model, we are encouraged to believe that 'there was/ is a discovery process which uncovers/ed "real" social problems as a prelude to state policy interventions'. It is this model in his view and in the view of some others (see, for example, Rose and Miller, 1992) which allows neoliberal governments to present themselves as deregulationists, as cutting back on 'interventions'. Watts, in contrast, emphasizes that governments affect people's lives and control populations through a range of 'indirect' measures and through the activities of other 'expert' groups, such as psychologists and social workers. It follows that there is a need to analyse a wide range of social institutions that encourage people to internalize their difficulties, or to act in ways that make more direct supervision unnecessary. This indirect exercise of control, labelled in some accounts 'governmentality', directs attention to the processes whereby subjects are constituted in policy in ways that make them self-regulating.

It seems appropriate at this point to offer an example to illustrate the different kind of thinking a What's the Problem? approach entails. If we were thinking about political discussions of pornography, we would ask not what is the problem with pornography, but rather, what kind of a problem is pornography represented to be within different policy recommendations? This question opens up a space for reflecting upon the competing understandings of pornography offered by moral conservatives, defenders of free speech, feminists who find themselves in sympathy at some level with one of these interpretations, and feminists who wish to contrast their analyses with each of the other approaches. Representations of a 'problem' can encompass two interrelated levels of analysis and judgement. There can be different impressions offered of what is a concern. There can also be different impressions offered of the causes of a 'problem'. So, with pornography, the concern may be expressed as moral degradation, *or* as an abuse of women, while the 'cause' could be described as a lack of moral restraint, *or* as men's desire to control women. This example indicates that a great deal is at stake in competing representations of 'problems'. As Deborah Stone (1988: 162) forcefully states, '[S]truggles over causal definitions of problems, then, are contests over basic structures of social organization.'

A little elaboration is required at this point. It might have occurred to some readers that, for defenders of free speech, pornography is *not* a 'problem'. As Merton (1966: 786) noted some years ago, 'the same social condition will be defined by some as a social problem and by others as an agreeable and fitting state of affairs.' However, those who call pornograpy a 'problem' provoke a response from those who dispute its problem status. A What's the Problem? approach insists that it is crucial to reflect upon the representations offered both by those who describe something as a problem and by those who deny an issue problem status. Its purpose is to create a space to consider *competing constructions of issues addressed in the policy process, and the ways in which these constructions leave other issues untouched*. The approach can be applied to debates surrounding policy issues in public venues such as parliaments or the media, to policy documents such as committee reports, and to policy proposals in the shape of legislative or judicial decrees. For committee-produced documents, it is important to note that several problem representations may lodge within a single document, causing tensions and contradictions (see Maddox, 1997: 3). Still, the key insight of a What's the Problem? approach remains – the need to uncover problem representations and to see where they, and by implication, where they do not, lead.

I suggest thinking about problem representations as nested one within the other, necessitating repetition of the question 'What's the problem represented to be?' at each level of analysis (see Fraser, 1989: 163). Thinking of pay equity, for example, the *concern* is often represented to be either the undervaluing of women's work or the low wages some women receive. However, the undervaluing of women's work is also often offered as a *cause* of the low wages some women receive. Causes of the undervaluing are commonly represented to be either discrimination or gender segregation of the labour force. Gender segregation itself can be represented to be a problem of discrimination or a matter of women's 'choices'. Discrimination is also represented to be different kinds of problems in different literatures. This example highlights the need to reflect upon the implications of different problem representations in successive layers of analysis. Examples of problem nesting will be highlighted where they appear in Part Two of the book.

A What's the Problem? approach looks to competing constructions of *issues*. This is because, as I have already hinted, talking about something as a 'problem' or as a 'social problem' has a whole range of implications which need to be thought about. At the most obvious level, calling something a 'problem' gives it a separate existence, separate that is from judgement. 'Problems' become something 'out there', something politicians or social workers or psychologists will 'fix up'. It is of course this whole effect which a What's the Problem? approach is meant to challenge.

Michael Shapiro (1992: 99) reflects upon the framing of the 'problem' of 'traffic congestion' as a way of illustrating the effects of 'the typical passive grammar of decision makers "faced with problems", rather than, for example, a more politically astute version that would inquire into the way public policy thinking tends to remain within certain narrow modes of problematization'. He describes 'traffic congestion' as a middle-class problem, which already accepts the 'segregation, housing, and shaping of the labor force that has arisen from the structures of real estate speculation, work-force creation, city planning, and so on'. This example illustrates that more is at stake here than offering yet another approach to the study of policy. I am suggesting that approaches to policy studies are inherently political and need to be treated as such. With Deborah Stone (1988: 194), I insist that '[P]ortraying a problem as a decision is a way of controlling its boundaries.'

There is some sensitivity in some policy analysis to the political implications of different approaches to studying policy. For example, Tony Dalton et al. (1996: xii) recently emphasized the negative effects accompanying the 'up there' or 'top down' view of policy, which has a depoliticizing effect by making people feel incapacitated or unable to affect decisions which come from 'on high'. The goal of these authors is undisguisedly to encourage activism and this, in my view, is a good thing. But in a perverse way their goal can be undermined by their characterization of 'policy contests' as the 'very stuff of creative life in a democratic society' (1996: xv). Here, as in Armand Mauss (1975: x), the fact that we debate and deal with 'social problems' is interpreted as a sign of the health of our democracy: '[W]e maintain that it is one of the attributes of a society characterized by relatively high levels of education, leisure, and civil liberties to generate a variety of social problems continuously. If this is true, our history suggests that we are a fortunate people indeed.' In contrast, it is possible to suggest that it is the very nature of the piece-meal approach to change encouraged by 'social problems' thinking which keeps change within limits and manageable.

Joseph Gusfield (1989: 431) reminds us that '[T]he idea of "social problems" is unique to modern societies.' Murray Edelman (1988: 13–14) elaborates this insight by pointing out that certain conditions – '[S]egregated restaurants, hotels, schools and toilets in the South [of the United States]' – existed for many years without being constituted 'social problems'. He pointedly states: 'it is evident that conditions that hurt people need not become problems'. On the other side, Edelman draws attention to a range of 'problems' – crime, poverty, unemployment and discrimination against disadvantaged groups – which have existed for long periods of time, and speculates that this may be due to the fact that '[A] problem to some is a benefit to others'.

At one level labelling something 'social' implies that we think there is a public responsibility to address it. Joseph Gusfield (1989: 431) describes the concept of 'social problems' as 'a category of thought, a way of seeing certain conditions as providing a claim to change through public actions'. But this tells us little about the kinds of public actions such labelling would involve. Moreover, in much public debate, calling something a 'social problem' carries a tone of moral condemnation. Think for example of the ways in which prostitution or homosexuality or single motherhood are at times referred to as 'social problems'. Gusfield (1989: 435), summarizing Edelman (1977), notes that '[T]o use the language of "social problems" is to portray its subjects as "sick" or as "troublesome".' Hence, the language of 'social problems' tends to individualize causal agents, precluding an understanding of 'social problems' as systemic.

For these reasons, a What's the Problem? approach insists upon a close scrutiny of the ways in which 'social problems' are represented and what follows from these representations. It challenges the common presumption that achieving social problem status for one's cause is in itself a sign of success, a commitment to important change. Rather, it depends upon the way in which the problem is represented. For example, describing racism as the product of individual prejudice provides little leverage to challenge structural discrimination. Similarly, seeing sexual harassment as the unruly behaviour of a few predatory men deters an analysis of the role played in sexual harassment by the greater social prestige attached to the status 'male'. While not wanting to discount the challenges and resistances posed by groups of people who mobilize to press for change, we need, in my view, to consider more closely the shape of the challenges they pose, the ways in which they perceive and represent 'problems', and the reasons for this. Here we need to reflect upon why certain reform responses get taken up, why others get dismissed, and what happens to reform proposals in the process of being 'taken up'. The recognition of 'social problems' is not in my view necessarily a sign of a healthy democracy nor of a 'fortunate people'.

Context is highly important in a What's the Problem? analysis. This is because 'problems' are often constituted differently due to location-specific, institution-specific and history-specific factors. Attention to these specifics will provide insights into why some versions of a 'problem' appear in one place and other versions appear elsewhere, and/or why an issue problematized in one setting remains unproblematized in another. Gabrielle Bammer and Brian Martin (1992) offer interesting insights, for example, into what we can learn from studying how repetition strain injury (RSI) became a 'problem' in Australia, but not overseas. From this observation we can proceed to investigate the factors which facilitated the emergence of RSI as a 'problem' in Australia, and the factors which inhibited its emergence overseas. Why, Bammer and Martin ask, did the pain and disability associated with repetitive work documented in many countries not surface as a protest in the way it did in Australia? In Christopher Bosso's (1994: 200) words, 'we need to ask more questions about the "dog that did not bark" posed by Sherlock Holmes in the "Mystery of Silver Blaze" [*sic*].' To assist in this project in Part Two I will draw upon my wide background and research into women and policy in several countries, including Australia, the United States, Britain, Canada, the Netherlands, Sweden and Norway, though the majority of my examples will be American, Canadian and Australian.

The shape of Part Two of the book requires some comment. Given my criticism of the tendency to present policy areas as separate and discrete, I wanted to force myself and readers to address the inter-relationship of a range of issues. Hence, I decided upon the unifying theme of 'The Problem of "Women's Inequality"'. This was for several reasons. In my teaching over the past few years, I was struck by how little thought had gone into discussing explicitly the ways in which 'women's inequality' was being thought about, or represented. There seemed to be an assumption that 'women's inequality' was on the agenda and that this had to be a good thing. There was some disquiet at the lack of change in a range of indicators, such as segregation of the labour force or wage rates, but there was a hesitancy to interrogate the meanings offered of 'women's inequality'.

This is somewhat of an overstatement. There are certainly many studies which ask questions about the meaning of the 'equality' women are being offered; I have written one such study myself (Bacchi, 1990). But there seemed to be the need to bring these analyses to a head-on confrontation with the kinds of policy recommendations which characterize a number of Western democracies. The way I have chosen to do this is to examine debates in a number of policy areas through the lens of a structuring question: what is the 'problem' of 'women's inequality' represented to be? I have also selected policy areas commonly represented as central to addressing that inequality – pay equity policy, antidiscrimination and affirmative action policy, education policy, child care policy, policy addressed to abortion, domestic violence and sexual harassment. It needs to be emphasized that by asking the question, what has the 'problem' of 'women's inequality' been represented to be? I am suggesting neither that 'women's inequality' has assumed a place of importance in policy making (see Bacchi, 1996), nor that legislation has been designed to reduce that inequality. Rather, the point is to examine the ways in which policy proposals produce 'women's inequality' as a particular kind of problem. That is, policy 'responses' need to be understood as part of a discursive construction of the 'problem'.

The topics selected for Part Two were chosen in part because of the existence of useful feminist research in the area, research which indicates, without so identifying, a What's the Problem? sensitivity. A good deal of feminist theorizing highlights the ways in which pre-suppositions about women and their roles influence policy. Feminists have been more attentive than most to the effects of the frameworks structuring policy debates. In a sense, then, a focus on women allows an exploration of the genesis of a What's the Problem? approach, while reflecting on its usefulness for policy analysis and for feminist theorizing as well.

In the quote above, Rob Watts (1993/4: 116) put inverted commas around the word 'real' in the phrase '"real" social problems'. The use of inverted commas here and elsewhere where they appear is meant to 'denaturalize the terms, to designate these signs as sites of political debate' (Butler, 1992: 19). With Watts, I challenge the existence of 'real' social problems but, for reasons I explore in Chapter 3, it has become crucial to explain precisely what one means when making this challenge. To put it briefly, I argue that it is impossible to talk about any social condition without putting an interpretation to it. Hence, all we as analysts have access to, are the interpretations. So, while I believe that there are a multitude of disturbing social conditions, once they are given the shape of an interpretation, once they are characterized as a 'problem' or as a 'social problem', they are no longer 'real'. They are interpretations or constructs of the 'real'. We can have no direct access to the 'real'. In the words of Bannister and Fransella (1977: 18), 'we cannot contact an interpretation-free reality directly'. This is what is meant by the sometimes misunderstood phrase that people do not 'discover' problems; they 'create' them. It is the particular shape, the problem representation, assigned a 'problem' which is created.

I feel the need to spell this out clearly because it is easy for some who see 'real' challenged in this way to conclude that this means that 'social problems' are unreal, are inventions. In fact, there are many in the community who would leap at such an interpretation – all those, for example, who would challenge the 'problem' status of issues like racism, sexism, or pollution. I hope it is clear that this is not my intention in saying that it is impossible to identify 'real' 'social problems'. A What's the Problem? approach accepts that there are numerous troubling conditions, but states that we cannot talk about them outside of their representations, and their representations hence become what is important – because of the shape they give to the problem, and because of what they imply about what should be done or should not be done.

Some recent contributions to policy studies recognize the role of values and competing interests in the shape of policy and policy evaluation. Many have moved on from the model of policy making as 'rational decision making and planning', about which more will be said in Chapter 1. The study by Dalton et al. (1996: 16), for example, explicitly elaborates a counter-model, which sees policy as 'strategic and political process'. A What's the Problem? approach agrees that policy is 'strategic and political process' but sees the battles not simply at the level of wanting or resisting a particular policy initiative, but at the level of *constituting the shape of the issues to be considered*. Values operate at this level also, though I prefer to use the language of presuppositions and assumptions. Part of the task undertaken in a What's the Problem? approach is teasing out the presuppositions and assumptions in competing interpretations, *and commenting on them*. While a presupposition may be implied by a representation, however, it does not necessarily follow that the one making the representation holds this presupposition (compare Hawkesworth, 1988 in Chapter 2). We need to keep open the possibility that a particular representation has been selected for purely instrumental reasons, to achieve a particular goal, and has nothing to do with the values of the one making the representation. None the less, because particular assumptions or presuppositions *appear* to lie behind particular representations, it becomes important to examine them. Even if the spokesperson does not endorse these presuppositions, she or he seems to be assuming, by so constituting a 'problem', that they will attract a following. Hence they need to be discussed.

I note above that a What's the Problem? approach requires *comments* on different and competing representations. That is, it is not adequate in my view simply to identify different interpretations of issues; it is absolutely necessary to *evaluate* them. How one does so will depend on the values, assumptions, presuppositions and political motivations of the one doing the evaluating. In this book I will be offering my evaluations of competing interpretations of a number of political issues. I will be assessing representations of policy problems by my judgement of desirable outcomes, tied necessarily to my political commitment to improving the lives of people, and in particular women. My insistence on evaluation marks my distance from a number of social problem theorists and from some versions of postmodernism, a position elaborated in Chapter 3. In brief, I argue that a simple listing of interpretations is itself evaluative and political, a species of pluralism which accords equal status to competing interpretations. Evaluation then is already going on in the language used to describe these interpretations, even or especially if this language attempts to imply neutrality. This is hardly a new point but one which, in my view, bears repetition. What then are the grounds for evaluations of competing interpretations? It is possible to direct attention to accuracy or inaccuracy, in places where there is agreed upon information. It is possible to emphasize problematic assumptions, for example, assumptions that housework is 'women's work'. I will be doing some of this but I will evaluate interpretations primarily by what I believe to be their effects. Nancy Fraser (1989: 173) makes a key point here that each interpretation, or representation, 'carries a distinct programmatic orientation with respect to funding, institutional siting and control, service design and eligibility'. The 'programmatic orientations', or effects of policy proposals, can and must be assessed. Other effects which demand attention are the impact of problem representations on the subjects/objects of policy, and the impact of problem representations on the shaping of political agendas more broadly, topics touched on earlier and elaborated in this text.

As mentioned earlier, the language, concepts and categories employed to frame an issue affect what is seen and how this is described. This is true of analytic approaches to any subject. The questions we ask of policy processes depend upon frames which affect what we see and how we see. To date, much policy analysis has worked within state/market, or state/capital frames. More recently, writers on governmentality (see Chapter 2) use a government/subject frame. I have selected a question – What is the 'problem' of 'women's inequality' seen to be? – to illustrate the different configurations of issues which appear when a gender frame is adopted. Frames, however, need to be considered the starting point for, not the end point of, analysis. Hence, they – and here I include a gender frame – need to be subjected to the kind of analysis recommended for policy in general by a What's the Problem? approach: asking how they shape issues and policy, and asking what they leave unproblematized.

The raw material for the analysis will consist of policy statements, media representations of issues, public addresses, parliamentary debates, and theoretical analyses. The last category, theoretical analyses, is crucial. What's the Problem? as an approach suggests that it is as important to ask how academics and other professionals reflect upon policy 'problems' as to enquire into the views of 'policy makers' in the strict sense. This is because academics and other professionals often structure arguments and issues in ways which affect the framing of 'problems' in the wider community. Nancy Fraser (1989: 11) usefully refers to the discourses developed in universities, think tanks, professional associations and social-service organizations as '*bridge* discourses, which mediate the relations between social movements and the state'. Crucially, an increasing number of these analyses are being produced by feminists. These contributions will be subjected to the same kinds of questions about problem representations and presuppositions as other contributions to policy debate. I will also borrow freely from feminist analyses which make this very point about the need to scrutinize feminist problem representations.

Part One of the book elaborates the theoretical premises of a What's the Problem? approach. Part Two has been designed as a guide to method. Its purpose is to illustrate, through the application of a What's the Problem? approach to a range of issues, the sorts of questions the approach prompts, the kinds of insights it can provide, and the implications of the approach for feminists and others pursuing structural change. Key methodological points will be drawn out in the course of the analysis – how to select issues, how to select aspects of issues, how to identify the nesting of representations and how to disentangle the layers, how to pick out structuring discourses and deal with them, how to incorporate a sensitivity to context, how to uncover silences and to construct new problem representations, how to deal with the discovery that one is working with or within a problem representation one deems to be problematic or inadequate.

I have no intention of attempting to be comprehensive in my treatment of any single issue, primarily because that would defeat the purpose of the approach. The goal of a What's the Problem? approach is to keep analysis open to other possibilities, not to close off discussion. There is no doubt in my mind that other theorists working in related or even distant areas will have interesting contributions to make to the problematizations I offer. They may well cause me to revise some of my problematizations. A particular example or counter-example from another context, or a particular sensitivity to the impact of race or class in structuring discourses, could easily add nuance and insight to the contributions I offer in these chapters. Consider these chapters then a starting place or suggestive examples rather than declarative conclusions. At the same time it will become clear that I do not shy away from imposing an analysis upon the issues. Anything less would leave the impression that no patterns are decipherable, that no lessons can be learnt, a position I contest. I emphasize for example a number of frames which appear across the policy issues under consideration, frames which structure discussions of 'women's inequality'. We will see for example how notions of choice and privacy figure in different ways in the debates around a range of topics and with what effects. Some of the insights here will unsurprisingly resonate with conclusions in other feminist analyses. That a What's the Problem? approach produces these insights, to my mind, confirms its usefulness as an analytical tool.

I wish to emphasize again that a What's the Problem? approach is useful for any policy field. It provides a way of studying policy which opens up a range of questions that are seldom addressed in other approaches: how every proposal necessarily offers a representation of the problem to be addressed, how these representations contain presuppositions and assumptions which often go unanalysed, how these representations shape an issue in ways which limit possibilities for change. It also offers a framework for examining gaps and silences in policy debate by asking what remains unproblematized in certain representations. Here I offer an elaborated set of questions which could be used to initiate a What's the Problem? approach of any selected issue, remembering the dangers of single-issue analysis and the need to reflect upon interconnections between policy areas:

- What is the problem of (domestic violence, abortion, etc.) represented to be either in a specific policy debate or in a specific policy proposal?
- What presuppositions or assumptions underlie this representation?
- What effects are produced by this representation? How are subjects constituted within it? What is likely to change? What is

likely to stay the same? Who is likely to benefit from this representation?

- What is left unproblematic in this representation?
- How would 'responses' differ if the 'problem' were thought about or represented differently?

While these questions directly target policy *proposals*, they can also be used to clarify the assumptions and implications of understandings of an issue offered by those who *deny* an issue 'problem' status.

No single book can perform all of the analyses of political processes which are needed to make sense of our social world. I am offering a book which performs one necessary analysis, providing the conceptual tools to interrogate representations, offered by members of policy communities, broadly defined, of a range of political issues . There is less of a focus on 'citizen' actors, on people making sense of problem-definitions in their daily lives, though this will receive some attention, and more of a focus on identifying competing interpretations of a range of issues and reflecting on what follows from them. Nor do I undertake to examine how particular problem representations become dominant, important as this task is (see Walker, 1990). There is also no direct analysis of something called, in conventional policy literature, 'implementation'. Rather, I suggest that here we are dealing with a necessarily prior question, the problematics of 'problem' representation. This does not mean that problem representations *precede* implementation, a position developed in the problem definition literature discussed in Chapter 2. Rather, the argument is that the processes of policy are a package constituted around problem representations. Recall, however, that we are not simply floating in the realm of representation; we are asking what follows from particular representations. Hence we are vitally interested in the *effects* of policy proposals and the problem representations they necessarily contain. This is indicated in the set of questions offered above.

Those interested in an elaboration of the theoretical premises of the study are invited to read Part One. Chapters 1 and 2 review traditional approaches to policy and some more challenging contributions, suggest what these leave out, and indicate how a What's the Problem? approach contributes to understanding political processes. Chapter 3 situates the approach taken in the book within the debates surrounding social constructionist approaches to 'social problems'. Those who wish to see a What's the Problem? approach applied to the 'problem' of 'women's inequality' could turn directly to Part Two.

PART ONE

WHAT'S THE PROBLEM? AN APPROACH TO POLICY

PREAMBLE

This first section of the book is designed to introduce students to relevant literature for thinking about policy and social problems. There are indeed a number of relevant literatures, generated by different disciplinary approaches. For example, there is the literature associated with the discipline most commonly designated political science or policy studies. Within this field the student will find books which talk about 'public policy' or 'social policy'. Related material will address administrative behaviour and decision making in public bureaucracies. A completely separate but directly relevant literature has been generated within sociology and is commonly characterized the sociology of social problems. This literature is large and has a long history. The interest generated by this approach to thinking about social problems resulted in the founding in 1952 of an association, the Society for the Study of Social Problems, and a journal entitled *Social Problems*, published by University of California Press.

When I describe the sociology of social problems as a separate literature, I do not mean that there have been no intersections with political science. In fact, there have been and it is important to reflect upon what these intersections have produced. This part of the book will deal with these as they arise. It is important to note also that both policy studies and the sociology of social problems have been affected by developments in social and political theory. Both for example reflect the shift to postpositivist and postmodern interests. Or at least these trends in intellectual thought have aroused debate within the fields, earlier in the sociology of social problems, more recently in policy studies. These debates and their significance for the approach developed in this book will be raised where they become relevant.

For simplicity's sake, Part One has been divided into three chapters, the first two dealing with political science and its sub-discipline, policy studies, while the third chapter engages with the sociology of social problems literature. The goal in each chapter is to identify and describe the varied approaches to policy problems and the implications of each approach. The larger goal is to clarify just where a What's the Problem (represented to be)? analysis fits in relation to these varied approaches, if and where it is similar, where it is different and how.

1

POLICY STUDIES: TRADITIONAL APPROACHES

There are a number of ways to organize and label approaches to the study of policy. Janice Dudley and Lesley Vidovich (1995: 16–18) offer a useful categorization for my purposes. They place contemporary policy studies in three categories: (1) the rational comprehensive model, (2) politically rational models of policy making and (3) public choice models of policy making. They describe the rational comprehensive view as a 'model of decision making [which] sees policy principally as a process of problem solving. The fundamental assumption of the model is that there is a best collective decision, the public interest, that can be rationally and analytically determined if the correct neutral procedure is followed.' In contrast, politically rational models stress 'the *political* nature of the policy process [original emphasis]'. Dudley and Vidovich offer the example of Charles Lindblom (1980) who challenges the view that 'policy is a matter of problem *solving* [original emphasis]'. Rather, he argues 'that for most policy decisions there can never be any final solution, and that the problem will remain unresolved whichever policy is implemented. The policy maker can attempt only to improve the situation.' Lindblom therefore offers a model of incrementalism in place of the 'scientific' rational comprehensive model. A key difference in the approaches is the attitude towards values. In the rational comprehensive model it is assumed that 'a stable set of values and objectives is clarified and specified at the first stage of the process – referred to as defining the "decision space"'. By contrast, the political rationalist sees this as a 'practical impossibility as negotiation and compromise between complementary and contradictory values and objectives is continuous throughout the decision making process' (Dudley and Vidovitch, 1995: 19).

The first category then lines up with approaches generally described as the 'rational approach to policy'. The approach embraces a positivist epistemology, endorsing the view that there is a real world which is accessible to objective description and analysis. The process of making policy is set out in clear-cut stages: formulation, implementation, evaluation. There is an assumption that there is some readily identifiable social/economic problem which needs addressing and that policy makers get together and do their best to come up with a policy which will address this problem. A further assumption is that they will approach this task rationally and come up with the best solution given cultural, political and economic constraints. The emphasis on measurement and technical expertise leads to the labelling, in some accounts, of this approach as 'technical rationalism'. Marshall Dimock is representative of this approach. According to Dimock,

> [F]irst, there are always the problems and the issues. Second, there are the facts and analyses that need to be applied to the issues. Third, there is the setting forth of alternatives and the pros and cons applicable to each possible solution – all this in the light of larger institutional goals and objectives. Fourth, there is the decision proper, which depends upon choosing among alternatives . . . . (1958: 140, cited in Braybrooke and Lindblom, 1963: 38)

Jan Tinberger (1956: 6–11, cited in Braybrooke and Lindblom, 1963: 38) illustrates the way in which these theorists assume that value decisions are relatively straightforward and need to precede policy analysis. He describes the opening procedures for an ideal analytical process as, first, '[T]he policy-maker should pursue an agreed-upon set of values', and second, 'the aims of policy should be clearly formulated in advance of choosing among alternative policies.'

The second category, political rationalists, are more generally described as incrementalists and pluralists. Theorists in this category object to the impression conveyed by technical rationalists that policy is a straightforward matter of finding technical answers to readily identified problems. They are much more sensitive to the give and take of politics, to the shifting of positions and perspectives, and to the role played by politics, meaning here party politics and bureaucratic politics, in decision making. Importantly, they address the need to talk about the role of values in policy making, and the most interesting in the group have tried to devise approaches which deal rationally with normative differences of opinion (Fischer, 1980; Fischer and Forester, 1987).[1] These authors insist that it is inadequate simply to see values as personal preferences which can be ignored because little can be done about them, which is one possible interpretation of some comprehensive rationalists. Rather, they insist that values can be dealt with in a rational way. Some in this group claim the label post-positivist and argue that they reject a fact-value distinction, and hence positivism. Writers in this group (Lindblom, 1980; Wildavsky, 1979) argue that a system of negotiation and compromise works well in democracies which, ideally at least, give voice to a number of groups. Their chief goal is to find ways to keep the system honest through concerted attempts to ensure that the process of decision making is as open as possible, and through measures to increase access to influence for less powerful groups. Hence, they are true pluralists. To quote Dudley and Vidovich (1995: 32) again: 'the assumptions of the model are that the openness of the process and the wide range of participants, together with the appropriate use of technical knowledge, will result in a satisfactory policy solution or settlement.' By way of contrast, for technical rationalists, '[T]he need is for expertise rather than for political participation.'

Public choice theorists are mainly concerned with improving political processes. In the main they accept that politics matters and that the task of analysts is to figure out the ways in which it matters so that less desirable aspects can be controlled for. For example, a primary concern is the way in which bureaucracies grow due to the self-interest of bureaucrats in keeping themselves employed and important. In the public choice scenario, this 'fact' calls for measures to curtail the growth of bureaucracy. The rational choice emphasis on rational self-interest as the determining motivation in human behaviour is obvious here (Sibeon, 1996: 28).

The limitation on the categorization produced by Dudley and Vidovich is that they do not offer a way to think about more recent developments in policy literature. They raise important themes – the relationship between policy, power, ideology, language and discursive frameworks, and indeed offer an analysis of policy making which resonates with the one offered in this book. They insist, for example, that '[P]olicy making is a struggle over meaning and significance.' But they do not canvass authors who offer analyses similar to their own. Others (Hawkesworth, 1988; Pal, 1996) have attempted to group these new approaches under the heading postpositivist or postmodernist. A problem here is that you can indeed call yourself a postpositivist and still hold positivist presuppositions (see Hawkesworth, 1988: 16–17, 65). For these reasons, and given the particular focus of the approach developed in this book, I intend to categorize approaches to policy *by the way in which different authors deal with policy problems*. Here there will be some overlap with the categories developed by Dudley and Vidovich, and I will indicate these when they become important. But I find this organization by *approach to policy problems* more useful because it allows us to draw some necessary distinctions within their categories, and to clarify what is at stake in calling oneself a postpositivist.

First, I will argue that both technical rationalists and political rationalists focus on *problem solution*. That is, they see policy as about *decision making*, finding *solutions* to *problems*. Dudley and Vidovich are certainly correct that Lindblom describes his approach as *opposed* to a problem solving model and insists that no final solution will ever be discovered. Still, his focus is on improvement in the situation, suggesting that policy is about making decisions to improve conditions which exist in the society generally. Braybrooke and Lindblom (1963: 123) describe their approach to problem solving as 'successive approximation'. This approach will be elaborated below.

This is not to deny the importance of the distinction between the ways technical and political rationalists approach 'problems'. The former, as we have seen, assume that there is a discrete phase at the outset of the policy process in which values and objectives are clarified. Commonly identified as a 'decision space', I describe the phase as *problem identification*. I use this term deliberately to indicate that there is a sense in these accounts that this is a relatively unproblematic process, and that the real work, as it were, begins in finding solutions, often technical solutions, to problems which have been identified. Political rationalists, by contrast, engage in-depth in analysis of *problem definition*. The extensive literature here (see, for example, Dery, 1984)[2] makes the case that this is indeed a difficult task and tries to make suggestions about how to do it better. This group is, as mentioned above, insistent that policy makers and analysts must confront normative decisions and that any pretence that this is not the case is itself an ideological position.

I see both of these positions as working within a *problem solution* model. That is, even those authors who talk about the difficulty of problem definition want to offer ways of 'doing it better' so that 'better solutions' can be produced, though clearly political rationalists state emphatically that no final solution will ever be found. The focus in each case, however, is on the analyst as functionary, and on deducing what needs to be known to help them function better. This is so even with those authors who recognize that analysts do not stand outside of the normative disagreements which figure in problem definition. Here, I agree with Mary Hawkesworth (1988: 13) that both technical and political rationalists tend to argue 'that the techniques of policy analysis can contribute to democracy by generating usable knowledge for decision-makers'. The principal source of antagonism, as she identifies it, is 'what sort of knowledge is most useful – technical or political'.

By contrast, a What's the Problem? approach is not interested, or at least not directly, in making analysts better at their jobs. There is a completely different rationale for this kind of analysis. Basically, the goal is to understand how policy decisions close off the space for normative debate because of the impression that indeed they are the best *solution* to a problem. The focus then is on the closure effected by a model of policy making as decision making, or policy making as solutions to problems or, even more specifically, of policy making as working towards making improvements in situations. In all these models, analysts are given a disinterested position, to an extent.

Moreover, there is some impression that they wish to improve the situation, whatever that might mean. Despite the talk among political rationalists about values, they seem to think that it should be relatively easy to decide what it means to make an improvement in a situation (see discussion below).

Much of what some authors say when they talk about problem definition is relevant to a What's the Problem? approach and I will illustrate this shortly. But, it is important to recognize the crucial difference in perspective and task between the approach developed by these theorists and that contained in this book. Those who talk about *problem definition* think it can be done better and that this will lead to *better solutions*. A What's the Problem? approach, in contrast, emphasizes the inability to separate 'solution' from 'problem definition'. Hence, it sets as a task, not identifying how to do problem definition better, but revealing the assumptions about the nature of the problem in any postulated solution. This focus, I argue, is more useful because it allows us to see just what is at stake in postulated solutions. It suggests that it is naive to believe that being aware of the stakes in problem definition will allow analysts to do it 'better'. This, I would contend, is the assumption which lies behind political rationalism. Put bluntly, a What's the Problem? approach highlights the interests and commitments at stake in postulated solutions, and suggests that analysts as well as other political actors have interests and commitments here which cannot be denied. Analysts cannot then be 'taught' to stand back and to 'balance' disagreements about values. They are in a direct sense 'interested'.

The best way to characterize a What's the Problem? approach, in order to clarify its relationship to the positions just described, is to say that it focuses upon *problem representation*. That is, it argues that every postulated 'solution' has built into it a particular representation of what the problem is, and it is these representations, and their implications, we need to discuss. Schematically then I would set up approaches to policy in this way:

1   Problem solution:
        (a)   problem identification (comprehensive rationalists);
        (b)   problem definition (political rationalists).
2   Problem representation (a What's the Problem? approach).

Before I elaborate what is involved in a theory of problem representation and the procedures of analysis it recommends, I will look briefly at some exemplars in the categories discussed above. The purpose here is to clarify what they have to say about policy problems and how a What's the Problem? approach differs.

No further comment will be made on public choice theorists. While this may seem odd given the popularity of the approach, public choice theorists have little to say about the nature of policy problems. Their focus rather is on the behaviour of electors or administrators and the role of self-interest in this behaviour. The more sophisticated studies mention things like 'preference-shaping strategies' (Dunleavy, 1991: 8), drawing attention to the ways in which political actors shape the preference of electors. The implication here is that it is too simple to talk in this case about pure self-interest. However, the range of preference-shaping strategies canvassed include only things like 'partisan social engineering' and 'institutional manipulation' (Dunleavy, 1991: 121–3). There is some discussion of agenda setting but we are left to conclude that the only motivation for any manipulation of this kind is retaining or regaining political or institutional power. A What's the Problem? approach identifies more complex motivations behind agendas. Given the difference in focus, it is not surprising that public choice theorists see little reason to probe the meaning of problem or issue representation.

Comprehensive Rationalists

In a sense, comprehensive rationalists are not all that concerned with the nature of a problem. They are more directly concerned with describing processes for effectively moving towards an objective. Herbert Simon makes it clear that he sees a sharp and necessary distinction between fact and value, a distinction which maps onto an administrative/legislative division. He insists that, in order for administration to function, objectives have to be set and the goal of rational administration is to establish procedures which enable the individual to approach as close as possible to meeting these objectives. The term 'rational behaviour' in this approach 'refers to rationality when that behaviour is evaluated in terms of the objectives of the larger organization' (Simon, 1961: 41). Simon is prepared to admit that every decision has an ethical component, but this stands outside what it is possible to measure and hence outside of his analysis. He argues that you can examine and judge only whether the appropriate means to particular objectives have been selected. Since values stand outside the decision making process, it 'must start with some ethical premise that is "given"' (Simon, 1961: 50). Stated in another way, 'the values taken as organizational objectives must be definite, so that their degree of realization in any situation can be assessed.' Simon therefore leaves it to legislatures to set or determine values or ethical premises, which then become the 'givens' of administrative behaviour. This model sets up a distinction between legislature and administration which many would challenge, and a distinction between values and efficient behaviour which many would find difficult to accept. Simon goes on to deal at a very superficial level with the processes by which values, to use his terms, are set. He (1961: 52, 56) tells us simply that 'final responsibility for determining objectives rests with a legislative body' and that 'principles gradually emerge to view from a given set of problems'. In this model, problems are exogenous to the process of decision making.

A later exponent of technical rationalism, Eugene Bardach, directly addresses 'problems of problem definition in policy analysis'. In a sense, Bardach can be seen as offering the technical rationalist reply to the political rationalists who will be discussed in the next section. He (1981: 161) opens his analysis by addressing the claim that 'definining the problem is the hardest part of the analytic task'. Rather, he insists at the very outset, 'the hardest part of the task is finding a plausible solution'. Bardach is useful because his analysis provides some purchase on the fundamentally contested political visions which emerge in the different approaches taken towards problems and problem definitions. Bardach (1981: 163) calls for the application of cost/benefit analysis to pre-policy satisfactions and dissatisfactions. He insists that 'there are limits to democracy' and that '[O]ne cannot simply take up the raw feelings of the population and allow them to define policy problems.' In his view, '[C]ognition and intellectualization must always be joined to emotion and evaluation in order to define a policy problem' and '[T]ypically analysts are better equipped than the public at large to do this strictly cognitive work . . .' (Bardach, 1981: 164). Here we see the sharp contrast between cognition and evaluation typical of technical rationalists, alongside a presumed tension between analyst and citizen. Bardach goes on to argue that not all problems, in the sense of citizen dissatisfaction, can or should be dealt with by government (1981: 167), and that an acceptable strategy in this situation is for analysts to define something as a 'nonproblem'. We will see a direct challenge to this approach among the pluralists in a moment (see Bachrach and Baratz, 1963 below).

A key question here is, where does the analyst get this warrant to so shape the problem agenda? According to Bardach, the analyst derives this warrant to say 'no problem' from a social consensus for which 'he [*sic*], in effect, is obliged to be agent and spokesman [*sic*]' (Bardach, 1981: 168–9). This social consensus, Bardach argues, accepts 'the rules of a capitalistic market economy and a belief in the benefits of social change that such an economy engenders'. This 'duty' to 'articulate and represent some sort of implicit consensus on the matters of political economy' is all the more necessary in the face of 'the explicit challenge mounted by an aggrieved citizen making claims for "justice" based on more particularistic considerations.' In a

sense then, Bardach is well aware of the politics behind the 'identification' of problems, but he sees the analyst as 'chosen' to take the
lead in problem identification and agenda setting. The rest of his
analysis offers policy analysts a few guidelines to assist them in this
role. These include minimizing errors of fact and doing their best to
avoid 'the inadvertent incorporation of causal theories into the
"definition" of the problem'. The goal here is to 'substitute a more
precise, but more cumbersome, definition of the problem for that
which is conveyed by the rhetoric of issues'. In direct contrast to
Bardach, a What's the Problem? approach starts from the assumption
that every description of a 'problem' necessarily incorporates causal
assumptions. Moreover, I would suggest that Bardach's recommendation here amounts to nothing less than recommending a rhetorical
strategy to analysts, suggesting that they frame problems in ways
which *disguise* their causal assumptions.

To summarize, Herbert Simon portrays administrators as func-
tionaries and deals perfunctorily with the value dimension of policy
making. Here he is prototypical of technical rationalists who see value
decisions as originating elsewhere and as extraneous to the process of
'implementation'. Bardach explicitly accepts a view of policy analysts
as experts and as spokespeople for some consensus about social
relations, specifically endorsing the model of a market economy. He
recognizes the role analysts play in shaping the problem agenda in a
way Simon does not, but sees this simply as an extension of the role of
analyst. If problems are value-laden and difficult to agree upon,
analysts need to be trained to hide this fact so that they can get on
with the more difficult task of 'finding a plausible solution'. The image
of democracy in both cases is of a technocracy and it is exactly this
image which political rationalists contest, as we will see shortly.
Importantly, for this book, we will see that different approaches to
identifying or defining policy problems illustrate most precisely the
conflicting political positions of the two groups. In a word, talking
about the ways theorists deal with the notion of 'policy problems'
provides key insights into their politics and their political agendas.

Political Rationalists

In a sense political rationalists represent part of the political revolt of
the 1960s which posed challenges to the established way of doing
politics. Here I am focusing on the United States and the anti-Vietnam
protests, Black demands for 'civil liberties', student demands for
participatory democracy and women's demands for 'equal rights'. In
another sense we can see the debate between technical rationalists and
political rationalists as a debate about what is to be done in the face of

the breakdown of consensus associated with these movements. We have just seen Bardach's response, which is to provide the warrant to policy experts to make the 'hard' decisions and to speak for some generally accepted values against the demands of 'aggrieved' citizens 'making claims for "justice" based on more particularistic considerations'. For theorists like Charles Lindblom (1980) this is quite simply inadequate, and he with others, including David Braybrooke (Braybrooke and Lindblom, 1963), David Dery (1984), Aaron Wildavsky (1979), Peter Bachrach (1972), Martin Rein and Donald Schön (1977), Joan Stringer and J. J. Richardson (1980), set out to offer an alternative. Crucially, as mentioned above, these theorists stress political participation rather than expertise. In Lindblom's (1980: 27) words, they 'substitute interaction for analysis'. And crucially for this book, they see as key to the difference in their approach the different ways in which the two groups, technical rationalists and political rationalists, approach policy problems.

Charles Lindblom (1980: 35) clarifies the difference between what he calls the scientific (or technical rationalist) and the strategic (or political rationalist) ideal. Proponents of the strategic ideal begin, he explains, 'with the limited cognitive capacity of the human being'. It follows that analysis should be simplified in all possible ways, 'for example, by proceeding step by step through trial and error rather than by trying to comprehend a problem in its entirety.' Here is the political rationalists' incrementalism. Further, he goes on, 'because proponents of the strategic ideal see problems as too complex for the human brain, their trust in any one analyst or policy maker does not go very far.' It follows that '[P]olicy making responsibility should be shared by a plurality of interacting policy makers and analysts.' Here is the political rationalists' pluralism.

The focus shifts in the political rationalists' account from the *analysis* which produces decisions to the *politics* which leads to decisions. The policy analyst is presented more as a conflict manager than as a technical expert. In the words of Martin Rein and Donald Schön (1977: 236), 'policy development is about problem setting, dilemma and tradeoff management, and consensus building via coalition formation.' And, according to Rein and Schön, 'policy researchers can go further toward conflict management and goal development if they attend systematically to problem setting.' Rein and Schön also clarify the different political starting place of political, as opposed to technical, rationalists. They are concerned by what they describe as the erosion in consensus which characterizes the United States at the point at which they are writing. To their mind, the erosion of consensus suggests that 'the nature of the problem is itself in doubt' and hence makes urgent 'the exploration of problem setting'. They ask (1977: 237), '[B]ut how are problems set in this period of doubt?' and

reply, '[W]e believe that problem setting requires the finding, building, or selecting a framework within which uncertain situations can be
organized.'

Lindblom (1980: 37) clarifies the different political visions which
accompany the two perspectives. Scientific or technical rationalists
press toward ever more formal scientific techniques and hence
towards 'the kinds of political and administrative organization supporting those techniques': '[T]hey tend toward centralized authority
within the executive and toward moving authority from voters and
legislatures into a highly trained bureaucracy.' In contrast, political
rationalists are pluralists: '[T]hey wish to keep authority diffused – in
Congress, for example, to many congressional committees.' They also
find merit in interest group activities. Where the former see planning
as 'analogous to scientific inquiry', the latter see it 'as the practice of
the usual partisan analytical strategies'. In a word, political rationalists
are democrats and technical rationalists are technocrats. This is clear
in Peter Bachrach's (1972) condemnation of 'democratic elitism', as it
is in Lindblom's (1980: 124) insistence that '[T]o improve the policy-
making process, a citizen must enter into policy making.' For Stringer
and Richardson (1980: 36), an 'improved' system of problem definition
would require a 'more open system of government'. They endorse the
study commission system in Sweden as a more 'objective information
collections system'.

A clear point of distinction between scientific and political rationalists, as was mentioned earlier, is differing attitudes to values. We
saw above that scientific rationalists either minimize the difficulty of
making normative decisions, or place the analyst above the process.
Political rationalists, by contrast, stress that analysts cannot resolve all
conflicts of values and interests (Lindblom, 1980: 22). The question
then becomes what to do about them. Importantly for the project in
this book, the way through the conflicting values dilemma resides for
political rationalists in 'problem setting' or 'problem formulation' or
'problem definition'. The language may differ but, as we will see, the
meaning of these terms is the same. Political rationalists base their
challenge to scientific rationalists on a challenge to the easy dismissal
of problem formulation among the latter. Rein and Schön (1977: 235)
criticize the image of the process of policy development as beginning
with 'a shared articulation of the problematic situation'. This, in their
view, excludes 'the most crucial aspect of the policy process': '[I]n
policy development one seldom starts from a consensual definition of
the problem to be solved . . .'. They go on: '[P]olicy development is
essentially about a process of *problem setting*; it is concerned with
developing new purposes and new interpretations of the inchoate
signs of stress in the system that derive from the past [original
emphasis].' So, we have moved from the 'problem identification' of

comprehensive rationalism to 'problem setting'; the shift is meant to capture the greater activism of the analyst in setting agendas and the necessary introduction of normative decisions as a part of this. The important paper by Bachrach and Baratz (1963) on decisions and nondecisions was meant to draw attention to the forces which prevented issues from becoming 'problems', from getting onto the agenda. Where Bardach (1981) felt it appropriate for analysts to ensure that some issues became 'nonproblems' in order to help them manage, political rationalists like Bachrach and Baratz wish to challenge this limiting of the agenda, or at the very least to draw attention to its occurrence.

It is also important to note that some political rationalists were reading and reflecting upon the growing literature in the sociology of social problems, which is the focus of Chapter 3. For example, Rein and Schön (1977: 237) introduce the 'construction of reality' perspective. David Dery (1984) devotes several chapters to this literature. Dery shifts the language from 'problem setting' to 'problem definition' and is crucially important as a focus for distinguishing between political rationalist and later postpositivist and postmodern approaches. He, with Aaron Wildavsky, allows us to identify more precisely the political rationalist project. Dery (1984: xi) begins by asking: '[I]f problems are defined (rather than identified or discovered), what sort of entities are they, and what sort of definition takes place when it is a problem that is being defined?' He proceeds to clarify his epistemological starting point and here he lines up with the social constructionists associated with the sociology of social problems: '[T]he very notion of problem definition suggests a constructionist (rather than an objectivist) view; that is, problems do not exist "out there"; they are not objective entities in their own right', but are rather 'the product of imposing certain frames of reference on reality' (Dery, 1984: 4). Given the use of this phrasing, in particular the reference to problems as not 'out there' and to frames of reference, phrasing I myself adopt in the Introduction, it becomes important to elaborate further on Dery, in order to clarify where we agree and where we differ.

Dery draws attention to an important insight, an insight foundational to a What's the Problem? approach. Referring to Kitsuse and Spector (1973; see Chapter 3), he notes that 'each solution seems to have a different problem in mind'. That is, it is only by examining postulated solutions that we can uncover the presumed problem and indeed the problem representation. Dery offers as an example increased water consumption. The problem is identified only in recommended solutions. So, for example, if the response is spring-driven taps, someone clearly believed or wanted to present the situation as a problem of user behaviour. By contrast, '[R]unning a check on the water-pipe system, needless to say, does not have users in mind, but only pipes and possible leaks.' This insight into the relationship between 'solutions' and 'problem definitions' (I would say 'problem representations') is crucial to the approach developed in this book. But Dery deduces very different things from the insight.

The difference is clearest where Dery (1984: 28) directly addresses the social problems literature. In his view the sociology of social problems approach lacks an appreciation for the 'interventionist perspective' and hence is often 'a study of "pseudo problems" – that is, social conditions that no known situation will ameliorate or will do so only at a justified cost'. He insists that for political science an approach 'not normally concerned with the production of administratively workable and politically realistic ideas for solving social problems' is, quite simply, inadequate. He declares (1984: 38), '[O]ur interest is unashamedly "applied". We want to see what happens when we look at the subject *only* through an interventionist lens [original emphasis].' The approach is explicitly pragmatic. Hence, in Dery's hands (1984: 40), deciding just what is a 'problem' takes on a specific slant: '[A]n intervention model requires a problem to be defined in one way only, one that will promote its solution (amelioration or transformation).' He goes on, '[T]his means, first, that one should avoid defining problems in a way that will render them insoluble.' Here, problem definition becomes a task assigned to analysts and they are advised to define problems which allow them to do something. Broader 'social issues' are simply, in this interpretation, 'pseudo problems', and should be left to sociologists, or left altogether. Beyond the defining of a problem in such a way that action becomes feasible, it should be defined, says Dery, only if it offers an opportunity for improvement. Lindblom (1980: 4) says something very similar, characterizing policy problems as 'opportunities for cooperative action'. For political rationalists then the 'ground rules for justifying or rejecting a certain [problem] definition' are that 'problems' must be defined so as to guide further policies. If they don't do this, problem definitions are considered inadequate.

Aaron Wildavsky (1979) clarifies this position and in the process lays the ground for distinguishing between political rationalism and a What's the Problem? approach. According to Wildavsky, 'policy analysis is better taught backward':

> [I]nstead of beginning by formulating a problem, considering alternative solutions, developing criteria, applying criteria to data, and so on, students' work improved when exercises went the other way around. The best way to begin learning was to apply strong criteria to good data, go on to create criteria and discover alternatives, and, after numerous trials, formulate a problem at the very end. . . . [F]ormulating the problem was more like the end than the beginning of analysis. (Wildavsky, 1979: 3)

The focus here is, as in Dery, pragmatic and interventionist: 'in public policy . . . creativity consists of finding a problem about which something can and ought to be done. In a word, the solution is part of defining the problem.' Wildavsky tells a story to illustrate his approach and, because it unambiguously identifies the political rationalist project, I repeat it here:

> Mike Teitz tells about a soldier in New Zealand who was ordered to build a bridge across a river without enough men or material. He stared along the bank looking glum when a Maori woman came along asking, 'Why so sad, soldier?' He explained that he had been given a problem for which there was no solution. Immediately she brightened, saying, 'Cheer up! No solution, no problem.'

So, with all their insight into the relationship between 'solutions' and 'problem definitions', and the way in which problem definitions set agendas, in the end the political rationalists put aside the conflict of values and suggest simply getting on with the job of management or government. The solution to the problem of problem definition is simply to define problems which can be solved: 'the task is not to compile a list of all unfulfilled human needs (or even the shorter list of those which deserve fulfilment), but to connect what might be wanted with what can be provided' (Wildavsky, 1979: 3). A What's the Problem? approach refuses this pragmatism, and insists that indeed it is important to draw attention to what is left out when problems are defined in this way. It is concerned, as stated earlier, not so much with the task of making the life of the policy analyst easier, but with the processes by which problem representations impose constraints on social vision. In this interpretation political rationalists *cum* pragmatists are participants in the process of constraining vision, simply by refusing to examine issues they believe to be unresolvable.

Political rationalists are then, by definition, reformist and this is clear throughout their writings. Dery (1984: 40) declares that '[W]e have little choice but to rely on the normal political process, rather than on "science", private values, or class interests, as the legitimate arena' for resolving conflicts of problem definition. While Donald Schön (1979: 251) is keenly aware of value conflicts or frame conflicts among policy analysts, he invests his hope in the possibility of enquiring into conflicting ends, subjecting frame conflicts to shared enquiry. The assumption here is a common agenda or, as in Wildavsky's account (1979: 7), a common culture. Despite the sensitivity to the 'erosion of consensus' then, political rationalists continue to place their faith in a degree of consensus. In their political vision, the system can be saved; the system works.

Similarly, Rein and Schön (1977: 238), who provide valuable insights into the roles of framing and naming in the realm of policy, identify the main task as working through the process by which 'worries, arising in problematic situations, can be converted into the orderly formation of problems'. They also feel that it is possible for analysts to discover the 'tacit frames' which organize their insights and to subject them to critical reflection, even to challenge them. The solution to value conflict becomes subjecting values to enquiry (1977: 248). They set as criteria for problem setting a principle of consistency and a principle of testability – 'the theory or model contained in problem setting should be subject to empirical test; it should be capable of disconfirmation' (1977: 249). The collection of information hence remains important. For Stringer and Richardson (1980: 35) this is necessary as 'problems still need to be identified and defined, otherwise they will be compounded'. The appeal to empirical tests indicates a lingering positivism, despite David Dery's insistence that a focus on problem definition necessitates a social constructionist perspective. Stringer and Richardson's comment indicates that, for these theorists, 'problems' remain 'out there' awaiting identification and/or definition.

This is confirmed in the insistence by Braybrooke and Lindblom (1963: 142) that policy needs to move 'away from an *identified ill* [emphasis added]'; Dery (1984: 6–7), as we have seen, wants problem definitions to provide opportunities for social improvement. In both these cases, there seems to be some belief that social ills or social improvement are uncontested notions and hence easy to identify and define. In the end, this analysis is circular, stating that problem definitions involve value conflicts but that analysts can avoid these by defining problems in ways which produce 'improvements'. Towards the end of his book, Dery (1984: 115) raises a key question – 'Improvement for whom and at what cost?' – but he does not attempt to answer it.

With all this, it is important to draw attention to some positive moves within the political rationalist approach. Dery is keenly aware of the dangers of leaving analysis of policy within the frames established by organizations and bureaucracy. Pointing out that organizations stymy creative problem redefinition is in fact central to Dery's agenda. As he says (1984: 10–11), '[A]n agency's formulation of a problem states the values that the agency wishes to serve by means of a solution. Unless the analyst is allowed or even encouraged to examine the agency's formulation, analysis will be restricted to an examination of means.' His solution here is to involve 'agents of change' within organizational settings. Political rationalists also draw attention to rhetoric and persuasion as part of the analysts' role, and occasionally to the ways in which language shapes agendas. These points are taken up and pursued in greater depth by postpositivists, who are examined in the next chapter.

To summarize, there are several important differences between a political rationalist and a What's the Problem? approach. First, a What's the Problem? approach sees the analyst as actively engaged in the value conflicts involved in problem representation. It questions the presumption among political rationalists that analysts can stand back from their values and commitments, and subject them to critical scrutiny. It also questions the adequacy of defining problems in terms of the possibility of intervention. Rather, it suggests that such an approach automatically removes from consideration issues of central importance, such as why intervention in some areas is deemed to be inappropriate or impractical. A What's the Problem? approach is designed then to draw attention to the very questions political rationalists consider irrelevant or inappropriate.

Notes

1 Any categorization of authors, such as this, is necessarily subjective and open to contestation. My reasons for placing Fischer among the political rationalists become clearer in Chapter 2.

2 A more recent contribution by Rochefort and Cobb (1994) offers a discussion of problem definition much closer to the one offered in this book. They also distinguish their approach from the applied approach associated with Dery (1984 in 1994: 8). I will deal with their contribution in Chapter 2, explaining why I feel 'problem definition' remains inadequate as a description of the process under consideration.

2

RETHINKING POLICY STUDIES

From Political Rationalism to Postpositivism

I have headed this section in a way that suggests transition because I will argue that some authors, despite claims to have left behind incrementalism and to have embraced postpositivism, retain the political rationalists' optimism about democracy and a positive role for the policy analyst. The basis of their optimism is very different, as is the role for the analyst. In these accounts, the technical expert of the comprehensive rationalists and the conflict manager of the political rationalists is replaced by the analyst as public critic. The authors I have selected as transitional, Frank Fischer (1980; 1990; see also Fischer and Forester, 1987), John Drysek (1990) and Giandomenico Majone (1989), also continue to insist on the need for both empirical and normative theory in policy design, lending doubt to the claim to postpositivism. Mary Hawkesworth is useful here. In her view, the test of a postpositivist is a complete rejection of the fact/value distinction. She suggests that many who claim this label do not live up to this test. As she correctly points out (1988: 6), those, like Fischer and Majone, who look to the need for *value identification* in decision making still assume that there are facts out there waiting to be discovered.

Frank Fischer provides a good example here. He locates the shift in policy studies from technical or instrumental rationality to postpositivism in the period of the Great Society and the Vietnam war (Fischer and Forester, 1987: 11) when, he claims, it became clear that policy advisers were not neutral. The discipline, he continues, was forced to face a 'troublesome reality' – 'Decision criteria are always political.' He offered a solution: 'To rescue the discipline from irrelevance, analysts had to incorporate a wide range of evaluative criteria into their analyses.' Fischer refers to the work of Martin Rein and Donald Schön (1977), signalling the connection to political rationalism. And there are indeed similarities in their projects – to create a space for analysts to continue to be useful, and to recognize values as unavoidable. Another similarity is the aversion to technocracy and a commitment to 'the emancipatory ideals of participation and empowerment' (Fischer, 1990: 7). Fischer (1990: 339) joins Peter Bachrach (1972) in the condemnation of 'democratic elitism'. The difference in the approaches is the insistence by Fischer that analysts cannot be neutral and what to do about this. Fischer's solution is something he calls 'participation research'. He takes his cue from Jürgen Habermas's (1972) theory of comprehensive rationality (sadly misnamed given the association of that label with technical and instrumental rationalism) and sets out to design a *'collaborative* research technique [original emphasis]' which engages 'workers' in an 'authentic dialogue about their own needs and interests' (Fischer, 1990: 216, 340). His position then is that it is possible to produce 'a more democratic set of expert practices' (Fischer, 1990: 8).

The major distinction between Fischer and political rationalism emerges in his criticism of the 'process approach' to policy (1980: 80). This is an approach which leaves the determination of goals to political processes and can be seen as implied in the view that problems need to be defined in ways which permit solutions. To Fischer, this is sadly inadequate. In his view, a procedure must be found to allow 'an assessment of the outcomes of the decision-making process'. For Fischer it would be unthinkable to 'do policy backward' as Wildavsky (1979) recommends. Rather, assessment must 'aim at determining the "right" or "good" decision'. When it comes to setting the criteria for making these judgments, however, some of Fischer's suggestions sound familiar. For example, he insists (1980: 193–212) that there must be a 'potential basis for normative consensus in policy deliberation'. Analysts are to be provided with a 'framework of ideals' which are considered to be uncontroversial, for example, economic progress and political freedom. And the analyst is then invited to try his or her hand at 'political consensus formation'. By contrast, a What's the Problem? approach considers ideals like economic progress and political freedom to be concepts that need to be analysed, as grist for the mill of analysis, rather than as presumed starting points for formulating policy. Hence, it would examine problems which are represented as threats to these ideals or as necessary to the defence of these ideals, and would conjecture on the outcomes of these representations. The goal here is neither to preserve a role for the policy analyst nor to prevent social conflict. The goal is to reveal what happens when these very presumptions – that the analyst must be useful or that consensus must be achieved – structure our understanding of the policy process.

John Drysek (1990: ix) has as his target, with Fischer, 'instrumental rationality and objectivism'. And, with Fischer, he emphasizes that '[I]mportant social problems are pervaded by conflicting values which instrumental action cannot resolve' (1990: 53–4). With Fischer he finds solace in Habermas's notion of communicative rationality which 'allows for reasoned consensus on normative principles' and which therefore 'can contribute to the resolution of social problems, especially complex ones'. However, Drysek is much less enamoured of the potential for policy analysts to assist in this task. His goal is to encourage the establishment of settings *outside normal political processes*, where free and open discussion on public issues can ensue. He therefore shares a profound suspicion of technocracy but believes that citizens can have an impact through institutions outside the state, his 'discursive designs'. Here he sees a role for academics who, in his view, have fewer direct interests in the existing political system (1990: 129). Drysek is concerned about the ways in which the financial support of foundations determines the kinds of questions research addresses (1990: 211) and, at this level, he talks about 'how political power can distort problem definition'. The interest here is in how issues get onto the agenda without looking deeper into the way in which they are constituted. In general, Drysek describes policy analysis as 'that knowledge-based activity concerned with social problem *solving* [emphasis added]' (1990: 23).

Giandomenico Majone has a similar agenda to Fischer and Dryzek. He (1989: 22–4) denounces instrumental rationality and uses the issue of problem definition to explain his complaint. For Majone,

> [T]he image of the analyst as problem solver is misleading because the conclusions of policy analysis seldom can be rigorously proved. Demonstrative proof that a particular alternative ought to be chosen in a particular situation is possible only if the context of the policy problem is artifically restricted. One must assume that there is no disagreement about the appropriate formulation of the problem, no conflict of values and interests, and that the solution is, somehow, self-executing.

So, with Fischer and Drysek, Majone emphasizes that 'to say anything of importance in public policy requires value judgments'. Moreover, he recognizes that the 'most important function both of public deliberation and of policy-making is defining the norms that determine when certain conditions are to be regarded as policy problems'. He also acknowledges that 'policy analysts and researchers are often deeply involved in the process of norm setting'.

From this acute sensitivity to the politics of problem setting Majone moves on to recommend that analysts learn rhetorical and dialectic skills (1989: xi, 1) since 'argument is central in all stages of the policy process'. Rationality in his account then, very similar to that offered by Fischer, is not technical expertise but 'the ability to provide acceptable reasons for one's choices and actions'. The emphasis, however, in contrast to Fischer, is less on providing a methodology for 'finding' the appropriate norms, than on learning the importance of reasoned argumentation as a part of policy analysis. Majone is also a pragmatist and on this issue seems closer to Lindblom and Dery, again illustrating the links across these groups. For Majone (1989: 76), 'feasibility, rather than optimality, should be the main concern of policy analysts.' And, while Majone is doubtless a democrat, his views on democracy and consensus again place him closer to political rationalism. In his view (1989: 163), the policy community must be open but not too open, and '[A] distinguishing feature of a well-functioning intellectual community is that every argument presented must relate to some point of view already present in the community.' Such a description presumes a degree of consensus and necessarily puts limits on what can be discussed.

In summary, Fischer, Drysek and Majone all wish to create space for discussion of normative goals. Fischer offers a model to assist analysts to do this, outlining a strategy for discussing values. Majone wishes to train analysts to recognize that they will be involved in the activity of setting norms and to equip them better to so engage. Drysek insists that the only real, in the sense of free, discussion can go on outside the state. Each is aware of the problem of problem definition but their concerns stop short. They wish only to draw attention to the inadequacy of the technical rationalist model which sees policy as about solutions, primarily technical solutions, to problems. Fischer and Majone leave the analyst in a privileged position as public critic. Drysek holds out hope that academics may fill this role. The preoccupation with the problem of technocracy means that neither Fischer, Majone nor Drysek is willing to look to the variety of reasons a person, be it an analyst or an academic, might have for offering a particular problem representation.

An example here is the way in which Drysek deals with abortion. He suggests (1990: 75) that his approach will 'do little to facilitate discourse on issues of fundamental moral conviction, such as abortion or capital punishment, whose zero-sum character is immutable'. A What's the Problem? approach would take this statement as the starting point for analysis, asking why abortion is placed in a category of issues characterized in this way. It would ask just what kind of a problem abortion is represented to be here, and with what effects and implications. This example signals the depth of questioning required in a What's the Problem? approach and illustrates the need to probe ethical presuppositions among theorists, in this case Drysek. In each case, what appear to be givens become starting points for analysis. This focus is achieved by analysing problem representations.

Problem Representation

Early in Chapter 1 I schematized approaches to policy problems in this way:

1   Problem solution:
    (a)   problem identification (comprehensive rationalism);
    (b)   problem definition (political rationalism).
2   Problem representation (a What's the Problem? approach).

Problem representation is meant to capture a primary interest in how problems are described, implied causations and the implications which follow. Deborah Stone (1988: 106–7) is most useful here. She explains that '[P]roblem definition is never simply a matter of defining goals and measuring our distance from them. It is rather the *strategic representation* of situations . . . [original emphasis]'. She is explicit about the goal of problem representation: '[R]epresentations of a problem are therefore constructed to win the most people to one's side and the most leverage over one's opponents . . .'. And, from these observations, she sets the task for policy analysis (1988: 183): '[I]n confronting any definition of a policy problem, the astute analyst needs to ask how that definition also defines interested parties and stakes, how it allocates the roles of bully and underdog, and how a different definition would change power relations.' Here, Stone sets the agenda for a What's the Problem? approach, though her analysis stresses intentionality more than I do. As mentioned in the Introduction, I am more concerned with unpacking the implications of representations of problems than with attempting to understand them as deliberate or less deliberate distortions of situations.

A recent collection of papers on problem definition edited by David Rochefort and Roger Cobb (1994) illustrates that the kinds of questions raised by Stone and myself are attracting increasing attention. In their introduction to the collection, Rochefort and Cobb (1994: 4–6) note the convergence of interest in these questions generated by social construction theory (discussed in Chapter 3), postmodernism and policy analysis. They distinguish between two tracks (1994: vii) in this 'emerging perspective', the first concerned with how the description of a social problem 'can affect its rise or decline before government', and the second which concentrates on examining the links between problem descriptions and 'the solutions that government devises'. The first, in effect, expresses a concern with agenda setting – what gets on and what fails to get onto the political agenda – touched on in previous chapters. The second concentrates upon the representations of those issues that reach the political agenda, what is recommended and what goes unproblematized. A What's the Problem? approach follows the second track.

Rochefort and Cobb draw on much the same literature as I do and many of their insights are similar. Specifically, they (1994: 3) state that 'every retrospective analysis in problem definition is also a look ahead and an implicit argument about what government should be doing next'. However, there are important differences in our analyses which will become clearer in the remainder of this chapter and in Chapter 3. In brief, Rochefort and Cobb see nothing particularly amiss with the conventional approach to 'social problems'. This shows up in their tendency to see the government as, in a sense, standing back from the problem definition process. They emphasize the competing interpretations offered by 'issue advocates', while the government is presented as 'responding' to competing problem definitions, offering for example a 'holistic approach', spreading resources thinly to satisfy contending parties (1994: 15), or reflecting upon alternative perspectives emerging from contending parties (1994: 16). The government in this account stands outside the process. Compare and contrast this description offered by Linda Gordon (1988: 27–8): '[D]eviant behavior becomes a "social problem" when *policymakers* perceive it as threatening to social order, and generate the widespread conviction that organized social action is necessary to control it [emphasis added]'. With Gordon, and in contrast to Rochefort and Cobb, a What's the Problem? approach sees those involved directly in the policy process as necessarily involved in problem representation. Rochefort and Cobb also offer a limited understanding of the constitution of subjectivities in problem representation, as we will soon see. They offer no analysis of discourse or of policy as discourse (discussion to follow).

I see the limitations of their analysis encapsulated in their use of the language of 'problem definition'. This language encourages a continuation of the view that indeed this is a separate part of the policy process, despite the occasional nod to the inextricable links between problem definitions and solutions. The continuing separation in their model is highlighted by the discussion of availability, acceptability and affordability of particular problem 'solutions'. By contrast, a What's the Problem? approach would draw attention to the contending representations at work at every level of discussion – about acceptability, affordability and availability. For these reasons, I distinguish my approach as concerned with 'problem representation'.

Speaking about problem representations has its own problems, however. It needs to be made clear that there is no assumption in the use of this language that there is a reality which stands outside representation. As Michael Shapiro (1988: xi, 26) explains, 'representations do not imitate reality but are the practices through which things take on meaning and value; to the extent that a representation is regarded as realistic, it is because it is so familiar that it operates transparently.' So, the task is to examine the ways in which 'public policy problems achieve their reality in language'. There follows the dilemma created by just this stand. If indeed all we have are competing representations, how can we defend one and challenge others? This of course is the charge of relativism frequently made against theories which talk about the construction of meaning, and we shall see it appearing again in the succeeding chapter on social problems theory. Zygmunt Bauman (1992: viii) puts it thus: [How] quixotic to debunk the distortion in the representation of reality once no reality claims to be more real than its representation.' This is a serious concern indeed and needs to be addressed. In the hands of some authors, this very argument is used to challenge the validity of any interpretation. For example, Leslie Pal (1996: 362–3) concludes that the postpositivist perspective makes it impossible to decide 'whose reality is right'. He uses this argument to undermine the authenticity of a Canadian 1992 federal government report on sexual harassment: '[L]ike any survey, this one had to be constructed and at a deeper level it contributed to the ongoing construction of the "reality" of gender relations.'

The question of relativism lies at the heart of disputes about post-modernism and surfaces most readily as the distinguishing feature of different postmodern approaches. We will see this again in the next chapter. Pauline Rosenau (1992: 76, 105), for example, distinguishes between affirmative and sceptical postmodernists and notes that, while 'no representation is ever authentic' in postmodernism, 'affir-matives still believe the effort to represent the social world is worthwhile while it will be inexact'. We will see how positions in this debate get tied into competing theories of language, with the sceptics arguing for no reality outside the text, while affirmatives insist on the ability to judge the impact of texts on a world in some way 'outside'. Rosemary Hennessy (1993: 5, 28) usefully develops a position she calls 'postmodern materialism' which, as she explains, reworks the decon-structionist notion that there is no meaning outside the text 'to denaturalize language as a referential system': '[F]rom a materialist vantage point, deconstruction helps make visible that the "real" is not given or unalterable.' She proceeds to argue that it becomes not only possible but necessary to 'rate' theories and on these grounds: 'theor-ies claim their truth on the basis of their explanatory power, that is, their effect on and intervention in the ideological construction of reality.' McHoul and Grace (1993: 35) make a similar point in their discussion of the meaning of discourse in Foucault, about which we will hear more shortly: 'if discourses don't merely represent "the real", and if in fact they are part of its production, then which discourse is "best" can't be decided by comparing it with any real object . . . . Instead discourses (forms of representation) might be tested in terms of how they can actually intervene in real struggles.'

The point here is that an analysis which focuses on problem rep-resentation does not leave us trapped in language. To quote Nancy Fraser (1989: 166) again, 'interpretations are not merely representa-tions – they are acts or interventions'. Hence, we can and must comment on the nature of the interventions which accompany particular representations. Such is the project of a What's the Problem? approach. It is also important to reflect upon which representations dominate and why, though that task is not pursued in any detail in this text. For this task, we need a theory of power which allows us to consider who become the problem representers, whose representations get taken up, and whose voices remain unheard.

Clearly an interest in representation produces an interest in discourse and the term has already appeared several times. Stuart Hall's (1992: 291) definition of discourse makes this connection explicit: 'a group of statements which provide a language for talking about – i.e. a way of representing – a particular type of knowledge about a topic.' A number of policy theorists are now describing 'policy as discourse' (see Ball, 1990; Goodwin, 1996; Phillips, 1996; Rose, 1993; Torgerson, 1996; Watts, 1993/4;), a sign of the postpositivist turn in policy studies. Unfortunately, 'discourse' and 'discourse analysis' are slippery concepts and there are in fact important disputes about their meanings, disputes tied to other disagreements we have already identified about the relationship between language and reality, and the question of relativism. Since a What's the Problem? approach accepts a description of policy as discourse, it is necessary to sort through some of these disagreements and what is at stake in them.

Policy as Discourse

The best way to describe the difference between theorists like Fischer, Drysek and Majone, and those associated with poststructuralism and variants of postmodernism, including a What's the Problem? approach, is as a shift in focus from the role of values in policy making to the production of meaning. Moreover, there is attention not only to the limitations of technical expertise in policy making, but also to the role of all experts, including theorists, in the production of meaning in the policy process. There were certainly indications of a shift taking place in this direction among some of the authors already discussed. Rein and Schön (1977: 239) drew attention to the role of language and concepts in shaping policy, noting for example the difference in addressing policy to 'single-parent families' rather than 'broken homes'. Dryzek (1990: 116–17) refers both to Edelman (see below) and to Foucault, noting 'how policy analysis helps constitute subjects in particular ways, as clients, or spectators rather than citizens or participants'. He uses the term 'discourse', but defines it as 'free and open communication in political life', the converse of the understanding of discourse employed in this text. Schön's (1979) work on generative metaphor is particularly insightful regarding the ways in which language works to structure the possibilities of policy proposals. Schön, however, feels that it is possible and necessary for analysts to become aware of the metaphors which structure their proposals and to 'stand back' to see how they work and to judge their adequacy. As in Fischer and Drysek, there is an assumption that all these things can be talked about and 'reasonable' compromises worked out. This reflects the Habermasian commitment to communicative rationality.

By contrast, poststructuralist theorists are concerned with the closure exerted by language and more specifically by discourse. Discourse, in this usage, refers not to free and open public debate but to the way in which language or, more broadly, bodies of knowledge, conceptual and interpretive schema, define the terrain and consequently complicate attempts at change. Here it is best to go directly to Foucault for a definition: discourses are 'practices that systematically form the objects of which they speak; they do not identify objects, they constitute them and in the practice of doing so conceal their own invention' (Foucault, 1977b in Ball, 1990: 17). In brief, discourse is understood as 'speaking' which sets limits on what can be said. To emphasize the distinction from language – that is, discourse is larger than language, more than words – it is useful to talk about discourses as frames, since they provide frameworks or ways of viewing issues (Bové, 1990: 56; Frank, 1992: 110). Words, of course, form parts of discourses and at times are deeply encoded by their place within discourses, complicating their usage (Reekie, 1994). This is true for example of the phrase 'domestic violence', which I analyse in Chapter 10.

Foucault speaks about disciplinary discourses, focusing in particular on medicine and criminology, but he also examines the Western discourse on sexuality (Foucault, 1981 [1976]). With the focus on frames and ways of thinking, it is useful to think of religious doctrines, political institutions, cultural myths as all taking a role in shaping discourses. So, for example, we can talk about the importance of a rights discourse in countries which have Bills of Rights, or the importance of a liberal discourse in countries which privilege constitutionally the protection of liberty. It is crucial, however, in identifying and describing key discursive components of political discourse not to fall victim to the tendency to see either institutions or political culture as immutable (Bacchi, 1992a; Bosso, 1994: 199). Discourses, we will see shortly, need to be recognized as multiple and contradictory.

The focus on discourse challenges notions of immutable knowledge or truth, since what is discovered is contesting claims to truth in different discourses. Genealogy is recommended as a technique to historicize claims to knowledge, indicating shifts in thinking and acting around particular issues. The uncovering of such shifts raises, as an effect, questions about what appears to be self-evident. Mitchell Dean (1992: 216–17) describes genealogy as 'the methodical problematisation of the given'. One way to do this, as he explains, is to constitute 'lineages' of 'assemblages' like madness, criminality, sexuality, poverty, the economic, the social, etc. The focus is upon the appearance of categories of analysis, such as 'poverty', 'the private', 'male breadwinner', identifying the conditions which led to their creation. In each case the presumption is that it is necessary to uncover and reflect upon what is said about a range of issues and problems historically and currently, rather than to assume that all that has to be said has been said – that what we have before us are fixed and immutable social situations. A What's the Problem? approach starts from the premise that problematizations ought to feature as a central focus of analysis. Hence, we will be using the genealogical technique throughout.

Terry Threadgold (1988: 50) usefully describes the Foucauldian problematic as twofold: what the subject is able to say, and what the subject is permitted to say. Theorists who describe policy as discourse generally employ this dual problematic. So, Stephen Ball (1990: 17–18) describes discourses as 'about what can be said, and thought, but also about who can speak, when, where and with what authority'. This necessarily draws attention to both the power *of* discourse to delimit topics of analysis and the power *to make* discourse. On the power *of* discourse, Ball contends, 'discourses construct certain possibilities for thought. They order and combine words in particular ways and exclude or displace other combinations. We do not speak the discourse. The discourse speaks us.' On the power *to make* discourse, he explains (1990: 18): '[M]eanings thus arise not from language, but from institutional practices, from power relations, from social position. Words and concepts change their meaning and their effects as they are deployed within different discourses.' John Codd (1988: 240–2) develops a similar position. He contrasts the idealist and materialist views of language in which the latter recognizes that 'words, whether in speech-acts or texts, do more than simply name things or ideas that already exist'. Rather, he calls for a conception of 'how the use of language can produce real social effects'. In this materialist theory of language, discourse embodies 'both the formal system of signs and the social practices which govern their use'. In this interpretation, discourse 'refers not only to the meaning of language but also to the real effects of language-use, to the materiality of language'.

Applied to the policy field, an interest in discourse becomes an interest in the ways in which arguments are structured, and objects and subjects are constituted in language. A What's the Problem?

approach turns attention specifically to the ways in which problems, acknowledged by political rationalists as key to the policy process, get constituted in language, broadly understood. Murray Edelman (1988) was one of the first to draw together a focus on discourse and policy problems. Edelman describes (1988: 12 fn 1) Foucault's analysis of madness, crime and sexuality as 'tracing changes in discourse that constitute problems'. In this view, problems 'are rarely solved, except in the sense that they are occasionally purged from common discourse or discussed in changed legal, social or political terms as though they were different problems'. For Edelman (1988: 16), the recognition of the construction of policy problems produces this definition of policy: '[A] "policy" then is a set of shifting, diverse, and contradictory responses to a spectrum of political interests.' We have moved some way from Herbert Simon!

Stephen Ball (1990: 23) brings a study of discourse to his interpretation of education policy under Thatcher in Britain. Without explicitly using a What's the Problem? approach, he notes 'the way in which these emergent discourses were constructed to define the field, articulate the positions and thus subtly set limits to the possibilities of education policy.' Disappointingly, however, in another place (1990: 22), he describes discourses as 'intended to bring about idealized solutions to *diagnosed* problems [emphasis added]'.

Maggie Maclure (1994: 285) describes 'taking policy texts apart', interrogating policy texts and public discourse, as one of the obvious uses of discourse theory. She notes the description of this activity as 'deconstruction' and challenges the applicability of the term, wondering if what these theorists are doing is nothing more than 'critique' or 'analysis'. Maclure's point is that those engaged in the study of policy as discourse seldom apply the philosophical premises of deconstruction to their own work. She asks pointedly: 'is it possible to deconstruct only in an "outwards direction" in this way?' I think not and will reflect further on this question in the next chapter. Maclure's comment highlights the need for theorists who describe 'policy as discourse' to elaborate more fully what they intend by this phrase. Three interrelated questions will be pursued here:

- Where do discourses come from?
- What does it mean to describe discourse as practice and to say discourse has effects?
- Is there room to move within discourse/s?

These questions unsurprisingly are those which have dominated social and political theory in some form or other for some time. They are also questions commonly raised when postmodernism is discussed. Is the turn to the construction of meaning a gospel of despair?

Or, is it possible to retain insights into the construction of meaning while endorsing programmes of political change? It is exactly this question which has created some tension for feminists interested in poststructuralist and postmodern ideas. Here I think it necessary to accept that postmodernists differ. Pauline Rosenau's (1992: 134) distinction between 'affirmative' and 'sceptical' postmodernists is useful, with the former committed to emancipatory political activities despite the acknowledged difficulties with claiming some undistorted access to knowledge, while for the latter 'truth, outside the individual, independent of language, is impossible'. The content of the affirmative approach is elaborated in books like *Social Postmodernism* (Nicholson and Seidman, 1995). In the main, feminists and those theorists who describe policy as discourse can be characterized as affirmative postmodernists. This is not surprising as those generally interested in policy have at some level as a goal an agenda for change. Sceptical postmodernists, by contrast, according to Rosenau (1992: 5), dismiss policy recommendations.

There are really two queries which must be addressed about the sources of discourses – first, do they originate somewhere? are there agents who create discourses? and secondly, how do they become a part of people's everyday understanding? On the former, policy theorists who describe policy as discourse generally convey an impression that indeed there are actors at work in the creation of discourse, but that we are not dealing with simple conspiracy or manipulation. For example, Edelman (1988: 36) describes the 'construction of problems' as 'as much a way of knowing and a way of acting strategically as a form of description'. The use of the term 'strategically' is at the very least suggestive of intentionality. Ball refers to the 'purposive actions of individuals' while insisting that (1990: 155) the discursive process 'cannot simply be reduced to the intentions and ambitions of a few key actors'. Attempts to smooth over any tension here tend to use the language of discursive and extra-discursive factors. This is meant to direct attention to the 'social-institutional context' in which discourse is located (see Bové, 1990: 57; Fraser, 1995: 287).

This produces two insights. Recalling that discourses consist of conceptual schema attached to specific historical, institutional and cultural contexts, it is clear that no agent is completely free to construct or reconstruct them (see Bosso, 1994: 189). At the same time, recognizing the institutional location of discourses draws attention to the differential power of some actors in their creation. Discourses are not the direct product of intentional manipulation by a few key political actors, but neither are they transhistorical structures operating outside of human intervention. In the end I decide that this question of *sources* of discourse is less useful than the examination of *effects* and this will be the focus elaborated in this text. With Peter Beilharz (1987: 392) I agree that 'the object becomes that of seeking to understand policy better than its authors, to locate and identify the meanings in the text, in its language or perspective, rather than in its (often instrumental) intentions'.

But if discourses are not simply 'creations', how do they work? How do people come to absorb and transmit them? Here, theorists in the field offer several explanations, explanations which in my view leave important points unaddressed. There is a tendency in the literature to see discourses as expressions of values, values picked up by the by through what can only be described as processes of socialization. In Jane Jenson (1988: 156), for example, discourses are assumptions, or at least this is all we can conclude given Jenson's insistence on the role of discourse in delimiting policy and the comment that '[P]olicy-makers' assumptions – along with those of other significant political actors – set limits on the alternatives considered feasible for policy implementation.' Similarly, Mary Hawkesworth (1988: 82) focuses on the influence of presuppositions in the shaping of policy debates and policy. These, we are told, are 'acquired through a process of indirect learning inseparable from immersion and socialization to a particular culture'.

Some poststructuralists, however, express dissatisfaction with socialization theory as it creates individuals as the helpless 'objects' of socialization (McLeod, 1993: 112; Thorne, 1993: 107). Bronwyn Davies (1994: 76) insists on the need to distinguish between 'the humanist concept of socialisation' and 'the poststructuralist concept of subjectification', about which more is said below. Marie Danziger (1995: 436) usefully draws on the work of Scialabba (1994) to identify two things in proponents which influence their views: *histories* – that is, their background and location – and *interests*. People in this account are not just passive receptors of discourses; they can be attentive to them and can marshall them for effect (see John, 1996).

In order to reflect upon what this means for the possibility of challenge and change, it is useful to consider more closely the content of discourses. Deborah Cameron (1990: 22) makes the commonly recognized point that 'every discourse incorporates elements of what it opposes and aims to replace'. Discourses are multiple *and* internally contradictory. Hence we need, in the words of Maria Black and Rosalind Coward (1990: 131–2), a politics of 'making new meaning'. Paul Bové (1990: 63) agrees: '[S]ince ours is a society which increasingly tries to insure its political order through discursive systems that discipline our language and culture, any successful resistance to that order would seem to require strong weapons aimed to weaken that discipline.' As to how that would work, Bové elaborates: by 'the critical examination of how, in relation to state and its largest institutions, power operates in discourse and how discourse disciplines a population.' Some of this work is being undertaken by governmentality scholars, discussed briefly below.

So, in a world constructed in discourse, discursive interventions are possible. But these are difficult and tentative. The point made above about every discourse incorporating elements of what it opposes and aims to replace draws to our attention not only the contradictory character of discourses, but also how difficult it is to move outside them. A What's the Problem? approach is intended to sensitize those seeking change to this difficulty, to caution social critics to examine their language, their concepts, their assumptions and the way they construct their case discursively (see Bacchi, 1996; see also Condit, 1990). Attending to the effects of the language used to frame issues means attending to rhetoric, and this forms part of a What's the Problem? approach. However, in contrast to studies which emphasize a historical agent's ability to frame proposals rhetorically, I insist upon the need to draw attention to the constitutive power of discourse, to the difficulty of stepping outside of structuring discourses. The tightrope we walk here is a familiar one – insisting that indeed social actors can use language in the service of particular goals while recognizing the embeddedness of actors in discursive systems constituted by tradition, religion and political institutions.

Above, Foucault describes discourses as practices, as events with effects. Most theorists who describe policy as discourse accept this focus. They tend to emphasize the material effects of discourse and to insist that it is inadequate to neglect these effects. Three general categories of effects can be identified: first, the ways in which subjects and subjectivities are constituted in discourse; second, the effects which follow from the limits imposed on what can be said – as an example, designating some areas of our lives as appropriate to public supervision, and some as 'private' (Fraser, 1995; Olsen, 1985); and third, the 'lived effects' (Bordo, 1993) of discourse.

The first of these marks an interest in the way in which groups are assigned positions and value within policy discourses, as 'needy' (Fraser, 1989), for example, or as 'disadvantaged' (Bacchi, 1996; Eveline, 1994a, b). This positioning leaves the power to define 'need' and 'disadvantage' in those designing the policy. It can also disempower groups who are thus created as supplicants. It is important to contrast this position with that developed by Rochefort and Cobb (1994: 23) and others (Schneider and Ingram, 1993), because the differences in approach on this issue highlight the fundamental distinction between a What's the Problem? approach and attention to 'problem definition'. According to Rochefort and Cobb, governments respond to different groups in the community differently due to '*societal* perceptions of the people who are going to benefit [emphasis added]'. Similarly, Schneider and Ingram see government responses to different groups *as affected by* the stereotypes attached to those groups, as either powerful and deserving, or dependent and undeserving. In these accounts, government is positioned outside the process, *responding to* images and stereotypes. By contrast, a What's the Problem? approach focuses on how groups are constituted *in* policy discourse. Gillian Fulcher (1989), for example, examines the way in which the 'disabled' are constituted the 'problem' in policy on disability.

The second effect has been discussed above. The third, an emphasis upon the 'lived effects' of discourse, directs attention to the limitations of strategies which focus *solely* on discursive interventions. In Foucault and some adaptations of him (see Marcus, 1992), once we acknowledge that the way we think about things is delimited by socially constructed meanings, the way forward appears to be simply to challenge those meanings. Regarding rape, Foucault insists that, since its power resides in the discursive construction of sexuality as integral to personhood, we need to encourage women to challenge this meaning, to think about rape as like shoving 'a fist in someone's mouth' (quoted in *Change*, 1977, in Plaza, 1980: 31). Foucault's attempt to challenge the constructed nature of sexuality produces the decision, on his part, to deny the sexual character of rape. Compare, in contrast, the position of Monique Plaza (1980: 36), who insists that 'we must confirm that rape is sexual, to the extent that it refers to social sexing, to the social differentiation of the sexes'. Whereas Foucault offers a purely discursive response, Plaza emphasizes the relevance of nondiscursive factors, such as the social location of women and men. To put not too fine a point on it, for the woman raped, the experience is *not* equivalent to having a fist shoved in her mouth. Her feelings will reflect the 'lived effects' of discourse and it is sadly inadequate to suggest that she simply start to 'think differently' about sexuality. There are real bodies and real people living the effects of discursive conventions, and it is essential to attend to the harms they experience.

Rob Watts offers a theory of policy-as-discourse close to the one elaborated in this text. Watts (1993/4: 116) challenges 'the deep-seated assumption found in both social liberal and radical readings of the modern state that in state policy intervention there was/is a discovery process which uncovers/ed "real" social problems as a prelude to state policy interventions'. Insightfully he points out that (1993/4: 117–18) this exercise 'deploys categories in such a way as to ignore the possibility that the "discovery" of problems requires the discursive constitution and abstraction of categories of social practice.' In his view, and in mine, 'uncovering this process is the real task of contemporary theorists and historians'. With me, Watts (p. 118) directs attention to 'the special role of the intellectually and professionally trained, whether in state employment or in civil society, who are implicated in processes of what can be called "constitutive abstraction"'. This is a wonderful phrase, emphasizing the role of meaning-making, specifically in the realm of policy and policy problems. Here Watts also acknowledges others – Kress (1985), Yeatman (1990) and Beilharz (1987) – who describe policy as discursive activity. Watts (1993/4: 119) elaborates 'the duality of the relationships between "reality" and discourse'. In one sense, he tells us, 'problems or issues only come to be that way when they have become part of a discourse'. At the same time, this opens up 'the possibility of continuing debate and contest about what it is that is being defined as a problem worthy of the interest of the state or of becoming the object of state policy.' To this I would add the importance of turning an eye to those conditions deemed unworthy of this interest. This is where the idea of policy as discursive activity comes into its own, because it promotes consideration of the ways in which the terms of a discourse limit what can be talked about.

One key focus in Watts and other theorists interested in policy as discourse is governmentality. Again, the progenitor of this interest is Foucault. Foucault (1991: 87–194) talked about rationalities of government, how they operated and with what effects. He referred to these effects as governmentality. In brief, this approach was intended to signal the complexity of modern systems of government and the ways in which systems of control operated. One of the most sophisticated of these was the operationalizing of self-control through discourses of autonomy. Foucault was interested in how individuals became self-monitoring while believing themselves to be free. His work on sexuality discourses (1981 [1976]) had this as its specific target – illustrating how the proliferation of discourses about sexuality produced people obsessed with sexuality and controlled by this obsession. This particular rationality of government Foucault calls 'liberal' and those who write about governmentality (see Barry et al., 1993) are most interested in understanding the processes at work in liberal regimes. There is an ambivalence in some of this writing about whether these processes are simply to be observed or to be condemned. Foucault himself was ambivalent (see Hinkson, 1995). Importantly for this book, there is a direct connection between governmentality and problematization. For Foucault, one of the chief means of instituting liberal rationality was problematization – that is, structuring problems in such a way that liberal outcomes, in this case self-monitoring under the illusion of autonomy, follow.

Many feminists are keenly interested in the governmentality approach (see, for example, Goodwin, 1996; Walkerdine, 1995). The emphasis on the state's concern with social order and the subtlety of the understanding of the processes by which this concern is operationalized make this a particularly fertile field for feminists to explore. The way in which governmentality scholars challenge simplistic dichotomies between agency and structure, regulation and deregulation are particularly appealing. I would offer only one small proviso, the limitations in the range of questions raised by concerns about self-regulation.

Here it is useful to apply a What's the Problem? approach to the kinds of problems particular analysts and groups of analysts see themselves facing. For example, I would suggest that political rationalist and value identification models of policy analysis have been constrained by their target – technocracy. Along somewhat similar lines, I would suggest that the 'problem' targeted by governmentality scholars – self-regulation – leaves important questions unasked. It is possible to suggest that the individual/society frame which guides governmentality enquiries limits the field of vision to particular kinds of issues and misses others. Specifically, there is a need to examine problem representations in terms of other structuring discourses, those affecting gender relations, those prescribing sexual roles, those categorizing people by skin colour or accent or sexual orientation. When we ask what a problem is represented to be, we need to attune ourselves appropriately to these intersecting dynamics. The point here is to create a technique which leaves us ever-sensitive to the limitations of our own problematizations. Applying this approach requires discipline, a constant requestioning of the salience of the questions we pose. In this text I start with a gender frame and ask what we can learn about the limited problematizations of much current policy from applying it. At the same time I retain a space for putting questions about the limitations of a gender frame.

Conclusion

To summarize, a What's the Problem? approach brings an interest in the presuppositions expressed in policy discourse together with attention to the active marshalling of discourses for political ends, broadly defined. It focuses on the discursive construction of policy problems and on the effects, including the lived effects, of the policies which accompany particular constructions. There is an insistence that no political actor, neither analyst nor theorist, stands outside these processes. Rather there is a recognition that we are all implicated in the structuring discourses of our era and our cultures. There is a scepticism about pluralist models due to this recognition. Since we cannot stand outside discourse, a model which presumes that political processes where different voices speak will produce something called justice is suspect.

Values are important in this approach. But these are not seen as separate from facts and hence open to scrutiny. Nor are they seen simply as presuppositions structuring arguments. Rather, values become a key ingredient in discourse, marshalled to assign meaning and to designate roles. Labelling abortion a 'moral' or 'ethical' problem is an example of this value labelling. Any description or representation of a problem becomes in this approach material for analysis rather than presumed truth or even presumed beliefs.

The approach therefore is clearly a social constructionist one – that is, it suggests, as stated in the Introduction, that it is impossible to contact an interpretation-free reality. There is, as already noted, a long social constructivist tradition within the sociology of knowledge, and a sub-branch specifically interested in the social construction of social problems. A key question, as anyone familiar with debates in this field is aware, concerns the difficulty of declaring a political stance within a constructed world. We have encountered this question in another form in this chapter. Its significance and how to deal with it get taken up in the next chapter.

3

RETHINKING 'SOCIAL PROBLEMS'

The boundaries between disciplines are historical artefacts; they reflect the preoccupations of an era. Disciplines also provide jobs for professionals who have a stake in the status of their particular discipline. At least part of the debate over the meaning of 'social problems' reflects territorial disputes over subject matter and methodologies. In Chapter 1 we saw David Dery (1984) engaging with the sociological approach to social problems. It is to his credit that he was reading this material at all, since scholars often wander little distance from their disciplinary base. We saw also how he dismissed the sociological approach as a concern with 'pseudo problems', due to sociologists' unwillingness to suggest what to do about them. Given Dery's pragmatism, this disillusionment is unsurprising. To him, as to Wildavsky (1979), a problem is a problem only if it can have a solution; to talk about anything else is a waste of time. Dery explicitly distinguishes his approach from that of the sociologists Spector and Kitsuse (1987, Chapter 5), a primary focus of this chapter, because they 'specifically urge us to set aside questions of "public concern"'.

As policy theorists have turned increasingly to the roles of discourse and representation, there has been more cross-fertilization with the sociology of social problems.[1] For example, many in both camps use the language of social construction. And the problems which accompany a social constructionist or constructivist perspective, most obviously the problem of relativism, engage both sociologists and postpositivist policy analysts. In a sense this cross-fertilization simply reflects general trends in social and cultural theory. Given the focus of a What's the Problem? approach on the construction and representation of policy problems, it is important to engage with the sociological literature. At the outset, however, I wish to make clear that I share many of the criticisms made of those frequently seen as representative of the social construction of social problems approach, specifically Spector and Kitsuse (1987), and Ibarra and Kitsuse (1993), and will use this chapter to explain my dissatisfactions with this literature. My book title deliberately refers to 'the construction of *policy* problems' not to 'the construction of *social* problems', to signal my distancing from the dominant sociology of social problems approach.

To prefigure the argument, I object to the concentration on 'social problems' and on those who constitute them through their claims, without reflection upon the narrowness of this enterprise and what it leaves out. I object also to the suggestion that social theorists can stand back from their material – the process of social problem construction – and frame it objectively, a claim made by some sociologists of social problems. Most fundamentally, a What's the Problem? approach focuses not on the processes or rhetoric of social problem construction, positions associated with the sociology of social problems, but on *deconstructing the social problem constructions on offer*. Raymond Michalowski (1993: 384) identifies the crucial difference in these perspectives:

> [A]s a way of naming a method for studying social problems, the term *social construction* places the author of the sociological tale being told in the background. *Deconstruction*, on the other hand, foregrounds what is done by those doing the studying, i.e., how those telling the sociological tale set about tempting social texts to yield up new meanings [original emphasis].

The History of 'Social Problems'

Comment upon and engagement with 'social problems' has a long history in the United States. It should be noted that this is not coincidental, that as disciplinary boundaries are historical artefacts, so too are the foci of disciplines in particular countries. In fact, we can learn more about the nature and meaning of the social problems approach by examining the historical conditions of its emergence than by examining its arguments.

A number of authors schematize approaches to social problems. Thomas Sullivan and Kenrick Thompson (1994) identify three theoretical perspectives: functionalism, conflict theory and interactionism. While Lee Rainwater's (1974a: 3–7; see also 1974b) categories (note that he takes his categories from Earl Rubington and Martin S. Weinberg, 1971) are similar, he usefully ties them to historical periods. Rainwater's first two categories, social pathology and social disorganization, are roughly equivalent to Sullivan and Thompson's functionalism. As Rainwater notes, the social pathology approach was typical of early sociologists, working in the period before the First World War. Here, commentators 'tended to see social problems as manifestations of one or another departure from "normality" in society'. Society was described as an organism and 'sick' people, be they feeble-minded or possessing criminal constitutions, were considered the source of the social disruptions sociologists called social problems. After the war, sociologists, primarily those associated with the University of Chicago (Rainwater, 1974a: 4), started from the same presumption that social organization was good and disruption was bad. However, they located the sources of 'social pathologies' in normlessness and cultural conflict.

The value conflict approach which Rainwater attributes to Fuller and Myers,[2] and which Sullivan and Thompson (1994: 12) trace to Marx, stresses that problems occur 'not because things fall apart socially but because different groups in society have different interests, these interests conflict, and these conflicts precipitate conditions that at least some people regard as undesirable' (Rainwater, 1974a: 5). This approach marks a distinct challenge to previous theory since it suggests that what may be a 'problem' to some could constitute a statement of challenge to some others. Here, we can see the incipient origins of a social constructionist perspective which suggests that what we perceive as social problems depends upon how we see the world.

Sullivan and Thompson's interactionists (1994: 14) illustrate another move towards social constructionism, since they stress the ways in which people in face to face contact construct their own realities: '[B]ecause of our abilities to use symbols, we live in a world that we create ourselves, through the meanings we attach to phenomena.' The emphasis here is on the response to symbolic and social meanings, rather than to 'actual physical objects or actions'. As an example, interactionists note the effects of labelling people as deviants of one form or another on our interactions with them, and on the behaviour of those so labelled, should they accept the label. The emphasis in this account remains upon the desirability of social order and encourages the creation of 'new consensus with different meanings and expectations' when dissensus occurs.

The hallmark of pre-1960s social problems theory is indeed this category 'deviance', which captures in its very name the aim of many social problems theorists, normalization. Rainwater (1974a: 5–6) elaborates the important contribution of Robert Merton (1961) on this topic. Writing in the 1930s and 1940s, Merton traced deviance to obstacles or shortcomings in the opportunity structure. The Depression invariably had an effect here: '[D]eviant behavior is seen as the product of strains built into society, stemming from a disjunction between what the culture offers as desirable and what the social structure actually makes available to all members' (Rainwater, 1974a: 6). The presumption here remains that integration into existing social structures is indeed a good thing and that those who wish to minimize deviance ought to increase the opportunities for 'deviants' to become 'normals'. This indeed can be seen as the underlying logic of equal opportunity policy.

Labelling theory developed as a response to this approach and is, in effect, a variant of social constructionism, which will be elaborated in the next section. Labelling theorists are more interested in the process of labelling individuals or groups as 'deviant', than in the behaviours of those individuals or groups. As with conflict theorists, there is an insistence that we examine the perspectives of those who see certain behaviours as problematic. The 'problem' then is not out there waiting to be identified; rather who we are and what our social goals are, be these either stability or change, will affect who and what we consider to be problematic. Problems are, in this view, very much in the eye of the beholder.

Despite this increasing sensitivity to the constructed nature of social problems, the continuing preoccupation with 'problems' that need to be resolved in order for society to function can be seen as necessarily associated with a reformist agenda. It is no coincidence, I would argue, that the growing popularity of a concern with social problems theory coincided with the political disturbances of the 1960s. In Ben Agger's view, and I have considerable sympathy with this position,

> [S]ocial problems analysis as a latter-day statist strategy arose not in order to ameliorate human suffering at all but as a way of addressing the systemic disturbances caused by urbanization, unemployment, poverty, discrimination and environmental degradation. (Agger, 1993: 291)

Indeed, as we have seen, the dominant focus in much of the literature has been on maintaining social order. Paralleling the insights of governmentality theorists, then, problems are defined as 'problems of system maintenance' (deHaven-Smith, 1988: 93). As Joseph Gusfield (1989: 436) says, '[I]n the very definition of situations as problems the social control elements emerge, whether or not the practitioners are aware of them.'

The Advent of Social Constructionism

Berger and Luckman's *The Social Construction of Reality* (1967) is commonly considered the starting place for social constructionism as a sociological approach. The emphasis in Berger and Luckman, as in interactionism, is upon the meanings individuals impute, rather than upon a 'reality' standing outside individual interpretation. It is a direct challenge to realist presumptions about the nature of the world and our understanding of it. Variants of the realist/anti-realist debate surface in every branch of the social sciences. Rhoda Unger (1989: 15) identifies two dominant paradigms in psychology, for example – the 'reality constructs the person' paradigm, and 'the person constructs reality' paradigm, with the latter representing the constructionist perspective. Peter Backhouse (1996: 183) notes that the context for the development of social constructionist ideas was the broader social, political and intellectual movements which emerged in the West throughout the 1960s, including radical science. The motivation, according to Backhouse, was to challenge the presumed objective status of scientific knowledge. More generally, it is possible to see in social constructionism a suggestion that things taken for granted as good and valuable, as law, as custom, could be challenged as 'perspectives' and as 'perspectives' which suited particular groups in society. Here, social constructionism merges with value conflict theory.

It is not necessary to see social constructivism as by its nature and origin committed to progressive change, however. This depends very much upon how it is elaborated and upon the kinds of claims which follow from it. In some versions, as I will be suggesting of Spector and Kitsuse (1987), and Ibarra and Kitsuse (1993), and many of their followers, social constructionist attention to social problems produces no political agenda and hence supports the status quo. Moreover, the position that all interpretations are simply constructions leads readily in some accounts to the view that one interpretation is as good as any other (Rosenau, 1992: 137). Some feminists are understandably wary of social constructionism given this possible use of the theory. In the previous chapter, I noted that it is not necessary to subscribe to this view if one emphasizes the implications which flow from particular representations or interpretations. As I argued there, these implications have effects on people's lives, effects which need to be commented upon and assessed.

While constructivists share the view that 'the person creates reality', a direct challenge to the realist perspective, it is not always clear what is implied by this. In some accounts, and here I would include Von Glaserfeld's (1995: 1) 'radical constructivism', and personal construct theory (Bannister and Fransella, 1977), the constructs are in people's heads. In a sense, this restores some idea of autonomous individuals shaping their own reality and unsatisfactorily recognizes the constraints upon the shaping process. I prefer the way in which Ian John (1996) places constructs in the 'discursive world', recognizing the impact of social attitudes on the shape of personal constructs and the ways in which people actively construct different responses in different situations (see here the discussion on discourse in Chapter 2). On this point, Michal McCall (1993: 181) notes that, in interactionist approaches, there has been inattention to 'the social structures within which people construct meanings'. She insists, and the case is a strong one, that feminist social constructionism developed independently and retained a dual emphasis on structure and agency. Gale Miller (1993: 254) agrees that many critical-feminist theorists and some other social critics 'treat public understandings of and orientations to everyday life as social constructions, but they also emphasize how the understandings and orientations are constructed within gendered and/or capitalist social institutions and relationships'. As Miller goes on to explain, with this perspective it is possible to retain the insights of constructivism without losing a political edge to one's analysis. McCall likewise insists that feminist social constructionists are not 'noncommital' but endorse 'a politics directed at changing existing power relations between women and men in society' (McCall, 1993: 183; quote from Weedon, 1987: 1).

As part of this political analysis, it is necessary to direct attention to why some constructions 'stick' while others receive little attention. Avery Gordon (1993: 309) makes this point clear: '[C]onstructionism, as an epistemological characterization of the fabricated nature of social reality, or social problems, tells us little about those constructions if it cannot account for why some and not others predominate.' As in the theory of discourse outlined in the previous chapter, it is necessary to direct attention, in the words of Heather Maroney (1992: 239), to who controls 'the enunciative position'. Hence, we are returned to Foucault's dual problematic – what one is able to say and what one is permitted to say.

The Social Construction of Social Problems

Malcolm Spector and John Kitsuse are generally credited with bringing social constructionism to social problems theory, first in their important 1973 (Kitsuse and Spector, 1973) paper and later in their book, *Constructing Social Problems* (1987; first published 1977). As Holstein and Miller (1993: 7) explain, the position Spector and Kitsuse developed was a response to the structuralist functionalist approach which saw societal problems as readily identifiable and in need of resolution. To Spector and Kitsuse (Holstein and Miller, 1993: 6), social problems are not 'objective conditions to be studied and corrected', but 'interpretive processes that constitute what come to be seen as oppressive, intolerable, or unjust conditions like crime, poverty, and homelessness.' The focus of analysis shifts from 'harmful conditions' to the processes of social problems claims-making. In Spector and Kitsuse, there is a clear challenge to the proposition that it is possible to study conditions 'objectively' or to assert that objective conditions are harmful. They also directed attention to the role of sociologists as claims-makers in their portrayals of 'real' social problems (Holstein and Miller, 1993: 7). Yet they maintained that 'constructionism provides a distinctively sociological approach that focuses on the social processes through which social problems are constructed', and that such a sociology would examine 'the diverse claims-making groups and activities, and *avoid its own claims-making activities* [emphasis added]'.

The work by Spector and Kitsuse generated considerable debate, producing response and counter-response. Understandably, it was attacked by realists. More surprisingly, it was attacked as not measuring up to its claims by sociologists who claimed postpositivist and postmodernist sympathies. Most important was the article by Woolgar and Pawluch (1985) which accused Spector and Kitsuse of 'ontological gerrymandering', that is, of retaining objectivist assumptions in the suggestion that they could compare claims against a presumed constant condition. Kitsuse teamed up with Peter Ibarra (1993: 25) to offer a reply. Here they restated the goal – to develop 'an empirically based theory of social problems'. They explain that some of the problems with understanding the earlier (Kitsuse and Spector, 1973; Spector and Kitsuse, 1987) position were generated by the use in that work of the term 'putative conditions'. In the more recent work, they replace this with 'condition-categories' which are 'the terms used by members to propose what the social problem is "about"'. The purpose in this change of language is to distance analysts from assumptions about conditions. In this vein, Ibarra and Kitsuse (1993: 31) insist that the 'strict constructionist never leaves language' and they turn their attention to the rhetoric used to frame claims about social problems. They identify rhetorical idioms, including the rhetoric of loss, the rhetoric of entitlement, the rhetoric of endangerment, the rhetoric of unreason, the rhetoric of calamity, and counter rhetorics and motifs. They repeat the fundamental constructionist claim (1993: 42) – 'claims-making activities constitute social problems'.

The suggestion that the constructionist 'never leaves language' disturbed some social constructionists in the field. Joel Best (1989) was one of these and he proceeded to elaborate a spectrum of social constructionist views. Best (1989: 245) identifies Spector and Kitsuse, and Ibarra and Kitsuse as *strict* constructionists who argue that 'social problems analysts should avoid making assumptions about objective reality'. At the other extreme is 'debunking' which takes, as the analysts' task, drawing attention to 'mistaken or distorted claims'. Between these poles, Best (1989: 246) locates *contextual* constructionists, a category in which he includes himself. Contextual constructionists remain focused on the claims-making process but 'acknowledge making some assumptions about social conditions', the very assumptions that Woolgar and Pawluch warn against. But to Best these assumptions are necessary to locate claims-making within social context. He elaborates that claims can and must be evaluated against evidence. While acknowledging that all evidence is itself a construction, contextual constructionists 'assume that such information can be used to (imperfectly) describe the context within which claims-making occurs'. So, for Best, it would be important to assess claims about a rise in the crime rate against existing measurements of crime rates and, if a discrepancy is found, to comment on the nature of that discrepancy and its possible meaning. Best (1989: 247) makes two important criticisms of the strict constructionist position. First, he claims that the goal of an analysis free of assumptions about objective conditions is impossible. Second, he claims that a move in this direction is undesirable, since it 'limits the kinds of questions an analyst can ask'. I agree with both these points.

On the first, it is clear that Ibarra and Kitsuse (1993) are actively involved in the creation of categories of analysis which are then imposed on public statements. It is no more possible then to gain 'objective' access to claims than to gain 'objective' access to 'social problems'. On the second point, Best is concerned that 'analytic purity can come at a terrible cost'. In his view (1989: 143), the implications of strict constructionism 'put the analyst . . . into a contextless region where claims-making may only be examined in the abstract'. Whereas the sociology of social problems, says Best, began 'with the assumption that sociological knowledge might help people understand and improve the world', strict constructionism 'sells that birthright for a mess of epistemology'. In his words, Ibarra and Kitsuse reduce social problems claims-making to a 'language game'. I would add that the declared determination to avoid political assessments is, in effect, an assessment itself. The view that all we have in the world of public policy are competing framings of problems is, I would argue, a species of pluralism which supports the status quo.

What's the Problem? and Social Problems Theory

In a number of ways, a What's the Problem? approach lines up with contextual constructionism. At the very least, use will be made of varieties of evidence, if only, as Best suggests, to ask questions about the way it is used or why it is ignored. Contextual constructionists also pay more attention to the important point raised earlier regarding who controls the 'enunciative position', who gets to make claims and who gets their claims heard. By contrast, the assumption in strict constructionism seems to be that this is an inappropriate or uninteresting question, leaving the impression that those with legitimate claims will get a hearing. I see this assumption also in the work of Mauss (1975) on social problems as social movements. Mauss stresses the origins of social problems in public opinion and traces the life-history of accomplished claims to resolution. As suggested in the Introduction, I find in Mauss a naive optimism about the openness of the system to claims, a position feminist social constructionists and some others would challenge.

Contextual constructionists also draw attention to the way in which constructions/representations of social problems constitute subjects, a project described as important in the previous chapter. Loseke's (1993) particular concern is the 'battered wife' and the implications which flow from being so labelled. There are clear links here with labelling theory and with Foucault's (1975, 1977a) project, to draw attention to the effects of naming 'criminals' and 'the insane'. Similarly, Joseph Gusfield (1989), with Patricia Morgan (1980), comments upon the creation of the 'troubled persons' professions which accompanies an understanding of social disruption as due to 'troubled individuals'. He also points out that this individualizing of social problems diverts attention from the institutional factors which create 'disturbances'.

Gillian Fulcher (1989) applies these insights in her analysis of education policy and disability, illustrating the links between those who study policy as discourse and contextual constructionism. Describing policy as 'merely an instance of a discursive practice' (1989: 12, 24–5) , she draws attention to the 'individualistic discourse which typically characterizes encounters between professionals and people called "disabled"'. In this discourse, disability is portrayed as a personal trouble, rather than a public issue. It follows that labelling people 'disabled' diverts attention from the 'disabling' structures which constrain them. Some of this individualizing of social conditions takes root *within* the subjects who are constituted as either 'troubled' or 'disabled' or 'disadvantaged'. Dawn Currie (1988: 248), for example, shows how the language of 'reproductive choice' encourages women to personalize 'their dilemma of choice rather than seeing how choices were shaped by structures'. Gusfield (1989) also examines the way in which groups become locked into a 'social problems' frame, so that once something is called a 'social problem', it is difficult to shift or relocate the frame. We will see, for example, how difficult it is to ask the question – is abortion the problem? Despite these commonalities in approach, What's the Problem? distinguishes itself from contextual constructivism in the way in which it distinguishes itself from social problems theory generally. That is, it sees serious implications in the limitations imposed by an agenda of 'social problems' which then become the focus of analysis simply because someone has made claims about them.

The starting point for the social constructionist perspective on social problems is that very point made by Murray Edelman (1988), quoted in the Introduction – that a whole range of troubling social conditions fail to achieve the status of a 'social problem', or only achieve this status at particular times. This is the insight which directed the attention of Spector and Kitsuse (1987) to the factors which accomplish the 'recognition' of a social problem. They concluded that the word 'recognition' was totally inappropriate to describe this process since those who worked to achieve 'recognition' of a particular 'social problem' invariably put their stamp upon it. That is, the very nature of the social problem was constituted in the description offered of it. Now, this is very much the position argued for in a What's the Problem? approach.

The difference between a What's the Problem? approach and that pursued by Spector and Kitsuse (and Ibarra and Kitsuse) is best understood by considering what follows from this insight. As we have seen, Spector and Kitsuse (and Ibarra and Kitsuse) were concerned to rescue the project of creating usable sociological knowledge and hence a viable social problems theory. This, they argued, could be achieved by establishing a distance between the researcher and the 'identified' social problem, focusing instead on the claims-makers and their arguments. This, they suggested, was *all that was available* for sociologists to study. By contrast, a What's the Problem? approach takes the insight that all we have access to are contested claims about the existence and nature of social problems to: (1) reflect upon the shape of claims made about social problems; (2) consider the implications which flow from the shape of these claims; and (3) reflect upon what is missing from the shape of some claims and what implications follow from this. To repeat the characterization of the approach made earlier, a What's the Problem? approach deconstructs the social constructions on offer, instead of describing them, which is basically what Ibarra and Kitsuse do. In addition, a What's the Problem? approach sees as limiting a project which defines its boundaries as 'claims-making'. In my account, the starting place for analysis is not those who achieve social problem status for their particular concerns and how they accomplish this. Rather, it is questioning the too easy assumption that the material for analysis should be limited to *accomplished* claims (see Collins, 1989).

A number of other authors share this concern. Jaber Gubrium (1993: 92–3) makes this point forcefully: '[W]here there is little publicity, the social problem under contention hardly exists.' Leslie Miller (1993: 353–4, 358) shows that it is not just claims which are actively suppressed which need to be considered. She offers an analysis of a house'wife' who could not *articulate* her position relative to her husband due to dominant views and the 'cultural repertoire of discourses'. Miller emphasizes therefore that all talk, not just that associated with political interest groups for example, makes claims, and that 'the "absence" of social problems talk in some situations is an achieved invisibility'. With Miller, I object to the overemphasis on public claims-making in the sociology of social problems literature, and seek a more comprehensive approach which considers how the contemporary organization of power, knowledge and discourse *precludes* the conceptualization and expression of some social problems claims. With Miller (1993: 360), I would assert that 'exclusionary practices are discursive at root'. It is discourse in this sense, not rhetoric, as it appears in Ibarra and Kitsuse (1993), which is the focus for a What's the Problem? approach.

As I stated in the Introduction, one of the major limitations of current policy approaches is that they are generally limited to what governments do or deliberately refuse to do, preventing considera- tion of what fails to get analysed or what gets analysed in ways that leave certain issues sequestered in domains considered nonpolitical. In my view, Ibarra and Kitsuse and all those who focus on *articulated* social problems are of little use in broadening this agenda. In contrast, a What's the Problem? approach has this as its principal aim. This emphasis may not at first sight be apparent in the demand that we direct attention to implied problem representations in *existing* policy proposals. The goal, however, is to take these as starting points for asking what does *not* get problematized, to draw attention to silences in existing political agendas, not simply to items which fail to get onto agendas. Here I am referring to silences about power relations, gender relations, the exigencies of intimate life, as a few examples. I also call for greater reflection upon the way in which attention to 'social problems' has come to represent a progressive response to societal ills. Again, in the Introduction, I noted how a number of researchers start from the premise that 'dealing' with social problems is the way toward a healthier society. There lodges in this view all those assumptions about discrete social problems and about an identification/response approach to social problems which have been challenged in previous chapters.

Postmodernism, Social Problems and Policy

Some commentators (Warren, 1993: 59) see Ibarra and Kitsuse as postmodern. Some (Troyer, 1993: 124) see them as attempting to be postmodern, and failing. It is fairly clear that their recent work (1993) is an attempt to respond to the postmodern challenge by Woolgar and Pawluch (1985) that their theory harboured objectivist assump- tions. But the response they offer, as I note above, continues to assume that sociologists can stand back and analyse something, even if in this case it is only the rhetoric of claims-makers. Here I wish to consider the impact that postmodernism is having on social theory in a number of areas. The case of Ibarra and Kitsuse provides an opening to reflect upon this development and its repercussions.

Raymond Michalowski (1993: 380–3) is helpful here. He describes two branches of deconstruction: first, literary deconstruction associ- ated with Barthes (1967) and Jameson (1972), and second, social deconstruction associated with Foucault (1970, 1977a, 1980), Bataille

(1985) and Bakhtin (1968). Literary deconstruction focuses on the text and places meaning-making in the hands of 'readers' rather than 'writers'. By comparison, social deconstruction 'approaches society less as an analog to the literary text and more as an integrated patterning of ritual performances'. In this position, '[S]ociety is more than an accumulation of private, subjective meanings.' A number of other writers have drawn distinctions within postmodernism, distinctions which line up well with Michalowski's. You may recall Rosenau's (1992) comparison between affirmative and sceptical post-modernists. While Michalowski seems to see the textualists as more optimisitic than the social deconstructionists since they institute a 'radical return of the subject to social enquiry', the rest of the dis-tinctions between Rosenau's 'sceptics' and 'affirmatives' – in their attitudes to representation, and to policy – parallel Michalowski's. Alex Callinicos (1985: 86) also draws a comparison between the textualism of Derrida (1983) and a second form of poststructuralism which he calls 'worldly poststructuralism', associated with Foucault's 'master-category' 'power-knowledge'.

The editors of *Social Postmodernism*, Linda Nicholson and Steven Seidman (1995: 8–35), draw a similar comparison. They insist upon a concept of the social that goes beyond 'textual meanings and sign systems' and demand theories which 'focus on social institutions and processes'. They explain their project as addressing the problems which 'seemed to emerge from those places where postmodernism overlapped with poststructuralism', in particular the way in which 'the social was collapsed into the textual'. They wish to show that 'it is possible for postmodern thinkers to focus on institutions as well as texts, to think about the interrelations of social patterns without being essentializing or totalizing, and to create constructive as well as deconstructive analyses of the social'. For them, there is no incon-sistency in adopting a postmodernist perspective on meaning pro-duction and stating a positive, transformative social and political project. Some of this discussion links up nicely with the discussion of meanings of discourse in Chapter 2, where I identified a tension between analysts who dissolved everything into discourse, and those who insisted on examining the relationship between discursive and extra-discursive factors, specifically the role of institutions and of powerful actors in influencing the shape and content of discourses.

Michalowski (1993: 383) describes the work of Ibarra and Kitsuse as 'an example of literary deconstruction reformulated as rhetorical (de)construction'. This is seen for example in the declaration that the social problems theorist cannot step outside language, or the text. Michalowski's hesitation to recognize their work as deconstruction (indicated by the insertion of brackets around 'de') stems from their refusal to foreground their own position in the study. To use the current jargon, Ibarra and Kitsuse display insufficient reflexivity to qualify as full-blown deconstructionists. You may recall, in Chapter 2, the query raised by Maclure (1994) as to whether it is possible for policy analysts to deconstruct only in an outward direction. There I stated that I think not. I think it crucial that all analysts reflect upon their own location, institutional and cultural, reflect upon their position in discourse, and discuss this in their comments on constructions of policy problems. The point is to recognize that there is no stepping outside of these influences and that in fact all analyses reflect current discursive constructions – it could not be otherwise. This is not to create a static picture, a world without change. Discourses, as we have seen, are complex and contradictory, and constructions can be challenged. If we accept that our world is socially constructed, then it can be changed by challenging – deconstructing – constructions which have effects we wish to reduce or eliminate. This is, in effect, a description of a What's the Problem? agenda.

The question then becomes: what are the grounds of one's challenge? What follows once we recognize the impossibility of creating objective analysis of either 'social problems' or the claims about 'social problems'? We return here to the dilemma posed in the preceding chapter: does this insight produce a counsel of despair? Does it leave us mired in relativistic claims which preclude the possibility of defending a political project? The key here, I suggest, is to recognize that competing social visions lie behind competing representations/ constructions of social problems, and behind the assessments offered of and by claims-makers. We need, I insist, to talk about these competing social visions and to discuss how particular problem representations, in our view, contribute to or undermine visions we support. Recognizing the impossibility of objectivism highlights the need for this discussion. The sociology of social problems therefore intersects at several important points with questions raised by a What's the Problem? approach. It illustrates and emphasizes the constructedness of social problems. It draws to our attention the roles of claims-makers in achieving 'social problem' status for particular concerns, and this is useful in thinking about the discursive authority of some groups (Weiner, 1994: 88–9). In some accounts (see Best, 1989; Gusfield, 1989), it draws attention to the role of discourse in shaping claims and in constituting subjects within claims.

However, in the main, the literature has been insufficiently self-critical. There needs to be more attention directed to the effects of focusing on 'social problems' – how this includes particular kinds of claims while silencing others, how the language of 'social problems' implies a response to disturbing conditions without analysing the nature of that response. A What's the Problem? approach creates the space to take up these issues. A sharp focus on problematization, rather than 'problems' (see Shapiro, 1992), it argues, encourages reflection upon the overall shape of policy initiatives, what they encompass and *what they leave out*. While retaining an interest in claims-making and the language used to make claims, it emphasizes a single question – What is the problem represented to be? – and assesses the implications of different representations. Further, a What's the Problem? approach moves outside the contextual-strict constructionist debate by accepting that objective information is unattainable while insisting that this produces the obligation to debate substantive social visions.

Feminists, Social Problems and Policy

In several places I have indicated that feminists do not agree about a number of issues raised in the preceding argument. Some are distinctly suspicious of postmodernism (Brodribb, 1992; Walby, 1992). Some are wary of constructionist approaches (Collins, 1989). Others (for example Stone, 1988; Hawkesworth, 1988; Fraser, 1989; Phillips, 1996; Jenson, 1988) work with both perspectives. Articles reviewing feminist approaches to policy (Ackelsberg, 1992; Hawkesworth, 1994) show that feminists, no less than others, embrace a variety of positions, often as Hawkesworth (1994: 105) notes, shaped by competing theoretical assumptions. Borrowing from Sandra Harding's (1990) typification, it is possible to identify feminist empiricists, feminist standpoint theorists and feminist postmodernists working in the field. Usefully, Harding stresses what these groups have in common rather than what separates them. She shows, for example, how feminist empiricists have taken empiricism to task for failing to recognize that the epistemic location of the author influences the shape and content of what is written. On the other side, she notes that feminist postmodernists retain space for political and ethical claims while questioning the attainability of 'truth'. The kinds of overlaps Harding identifies, I would suggest, makes constructionism – as I have developed it here – a natural home for feminists. Feminism as a political perspective emphasizes exactly the two key points of constructionism: first, that who we are influences our comments on and claims about the world; and second, that political stakes are involved in these claims. This will be illustrated in succeeding chapters which draw upon a large number of feminist contributions.

The discomfort some feminists have felt with a social constructionist approach is associated with the twin concerns I have addressed in this chapter – a concern that constructionism prevents or undermines political activism by undermining the legitimacy of political claims, and a concern that constructionism generally concentrates on articulated claims and ignores silences. Feminists are most attentive to the latter as women have never been well represented among political claims-makers, and as dominant discourses often position women as 'other' (see Bacchi, 1996), silencing them in particular ways. I hope that I have shown in this chapter that a What's the Problem? approach retains the insights of constructionism while obviating the problems just identified. I have done this by aligning a What's the Problem? approach with a variant of postmodernism, described in some accounts as 'social' (see Nicholson and Seidman, 1995), or 'worldly' (see Callinicos, 1985), or 'affirmative' (see Rosenau, 1992), or 'material' (see Hennessy, 1993). This variant is counterposed to versions of postmodernism which reduce everything to texts and 'readings' of texts. It resurrects the social and the structural by drawing attention to the relationship between discursive and non-discursive factors (see Barrett, 1991). It describes discourses as practices and insists that we attend to their material effects. It emphasizes the limits placed on constructions by structural factors, including the power of institutions and individuals to shape discourse, while insisting upon the possibility of challenging constructions which have effects we despise (see Loseke, 1993: 207). It does this through an insistence upon the need to attend to the implications of problem representations. In this view Dery's (1984) 'pseudo problems' become the stuff of policy analysis. Part Two of the book applies the approach outlined here.

Notes

1 Roger Sibeon's (1996) book integrates insights across the disciplinary boundaries between sociology, social theory and political science. Despite some differences in our emphases and conclusions, his work is a useful introduction to the implications of postmodernism, Foucault and discourse analysis for policy studies.

2 Rubington and Weinberg (1971: 83) note that Fuller and Myers wrote five papers between 1936 and 1941 in which they 'held that conflict of values figured in all phases of most social problems'. The two papers reprinted in Rubington and Weinberg are listed in the bibliography.

PART TWO

THE PROBLEM OF WOMEN'S INEQUALITY

PREAMBLE

As mentioned in the Introduction, in Part Two of the book a What's the Problem (represented to be)? approach will be applied to a selection of issues frequently identified as crucial to ending 'women's inequality'. The purpose is not, however, to attempt a comprehensive treatment of any single issue but to provide a guide to method. Each chapter is written in such a way as to draw attention to methodological pointers and each will highlight one particular aspect of a What's the Problem? approach. In the process, an analysis of the issue will be offered with all the provisos mentioned in the Introduction – that other authors could well use the methodology developed in this book to make new, interesting and challenging points about the interpretations of issues it presents.

Here I offer a summary and forecast of the kinds of methodological points which will be illustrated. The chapter on pay equity (Chapter 4) applies a What's the Problem? approach to feminist battles for fair remuneration. It illustrates the recommendation that competing representations be assessed by their likely effects. In the chapter on antidiscrimination and affirmative action (Chapter 5), I will concentrate upon what it means to refer to the way in which subjectivities are constituted in policy. The education chapter (Chapter 6) offers an example of the nesting of problem representations and how to deal with this phenomenon. Child care (Chapter 7) presents a different kind of example, where several problem representations operate simultaneously. In the abortion chapter (Chapter 8) I illustrate the usefulness of a genealogical approach. In the violence against women chapter (Chapter 9) I concentrate upon language and the relationship between terminology and discourse. Sexual harassment (Chapter 10) rounds off the exercise, providing the opportunity to reflect upon several methodological points, the constitution of subjectivities, genealogy, nesting and language. Each chapter will follow the model recommended, in the Introduction, for the application of a What's the Problem? approach: identifying problem representations, reflecting on their effects, probing alternative problem representations and where they might lead.

The approach developed in this part of the book requires a certain amount of rethinking. In keeping with the project outlined in the Introduction, the heading does not imply that there exists an easily identifiable and measurable 'something' called 'women's inequality'. Rather, the point is to draw attention to the ways in which 'women's inequality' is discussed or described. This does not mean that I am questioning the reality of women's subordination or oppression, but that I am insisting that we examine the interpretations which describe that phenomenon. Again, in keeping with a What's the Problem (represented to be)? approach, the suggestion is that policies addressing 'women's inequality' assume particular interpretations of the problem. And, if the interpretations of the nature and/or causes of the problem miss the mark, so to speak, we can expect little to change.

The next point to remember is that it is inappropriate to think of interpretations of the problem as somehow standing outside of or as prior to policy proposals. Rather, it is necessary to see that policy proposals have in-built problem representations. That is, whatever is proposed creates in its formulation the shape of the problem addressed. As one example, plans to increase the representation of women in managerial positions which emphasize training programmes for women create the problem as women's lack of training. And again, education programmes which encourage girls to choose nontraditional occupational study areas create the problem as girls' unwillingness to select these areas. In both cases, women and girls are the ones who are expected to change. We will be discussing in Chapters 5 and 6 limitations with these approaches. The point here is to recognize that policy 'responses' need to be understood as part of a discursive construction of 'problems' (see Chapter 3 for a discussion of discourse and policy).

Following from the discussion of genealogy in Chapter 2, I also wish to highlight the historical creation of a 'problem' called 'women's inequality'. Note, I am not suggesting that women have ever been 'equal', but that we can identify, at least in Western democracies, a more or less precise period when the 'problem' was named and addressed in policy. With some variations this took place in the 1960s and 1970s, and coincided with the resurgence of feminist mobilizing. It is possible to see a forerunner of the 1960s formulation in discussions earlier in the century of 'The Woman Question', which was primarily concerned with the rising numbers of 'unattached' women, unattached, that is, to supporting male partners (Bacchi, 1986). Whereas in this earlier period the problem was represented to be disruptions to traditional mores caused by unmarried women and the prospect that they might become financially independent, in the 1960s the problem became women's lack of access to the labour market.

There is of course a vast sweep of history between these two periods, a sweep which included two world wars that had important impacts on both women's participation in paid labour and their acceptability in that role. However, the 'problem' of 'women's inequality' was fully articulated only in the 1960s. It is in this period that Americans organized a Presidential Commission on the Status of Women (1963), with the Canadians following suit (1967). In a sense these events signal a kind of culmination of interest in the subject. But, in another sense, they are markers of 'women's inequality' as a new 'social problem category' (Morris, 1980). A number of countries, as we will see in the next chapter, had already passed legislation calling for equal pay for women. But by the 1960s the 'problem' had broadened beyond pay issues. Alongside Blacks in the United States, 'women' was constituted a 'disadvantaged' group and policies were designed to 'address' this disadvantage. A sign of this achievement is the appearance of 'the status of women' in the social problems literature from this point onward (see Rainwater, 1974a for example). Today it would be considered remiss to produce a social problems anthology which excluded the 'problem' of 'women's inequality', which is not to presume that this always happens nor that this will always be the case. Social problem status can be lost, as well as won.

Because of the ease with which it is possible to slip into a discovery/response approach to the situation, recall that policies necessarily constitute the problem they address. Hence, in order to understand what the problem of women's inequality was represented to be in this period and onwards, we need to look to the policies which addressed and address it. This we will be doing in the chapters to follow. The primary foci of change were and are anti-discrimination laws (Chapter 5) and equal pay laws (Chapter 4), with education policy (Chapter 6) and child care policy (Chapter 7) as supplements. The presumption underlying policies in these areas was/is that women become equal to men when and only when they have equal access to the labour market. Antidiscrimination laws and affirmative action have women's labour force participation as their goal. Equal pay laws and their derivatives, equal pay for work of equal value or comparable worth, address their fair treatment by the market. Educational reforms aim to better prepare girls for labour force participation. Child care provisions aim to facilitate women's engagement in paid labour.

It is interesting to reflect upon the subsumption of reforms like these beneath the rubric 'status of women'. Just what kind of a problem is 'lack of status'? While some might conclude that the term was meant simply to highlight legal status, Lee Rainwater (1974a:

215), writing in the period under consideration, specifies the link with a Weberian notion of 'social estimation of honour' and how this impacts upon 'self-realizing possibilities of individuals'. In this understanding, 'women' was characterized as a group lacking in social status and this status was to be achieved through participation in paid labour. That social honour and self-actualization were possible only through labour force participation was implied, if not spelt out. This characterization of 'women's inequality' as a labour market phenomenon has become so much a part of the thinking about the subject that it is difficult to think beyond it. The most common indicators of 'equality' are rates of labour force participation, accompanied by comparative pay rates and job segregation rates, both linked directly to labour market status. As a specific example, Wendy Weeks (1996: 81) describes how the Gender Equality Indicators produced by the Office for the Status of Women in Australia focus on women as citizen workers. The language which talks about 'women as a national resource to be tapped' and women's need for financial independence sounds like so much common sense. Though many feminists at different times have insisted that important structural changes, including the 'sharing' of domestic responsibilities with men, would need to accompany equal pay laws and the like, to suggest, as I am doing, that this particular problematization of 'women's inequality' requires scrutiny may sound like heresy.

Allow me here to hint at the case to be developed in this part of the book, by asking what is left unproblematized by formulating 'women's inequality' as lack of access to the labour force. Asking what remains unproblematized in different problem representations is, as outlined in the Introduction, a key focus in a What's the Problem? analysis. For one, such a formulation neatly ignores the numbers of women who have long had access to labour market participation, and who have not been 'freed' by the experience. This is emphatically so for women in so-called underdeveloped or Third World countries. The seemingly obvious equation of 'liberation' and 'labour force participation' bypasses questions of class and colonialism. The suggestion that labour force participation is a necessary 'good' also leaves unaddressed the 'good' of the lives we lead when we are not in paid labour. Despite all the rhetoric about reconciling family responsibilities and paid labour in many current policy proposals (see Chapter 5), the emphasis remains upon minimizing the former in order to maximize the latter, or upon transforming the former into marketable activities. Ruth Levitas (1996: 18) emphasizes that this ignores 'the fact that society is – and certainly should be – more than a market'. The equation of 'women's equality' with 'labour force participation' also ignores or subsumes questions of violence and sexual exploitation, and how women's bodies are policy targets in ways men's bodies are not.

Feminists active in the 1960s insisted that a whole range of issues, focusing upon violence and bodily integrity, be included in the 'equality' agenda. To an extent they were successful, as we will see in Chapters 8, 9 and 10, which deal respectively with abortion, domestic violence and sexual harassment. Asking in each case What's the Problem (represented to be)?, we will identify links with the labour market problematization and how this affects issue representation in ways that limit change. Other problematizations which leave these problems entrenched will also be examined. It would be a nonsense to suggest that the sole limitation to the agenda addressing 'women's inequality' is the focus on labour market participation. Just as it is inadequate to see 'women's inequality' as due to their lack of access to paid labour, it would be inadequate to trace the limitations of the agenda to this characterization of the 'problem'. Rather, we need to break out of monocausal formulations of problems wherever they appear. Monocausal explanations suggest simple 'solutions' and this, I will argue, is part of the problem.

Let us take a moment to explore the implications of a problem characterized as *'women's* inequality'. Of necessity, this imposes a man/woman frame and I will be drawing attention to problems with this framing throughout the chapters to follow. Most obviously, and as a number of feminist authors have argued, this framing takes as the measure of success the status of men (Bacchi, 1990; Eisenstein, 1988). So, we are encouraged to think, women will be liberated when they have work conditions like men, or pay comparable to similar groups of men. It is difficult in this framing to challenge the appropriateness of those work conditions or those male pay rates. There is also an unexpressed assumption that women are all equally 'unequal' and hence that measures to address the needs of some will address the needs of all. Within the last decade, a number of feminists have been at pains to draw attention to the ways in which this configuration of the problem ignores the class, race, sexual orientation, ability and age differences among women. Imposing a man/woman frame may then leave a whole range of issues unproblematized. Some of these will be highlighted in the chapters to follow.

If, as I argue, the characterization of the 'problem' of 'women's inequality' as a labour market problem is lacking in its explanatory value, some may ask how this characterization has gained its ascendancy. Though this is not the primary focus of this book which, as explained in the Introduction, is looking to the *effects* of particular problem representations, a few words on the subject are necessary. Looking to causes is an increasingly unpopular theoretical exercise, not least because of the tendency to oversimplify. The tendency to demonize must also be resisted. None the less, it seems apparent that economic conditions in the 1960s suited a configuration of 'women's inequality' as a labour market problem. Western democracies were experiencing boom economic conditions and there were fears expressed about labour shortages. Women then could be 'liberated', all the while solving an impending economic crisis. In subsequent decades, with recession, unemployment and restructuring, women suited ideally the need for flexible, meaning part-time, labour. The focus on the needs of the market in the formulation of the 'problem' of 'women's inequality' is not therefore unsurprising. The needs of the market helped shape the characterization of the problem. The fact that this characterization matched a feminist insistence on the desirability of women's economic independence guaranteed its dominance.

From the 1960s and on to today, feminists have highlighted the links between women's oppression and their financial dependence on men. The achievement of financial *independence* seemed to be and continues to appear a logical goal. Social structures, currently in place, penalize the dependant, and many of these are women. Still, we need to think through the full implications of a model of human existence predicated on 'independence'. Some of us will never achieve that status. Children and the elderly will always need forms of support. What is achieved by a model calling for independence? Are other models available and untested? The implication of this discussion is not that feminist mobilizing had no effect on policy, nor that feminist analyses were simply co-opted. Rather the point is to draw attention to the shape of reforms and what they leave out. Drawing attention to the implications and limitations of problem representations, which is what a What's the Problem? approach is intended to do, in no way diminishes the efforts of those who have campaigned for change and won. Rather the point is to press home the need to continue to analyse our 'victories' to see what remains unchallenged.

Some may find it odd that a chapter on welfare regimes is not included in this part of the book. This is not simply because the topic is so well covered by other feminist authors (Lewis, 1993; Sainsbury, 1994, 1996). The reason for its exclusion is that this was *not* an area which was targeted to 'achieve' something called 'women's equality'. In fact, the converse is true. Welfare policies have embedded within them assumptions about women's traditional roles. The move to 'equality' has meant removing these assumptions (Shaver, 1993). Where this shift has occurred, the model of equality introduced is premised on the independent male worker, substantiating the argument that 'women's equality' is equated with a model of independence and self-sufficiency achieved through labour force participation. This agenda suits political regimes intent on reducing welfare spending. It is no coincidence that a primary target is single mothers, with the goal of getting them off welfare and into paid labour. The presumption in each case is the same – dependence is bad (see Fraser and Gordon, 1994), independence is good. The linking theme then is the way in which 'women's inequality' became characterized as a 'problem' of their dependence, a problem which would be resolved by their participation as 'equals' in the labour force.

It may have occurred to some readers that, as with the 'problem' of pornography mentioned in the Introduction, there are vocal sections of the population who do *not* voice concern about 'women's inequality', who do not see it as a problem. There are also strong and vociferous *critics* of women's increasing labour force participation – groups like R.E.A.L. Women in Canada, Women Who Want To Be Women (now called Endeavor Forum) in Australia, and groups calling themselves 'pro-family'. While it is critical to reflect upon the nature of their challenge to the problem representation described above, their existence does not wish away the numerous pieces of legislation, the equal pay laws, the anti-sex discrimination acts, the education policies which *create* the problem of women's inequality as 'absence from the labour force'. At the same time I do not wish, by challenging this characterization of the problem, to be seen to be endorsing the views of these groups. Drawing attention to the inadequacies of this characterization, showing for example how it reduces family responsibilities to 'burdens' to be 'relieved', in no way suggests an endorsement of the traditional division of domestic responsibilities – which these groups invariably endorse.

The purpose of a What's the Problem? approach is to unpack problem representations in order to see why change takes place in certain ways, but not in others, or not at all. It is a tool to be applied to every area of analysis and to our own thinking. Some doubtless will challenge its utility. It will be described as utopian, as unconnected to the realities of women's lives. On the contrary, I insist that it is possible to use What's the Problem? to promote policies which avoid *some* pitfalls. It makes those of us who wish to use it sensitive to the problem representations which underlie current policies and to the problem representations which underlie our own policy recommendations, problem representations which may not be immediately visible to us. Of course, it is completely possible that some feminist reformers may be aware of the limitations of the problem representations in their proposals but press on regardless, for pragmatic reasons. But for others, thinking about problem representations in the way recommended here produces insights which are sometimes disconcerting, and sometimes downright disturbing. That seems all the more reason to endorse its use.

4

PAY EQUITY: ON WHOSE TERMS?

The first chapter in this section looks at equal pay because, in the modern period following the Second World War, this was the first area in which legislative reforms targeted the 'problem' of 'women's inequality'. Given what has been said in the Preamble to this part of the book about the characterization of this problem as lack of access to the labour force, this is not surprising. We have already touched briefly on some of the limitations of this problem representation – the assumption that paid work produces freedom, the emphasis on independence at the expense of those who are and must be dependent, and the effects of a focus on jobs, displacing consideration of nonmarket activities. More will be said about these themes in due course.

In this chapter we will examine initially the genealogy of *equal pay for equal work*, the shape of the debate around this issue and what this tells us about the character of the reform. We will proceed to examine post-1980s proposals for *equal pay for work of equal value*, referred to as pay equity or comparable worth in some countries, explaining its relationship with the earlier demand for equal pay for equal work pure and simple. A focus on proposals permits, as explained in Part One of the book, the elaboration of problem representations which in turn provide insights into the kinds of claims being made and the effects these claims tend to produce. Here I will draw upon the extensive literature which examines comparable worth as a strategy for equalizing wages between women and men. As a guide to method, the chapter will offer examples of the kinds of questions which lead to the uncovering of problem representations. It will also emphasize the importance of asking questions about the effects of these representations. Finally, the chapter will suggest the usefulness of a What's the Problem (represented to be)? approach for feminist interrogations of policy. It needs to be noted that, while chronologically it makes sense to begin this part of the book with an examination of equal pay proposals, developments in this area become inextricably intertwined with discussions of discrimination and affirmative action. Because of these links in subject matter, there are necessarily a number of cross-references to the next chapter.

The size and complexity of the issues addressed in this chapter demand that a simple framework be provided to facilitate analysis of the contending positions. Here it is helpful to employ the distinction between concern and cause mentioned in the Introduction. Using the language of a What's the Problem? approach, in *equal pay for equal work* initiatives the problem (that is, the concern) is represented to be the unequal wages of individual men and women doing the same or similar work. This, as we will see below, became a concern largely because of the fear that 'cheap' women workers would be hired by unscrupulous employers, driving men out of 'their' jobs. By contrast, *comparable worth and pay equity* proposals target as the problem (that is, the concern) the *wage gap* between male-dominated and female-dominated occupations. They emphasize the existence of job segregation in the labour force, with women dominating numerically three low-paid occupational categories – clerk, sales and service personnel – and the low wages attached to these occupations. Feminists who endorse these reform approaches are motivated in large part by an increased recognition of poverty among women, commonly referred to as the feminization of poverty (Berger, 1986: 14; Hutner, 1986: 4–7). A number of other feminists and non-feminists concerned about 'women's poverty' prefer reforms such as affirmative action, designed to place women in higher paying jobs, or wage solidarity, designed to increase the wages of those at the bottom of the wage hierarchy, who tend to be women predominantly.

Different reform responses indicate a range of different causal explanations of the 'problem', and hence construct the problem quite differently. Equal pay for equal work initiatives which target wages for women and men doing similar work construct the problem as direct employer discrimination. Sex segregation of the labour force and the low wages attached to female-dominated occupations are not problematized in this approach. In pay equity accounts, by contrast, the problem is described as *wage* discrimination, rather than *employment* discrimination (see Burton et al., 1987: 27–8). The problem is represented to be devaluation, either conscious or by tradition, of 'women's work' relative to 'men's work'. As we will see shortly, pay equity legislation constructs the problem as either incorrect evaluation of all jobs or as undervaluation of women-dominated jobs.

Equal pay for equal work initiatives imply, by lack of discussion, that the sex segregation of the labour force and the low wages attached to female-dominated occupations are due to women's 'choices'. There is a presumption that women take up jobs which are less demanding in terms of 'skill' or time commitments due to domestic responsibilities. In this account, the lower wages in women's jobs become the result of their lower human capital. Those who look to affirmative action or equal opportunity for change also accept that women are trapped in 'dead-end' jobs, but they describe *employment* discrimination as structural, not direct and individual. Wage solidarity advocates (a shorthand for those who endorse a range of strategies which target the wages of those at the bottom of the wage hierarchy) agree with

affirmative action advocates that the problem is structural employment discrimination, but are more concerned with exploitation of
all workers, not just women. Pay equity advocates, in contrast with
these analyses, want to challenge the view that women are paid low
wages because the work they do is low skilled or less demanding.
Instead, they contend that women's work is low paid because women
do it.

Those who accept one of these versions of the problem sometimes
contend that other versions misread the situation and hence will
cause more harm than good. For example, some of those who
endorse versions of affirmative action and equal opportunity argue
that we need measures which impel employers to advance women
into higher status and higher paying jobs. They fear that comparable
worth will freeze job segregation patterns, leaving women content
with their current jobs and in some accounts (see Paul, 1989: 7)
inadvertently increasing female unemployment. On the other side,
some pay equity advocates suggest that reforms like affirmative
action will only assimilate women into male job categories and will
never recognize the value of the work women in the main tend to do.
Those who propose campaigning for a higher minimum wage or
other reforms which target the wages of those at the bottom of the
wage hierarchy believe that focusing upon job comparison, which
necessarily accompanies proposals to revalue upwards 'women's
skills', will serve only to strengthen employer control over job classifications and wages, and reinforce job hierarchies (Lewis, 1988). I am
not suggesting that feminist reformers are always at loggerheads over
approaches to reform; most indeed are willing to countenance the
need for multiple forms of intervention. Still, the tensions over problem representation which I here identify are sometimes sharpened
when feminists become wedded to a particular approach. This issue
will be revisited in the conclusion to this chapter.

Schematically, this produces the following mapping of problem
representations in the area of equal pay:

1   Equal pay for equal work legislation: concern – women's lower
    wages in 'men's jobs'; cause – direct employer discrimination.
2   Equal pay for work of equal value (comparable worth or pay
    equity) legislation: concern – the wage gap between female-
    dominated and male-dominated occupations; cause – (a) incorrect
    evaluation of all jobs, (b) undervaluation of women's jobs.
3   Affirmative action legislation: concern – women's lack of access
    to high paid and high status jobs; cause – structural discrimi-
    nation (see Chapter 5).
4   Higher minimum wages and forms of wage solidarity: concern –
    women's lower wages *tout court*; cause – exploitation of workers.

Equal Pay for Equal Work

I mentioned in the Preamble to this part of the book that reforms in the area of equal pay were some of the very earliest reforms indicating the arrival of 'women's inequality' as a 'social problem'. Discussions about what remuneration women ought to receive when they engaged in paid labour occurred in the middle nineteenth century and attracted a good deal of interest even in that period. The framing of the issue at that time stayed with us until the 1970s. This was a framing which said that the problem was that women who worked *alongside men* in some occupations were being paid less than the men and that this was inappropriate. Some critics of the practice said it was unjust. The fact that these jobs – where women worked alongside men – were few and far between was not at this stage represented to be part of the problem. In fact, the congregation of women in a range of occupations where men were almost completely absent was seen to be entirely 'natural'.

Here it is necessary to reflect upon the variety of positions taken in these discussions and the reasons for them. It is also necessary to remain sensitive to context. A number of women activists in this pre-1960s period in Britain and the United States campaigned to secure equal pay for equal work. One example is the Women's Bureau in the United States which campaigned for equal pay for equal work throughout the interwar years. Others, however, opposed equal pay for women in jobs where they competed with men because they feared that this would mean simply that women would be driven from those jobs. Some others thought that this would be desirable. The British Fabian, Beatrice Webb, for example, in her Minority Report to the War Cabinet in 1919, defended equal pay on the grounds that it would lead to female unemployment because women were less efficient workers, but this was no bad thing since women could always return to the home (Lewis, 1984: 203). At the same time a major impetus for equal pay for equal work came from male unionists who had precisely as their intention driving women from their trades (Gregory and Duncan, 1981: 407 in Hutner, 1986: 22). The assumption was that women were indeed less efficient workers and that, if employers were required to pay them a full wage, they would clearly prefer men. A number of women reformers, who invested their hope for a better standard of living for numbers of women in higher wages *for their husbands*, agreed with this analysis. Lady Emilia Dilke, who headed the British Women's Trade Union League in the 1890s, welcomed minimum wage legislation for women because 'it would stop women dragging down wages and raise male incomes, thus making the work of married women unnecessary' (Lewis, 1984: 201).

We can see in these differences of opinion that, within the framework described above – what to do about women working in 'men's' jobs – some women activists put the more contemporary feminist line that women simply deserved the same wages and damn the consequences. Others were highly sensitive to the fallout for some working women which almost certainly would accompany this reform. And still others, in this case a male sympathizer, Victor Gollancz (1917: 217), expressed the view that the real interest of working women was not in their own wages but 'in the general wage and more particularly in the wages of their men folk'. For some, unequal pay for women was a problem; for others, it was a necessary evil. Among those who considered unequal pay a problem were those who hoped equal pay would *reduce* women's labour force participation. The real problem, in their view, was not sex inequality but low wages for many men and their families. This tension between women reformers who placed a priority on working-class solidarity and those who targeted women's wage inequality appears in a modified form in disagreements between contemporary wage solidarity and pay equity advocates (discussion below).

Two court cases in Australia clarify the parameters within which the issue was being considered in the early twentieth century. Australia had initiated a number of progressive reforms in this period, winning the title of 'Social Laboratory of the World'. In 1907 the Deakinite Liberal judge Henry Bourne Higgins instituted in the Harvester judgment a 'basic family wage' of seven shillings per day. The amount was supposed to provide the basic necessities for a man, his wife and approximately three children. Women were presumed to have no dependants and could thus be paid less. How much less was decided in the subsequent *Mildura Fruit Pickers* decision. In 1912, the Rural Workers' Union put in a claim for men and women casual workers in the fruit picking industry to be paid the same rate. The Union was disturbed that, because women could be paid less, they were being hired *instead* of men. Higgins generally agreed that this was a problem. He decided in the *Mildura Fruit Pickers* decision that, if a job was a *man's* job, that is mainly filled by men, an equal wage would have to be paid to women but, if a job were mainly a *woman's* job, filled by women, a *woman's* rate would be set and this would generally be 54 per cent of the basic wage. This decision set the pattern for the next 60 years. A barrier was erected between men's work and women's work. As long as this barrier went unchallenged, equal pay for women was a mixed blessing and a dubious rallying cry. The problem, as set out clearly in the Mildura decision, was not represented to be unfairness to women but *the undercutting of male wage rates*. And for many women, especially for those who depended on a male wage, doubtless the vast majority of women in this period, this was a very real problem indeed.

But what remained unproblematized in this particular representation of the problem? First, there was that very divide between men's jobs and women's jobs. Second, there was the assumption that all women were and would stay dependants and have none of their own. Third, there was the assumption that if the family, read husband's, wage rose, dependent wives would necessarily benefit. The presumption that women, or at least a particular class of women, ought not to participate in waged labour and that men needed to be encouraged to fulfil 'their' family-support obligations underlies the whole problem representation. Higgins put this presumption into words: '[F]ortunately for society, the greater number of breadwinners still are men. The women are not all dragged from the homes to work while the men loaf at home' (in Ryan and Conlon, 1989: 95).

Jane Jenson (1986, 1987) alerts us to the importance of context in relation to equal pay. She shows how in France women's high workforce participation from the turn of the century, combined with pronatalist concerns, produced policies, including maternity leave, tailored to allow women to combine paid work and maternity. While not wanting to underestimate the importance of the struggles of women workers around the issue of equal pay from the 1930s (Hoskyns, 1996: 54), the problem targeted in the French government's early (1950s) endorsement of equal pay was family poverty. The goal was to save the family while, or even through, allowing married women to engage in paid labour. Moreover, the motivation of protecting 'men's jobs', which we have seen in Britain and Australia, was replicated in France: '[I]f capital could no longer pay women less than men, women would not threaten men's jobs' (Jenson, 1986: 37). This is the context which needs to be remembered when examining equal pay initiatives in Western democracies.

Changing workplace demographics set the scene for the introduction of equal pay for equal work legislation. Women were joining the workforce in greater numbers. The concern that equal pay would drive women out of some occupations was a lesser, though lingering, concern. And, for many people, the idea that it was preferable or even possible for a family to live on a single, male breadwinner's wage had begun to wane. For many of these people the wage gap, which had begun to appear in assessments of women's labour market location, had to be addressed. Calculations showed that, in the United States for example, the median wage for full-time women workers was 60 per cent of that for full-time men workers (Berger, 1986: 24). In the lead-up to the Equal Pay Act of 1963, amendments called repeatedly for the extension of the reform to consider equal pay for work of equal value (Hutner, 1986: 27), a phrase used in the

International Labour Organisation Convention 100 (1951). However, the Act stated explicitly that equal pay would be awarded only in those cases where women did the same or similar work as men.

Here it is useful to look at the precise shape of the 1963 Equal Pay Act to tease out the problem representation it contains and the limitations in this representation. The limited scope of the legislation is indicated in the four defences made available to employers for unequal pay practices – seniority, merit, differences in quantity or quality of production, and 'a differential based on any other factor other than sex' (Hutner, 1986: 13). These four defences were retained in Title VII of the Civil Rights Act through the Bennett amendment. The first three defences provide ample room to differentiate among the value of workers and many would argue that these factors disguise forms of sex bias. For example, meanings of merit are contestable rather than objective, and historically have been defined by and for male incumbents of jobs (see Chapter 5). The fourth defence, 'a differential based on any other factor other than sex', opened the door for employers to argue that they were setting their pay rates according to what the market had decided was appropriate; to do otherwise would put them out of business. In *Christenson* v. *Iowa* (563 F. 2d 353 [8th Cir. 1977]) the Eighth Circuit Court of Appeals held that market factors could be considered by employers 'when the work classifications are *different*' (Heen, 1984: 210). The Supreme Court (Section 703[h], 42 U.S.C. §2000e–2[h]), in passing the Bennett amendment, specified that the fourth defence was added to the Equal Pay Act because of 'a concern that *bona fide* job evaluation systems used by American businesses would otherwise be disrupted'. Elaine Sorenson (1994: 134) notes that appellate courts are accepting market forces as a legitimate defence in Title VII wage discrimination cases. Put simply, this means that assumptions about the value of women's work already present in market rates cannot be touched through equal pay for equal work legislation or, for that matter, through equal pay for work of equal value legislation as it is currently conceptualized. Legislation which refuses to problematize 'market rates' assumes that these are either fair or unavoidable.

The way in which market forces are being accepted as defences against the charge of sex discrimination highlights the different meanings of discrimination being used in discussions of wage differentials. Elaine Sorenson (1994: 43) explains that different disciplines define discrimination differently, and that '[E]conomists generally define discrimination as the pay difference between two groups of workers that is not accounted for by productivity differences.' In this kind of explanation, it is accepted that worker productivity can be assessed objectively and that workers in many cases 'choose' to undertake 'less productive' work. For women, it is commonly argued that, due to the demands of domestic responsibilities, women invest less in the 'skills' required to undertake 'demanding' work and also 'choose' jobs which place fewer demands on their time and commitment. Such human capital explanations for different wage rates analyse the impact of age and education on wages and estimate 'the portion of the wage gap that is related to differences in these characteristics among men and women workers' (Hallock, 1993: 28). Discrimination is held to be the difference in wages *not* accounted for by human capital explanations (see Gregory and Ho, 1985: 8–9).

In tune with this kind of analysis, equal pay for equal work legislation sees nothing problematic about the lower wages accorded women in 'women's jobs'. The assumption here is that these jobs demand less skill and should be paid less. A study prepared for the Economic Council of Canada (Boulet and Lavallée, 1984: 2–3) argued, for example, that 'the earnings gap between men and women is not necessarily an economic problem; it could be the result of different choices being made voluntarily'. Pat and Hugh Armstrong (1988: 74) capture concisely the problem representation in equal pay for equal work proposals – 'too many women with too few skills – and perhaps some employers who discriminated against them'. As they say, the problem was defined 'in terms of people, not jobs' (Armstrong and Armstrong, 1992: 297). Along similar lines, there is the assumption in human capital explanations that women 'naturally' assume responsibility for domestic needs. Human capital explanations, moreover, generally feel it appropriate to deny the relevance of family responsibilities to the determination of working conditions and job worth. For Steven Rhoads (1993: 256 fn 4), for example, '[W]hile taking time off to attend to sick children seems desirable from the perspective of society as a whole, employees who take more sick leave for whatever reason are less productive, and on either worth to the employer or job factor-based criteria they could be seen as deserving less pay.' Alternative definitions of discrimination draw attention to the way in which education levels and sex segregation of jobs reflect historical discrimination against women. In these accounts, 'discrimination is built into the factors that explain the gap' in human capital explanations (Hallock, 1993: 28), including the assumption that the market does not need to recognize the 'private' lives of workers.

The understanding of discrimination embedded in equal pay for equal work legislation therefore served, rather than challenged, the rule of the market. The target was the discrimination of individual employers who deliberately paid women less for work judged similar to the work male employees performed. The concern was that such inequity would cause unrest in the workplace largely because men workers would be displaced by cheap female labour. As Debra Lewis (1988: 23) maintains, both trade unions and governments were 'motivated primarily by their desire to protect male workers rather than by an interest in the economic rights of women'. It is debatable to what extent equal pay for work of equal value claims seriously broaden the parameters of what is contested (problematized) and accepted (unproblematized) in equal pay for equal work reforms. I proceed to examine this question in the next section.

Equal Pay for Work of Equal Value

ILO Convention 100 (McCrudden, 1986: 399), passed in 1951, first used the language of equal pay for work of equal value. This phrase altered dramatically the problem representation in the area under consideration. The alteration of the problem representation, it should be noted, was quite deliberate. Comparative wage statistics indicated that equal pay for equal work legislation, where it existed, had not altered significantly the wage gap between women and men. Those who wished to address this phenomenon pointed out that the reason this was so was that jobs were dramatically segregated by sex, with women clustering in three low-paid categories, mainly clerical, service and sales. Because the equal pay principle accepted, indeed was premised upon, this segregation, it left the pay rates in these occupations untouched. In addition, it was becoming apparent to some women activists that, even within occupations, job categories, which ensured that women and men would be seen to be performing different work, were making it difficult for women to achieve equal pay. The phrase 'equal pay for work of equal value' was meant to draw attention to this fact and to insist that, regardless of categorization, women ought to be paid according to the value of their labour.

It is important to remember that, by the time of the appearance of the first equal pay for work of equal value claims (hereafter referred to as pay equity claims for ease of reference), understandings of discrimination had become contentious and had evolved to a certain extent. The next chapter describes the advent of the recognition of indirect discrimination which attempted to target for change structures and practices which discriminated against women, even if there was no intent to discriminate. The concept of structural or systemic discrimination began to be used to capture this broader understanding of discrimination. Affirmative action reforms represent a proactive response to structural discrimination, encouraging women to move into jobs traditionally dominated by men. Pay equity, by demanding re-evaluation upwards of the work women perform in female-dominated jobs, also constructs the problem to be structural discrimination. But, in some accounts, pay equity indicates a degree of dissatisfaction with some of the assumptions and effects of affirmative action proposals. The suggestion here is that, instead of seeing the problem as a matter of getting women into men's jobs, which appears to be the goal of affirmative action, the value of the work women already do needs to be recognized.

It is possible to see in this interpretation of pay equity a reflection of developments in feminist theory in this period. I am referring here to writings by authors like Adrienne Rich (1976), Nancy Chodorow (1978) and Carol Gilligan (1982), who can be clustered in a category of 'pro-woman' writers. All these authors stated directly or implied that it was time to look anew at the male standard of work. It was suggested that the aggressiveness and careerism associated with this model were undesirable templates for human development, and that women's traditional 'virtues' of caring and family-centredness ought to replace them. In sympathy with this analysis, pay equity advocates insist that women's work, which tends often to be caring work, ought to be given due recognition. There is also the feeling that, in affirmative action schemes, women are being held responsible for change, that they are represented to be the problem (de Bruijn, 1997: 155). Rather, according to pay equity advocates, we need a way to problematize men's styles of work.

Defenders of equal pay for work of equal value (Hutner, 1986; Remick, 1984) argue that the characteristics associated with women's work tend to be ignored or devalued. For example, they point out that jobs which require heavy lifting, when men do them, are recognized as demanding jobs, but 'skills' like manual dexterity, associated with many women's occupations, are commonly ignored. They direct attention to jobs like secretary, described as lacking complexity simply because the wide variety of tasks performed is unacknowledged. They emphasize how more value is assigned to work with machines than to work with people, noting that women are more likely to cluster in people-serving jobs. Some of this analysis insists that women's 'caring skills' are being ignored, often because these are considered to be 'natural' to women rather than acquired. To counter this assumption, it is claimed that women 'learn' how to care while fulfilling domestic obligations (Hartmann et al., 1985: 28).

To get these kinds of claims onto the political agenda, pay equity reformers turned to job evaluation as a tool for job comparison. These reformers were well aware that job evaluation was a well-established management tool for rationalizing and justifying job and wage classifications; however, they felt that it provided a means to identify the ways in which women's 'skills' are unrecognized. A number of job evaluation approaches are available for use and these construct the problem quite differently. Policy-capturing models (Rhoads, 1993: 20–1), which use employers' internal job evaluation schemes, represent the problem to be inconsistency in the application of the employers' own standards. *A priori* schemes, which delineate job factors and assign them points – the Hay standard (Burton et al., 1987: Chapter 2) is the most commonly used – construct the problem as under- or overevaluation of jobs across the board. The problem here is still constructed as inconsistency, but of a more deep-seated kind. In Johanna Brenner's (1987: 451) words, the demand for equal value 'is essentially a campaign to rectify distortions of the market'.

Job evaluation schemes which assign points to factors are based on the assumption that 'jobs dissimilar in nature can be compared in terms of knowledge, skill, effort, responsibility and working conditions, and that jobs equivalent in value in these terms would be paid equally' (American Association of University Women, 1987: 5). Claims like this one accept at some level that different kinds of jobs deserve different pay. As one woman interviewed for the study into pay equity by the Vancouver Women's Research Centre (Lewis, 1988: 34, 47) pointedly put it: '[T]he reason why I won't use the phrase "equal pay for work of equal value" any more is that it accepts the premise that different work has different value. Which I don't accept.' Another woman made the same case: '[I]f you really look at it, what's equal to what? What we're really saying is that a clerical worker is as good as a garbage man. Why isn't a garbage man as good as a doctor?'

This last quote alludes to a key limitation in the problem representation in pay equity proposals. Every legislative response to date targets single establishments. This, as mentioned previously, constructs the problem to be employer inconsistency of one form or another. This problem representation has a number of effects. For one, it prevents comparisons with jobs outside the particular institution. Attempts to draw attention to broad patterns in the undervaluation of women's jobs are thereby thwarted. Some authors (Findlay, 1991: 81) point out how focusing upon single employer establishments means difficulty finding male comparators, making it impossible to touch the wages of many women involved in women-dominated jobs. There is also the question of which men are to be used as the basis of the comparison. Since the problem is represented to be the difference between the wages assigned men and women, employers are free to choose particular men as the basis of the comparison. Employers confine assessments to comparisons between women clerks and men blue-collar workers, or between women clerks and low-paid Black men workers (McDermott, 1992: 26), but do not compare women clerks and men managers. A What's the Problem? approach suggests that this is not an implementation difficulty but an effect of the construction of the problem as male versus female wage rates. The construction of the problem as the wage gap between men and women makes it difficult, if not impossible, to problematize the wages men receive, be these high or low (Armstrong and Armstrong, 1992:

302; Lewis, 1988: 27). These, by implication, are assumed to represent 'value'. The way in which the man–woman frame employed in this analysis bypasses issues of race will be taken up again in the conclusion to this chapter.

A number of authors (Brenner, 1987; Lewis, 1988; Warskett, 1990, 1993) have pointed to the dangers in employing job evaluation – that it in effect strengthens employer control of job classifications and reinforces job hierarchies. The point here is that any scheme which details what is required in jobs gives knowledge to employers which can then be used to demand certain kinds of job performance (Armstrong and Armstrong, 1990: 124). Isabella Bakker (1991: 256) makes the point that employers' increasing knowledge of job content may facilitate a downward re-classification of jobs. Moreover, it has been argued that employers like job evaluation because the existence of formalized job classifications with wages allocated to different job descriptions lessens the scope for collective bargaining (Acker, 1989: 168). This claim is supported by the fact that pay equity as a reform is popular in places like the United States, where trade unions are weak. In Sweden (Acker, 1991: 248), until recently, women reformers have been able to rely upon wage solidarity schemes to increase women's wages, since women dominate the lower wage scales. It is only since the swing to the right in Swedish politics and the consequent weakening of trade union structures that women reformers have expressed an interest in pay equity. Ontario's path-breaking Pay Equity legislation introduced in 1987, which targeted private as well as public enterprises, contained an important silence on this issue – whether or not compliance with the legislation pre-empted the possibility of strikes (McDermott, 1991: 127). It is this history which has made some Australian feminists (see Ryan, 1987 cited in Burton et al., 1987: vii) wary of 'comparable worth', high-lighting the contingent and context-dependent nature of reform efforts.

In places where the focus is on factor point evaluations across the board, some jobs may be found to be over- rather than undervalued. This possibility has produced hostility and opposition from some men workers and their unions (Acker, 1989: 168). Ontario's 1987 legislation prohibited reducing men's wages but said nothing to prevent employers diverting part of general wage increases to pay equity adjustments. As Carl Cuneo (1991: 55) says, this silence 'perhaps goes a long way to explain why business, after so vociferously opposing proactive pay equity legislation, has now, on the whole, gone along with it.'[1] Silences like this one are partly responsible for the way in which job evaluation pits worker against worker. In practice, the refusal to lower men's wages has meant that compromises have been struck, extending salary increases to all undervalued jobs rather than targeting female-dominated jobs (Sorenson, 1994: 75). This, of course, is possible only where comparable worth is defined to mean the need to re-value all jobs, defining the problem as inaccurate assessment of job values overall. Hence, some of the most deleterious effects of pay equity derive from particular framings of the reform, framings made explicit in the proposals. As an alternative, Pat Armstrong and Mary Cornish (1997: 81) outline a wage line approach to job evaluation which allows 'relative comparisons based on a line plotted through wage rates for job comparison'. This approach targets not all jobs, but the discrepancy between female-dominated and male-dominated occupations, reducing 'hostility among workers by eliminating or reducing the need to compare specific jobs'.

Some authors (Blum, 1991; Magid, 1997) have pointed out that pay equity plays an important role in mobilizing women workers on their own behalf. Michael McCann (1994: 295, 282), with his emphasis upon the 'practical dynamics of social movement organization', describes, for example, how pay equity battles 'greatly fortified organizational ties among women workers and their allies'. While this is an important effect, the increase in tensions between women and men workers caused by some framings of the 'problem' suggests the importance of paying close attention to the shape of proposals. At the same time, it needs to be acknowledged that pay equity legislation is likely to benefit some women rather than others, usually those who are unionized (Armstrong and Cornish, 1997: 71) or those higher up the wage ladder. The reform therefore tends to increase wage differentials among women (Armstrong and Armstrong, 1991: 117); immigrant women are least likely to benefit (Armstrong and Armstrong, 1992: 308). Reductions in the wage gap between women and men hide the fact that earnings are becoming more unequal among women.

Representing the problem to be job segregation and the wage gap between female-dominated and male-dominated occupations also makes it difficult to recognize and factor in the impact of restructuring which has characterized Western economies in the past ten years. Pat Armstrong (1996) points out that men's jobs are becoming similar to women's jobs, and similarly 'bad' to the extent that they are insecure and have few promotion prospects. Any decrease in the wage gap between women and men, says Armstrong, is likely to be a result of a harmonizing down of men's wages. As a consequence, women are likely to find themselves equal in poverty (Bakker, 1991: 271). And, while job segregation rates may be reduced as a result of some of these changes, one suspects that the increase of men's representation in 'bad jobs' is not what pay equity reformers have in mind as a goal. This notion of 'bad jobs' directs us to consideration of important differences of opinion between pay equity and wage solidarity advocates about whether the problem is the devaluing of women's 'skills' or the confining of women to 'dead-end jobs'. The ways in which these views intersect with understandings of skill need to be understood in any attempt to reflect upon the effects of different problem representations.

Skill and Work

Pay equity as a reform was in large part a response to the common characterization of women's attributes as natural and hence as undeserving of wage recognition. For example, in one reevaluation study for salaried New York public employees (Rhode, 1993: 266), child care workers were contrasted to zoo keepers and the latter were deemed to deserve recognition for the 'learned' skills involved in caring for wild animals. By contrast, women were deemed to be 'natural' child carers. In response, pay equity advocates insisted that the 'skills' of child care were 'learned' also, often in the process of women performing domestic labour in their own homes (Hartmann et al., 1985: 28), and hence should be acknowledged.

As Wendy Bastalich[2] argues, the felt need to justify women's 'skills' as 'learned' buys into a vision of human nature which is problematic and has a number of regressive effects. The implication here is that individual human beings are responsible for acquiring skills and that this should form the basis of the evaluation of their work. Hence, while pay equity focuses on jobs rather than individuals, individuals remain the ones responsible for *earning their place in a job category*. The underlying premise is that individual workers are at some level responsible for the wages they receive because these depend upon employee 'skills'. This same premise provides the backdrop to the claim that the unemployed need training or retraining, or that the key to international competitiveness is multi-skilling (Butler, 1998). In each case individuals are held responsible for their designation as either unemployable or underemployable. This produces subjects intent on skills acquisition who would be likely to blame themselves, rather than the structures, if they fail to achieve. Skills discourse is thus heavily implicated in the kind of self-regulation which interests governmentality scholars (see Chapter 2). Given this, feminist reformers need to negotiate carefully how they choose to engage with it. The problem may not then be the obscuring of skill, as Joan Acker (1989: 212) suggests, but the very notion of skill.

I am not implying that feminists can or should refuse to use the concept 'skill'. This is hardly an option given that it is taken for granted as the way of measuring human talent. I am suggesting that, given its key role in creating self-regulating, work-motivated subjects, we try to find ways to undo or minimize some of its effects. The invocation of women's 'caring skills' can be seen as one attempt to do just this. However, characterizing 'nurturing' as a 'woman's skill' produces a number of undesirable effects. First, it constructs men's work as 'uncaring' and threatens to homogenize the categories 'women' and 'women's work', locking women into traditional representations of what women should be. Second, it leads to the necessary conclusion that indeed we wish to put a monetary value on care and consideration, encouraging what Arlie Hochschild (1983) describes as the 'commercialization of human feeling'. Consider, for example, the suggestion by Davies and Rosser (1986: 103) that what is needed is the formalizing of 'caring work', seeing it 'as part of the job rather than as a quality of the person'.

Here it is interesting to see how similar sorts of claims can be mounted in ways which attempt to alter fundamentally job content. Burton et al. (1987: 90–4) offer a reworking of the category Human Relations skill which does more than suggest that women ought to be rewarded for caring work. They point out that responsibility for people is not as highly regarded as responsibility for material assets, 'yet it can be highly regarded if it involves motivating and controlling other people'. The problem then is not that 'working with people' is devalued; the problem is that 'working through other people in the pursuit of organisational objectives is highly valued, but working for people, or contributing to the quality of working relationships in other ways (more typical of female jobs) is not'. By drawing attention to the way in which 'the exercise of authority', 'working through and down the hierarchy', is highly rewarded while working 'laterally and up' is not, Burton and her colleagues are looking for a way to problematize the value accorded 'authority over others'. Their careful framing problematizes hierarchy, not the devaluing of care, and hence promises more in the way of transformative job relations.

The way in which skills are seen to be a desirable human achievement, accomplished through paid labour, also complicates attempts to get domestic responsibilities factored in or acknowledged in any way. I want to offer as an example the job factor 'working conditions'. This is the category constructed to allocate points to those who do work others consider unpleasant. Feminists have pointed out, correctly, that what is unpleasant work has been judged by the kinds of work men find unpleasant – dirty, heavy, etc. Some have tried to get acknowledgement that dealing with human waste, for example changing nappies in child care centres, qualifies as unpleasant. There has been mixed success in these efforts. Here, however, I want to make a different kind of point. The starting place for the recognition of working conditions is that they have nothing to do with what people do when they are not at work. The problem is represented to be *what people do at work*. Hence, when women receive lower wages, these are often seen as due to the fact that women receive 'non-monetary benefits' (Rhoads, 1993: 14) such as 'shorter commutes' or 'easier time off for personal reasons'. The suggestion that the *absence* of these 'benefits' should indeed be construed as making work 'unpleasant' and hence as *compensable factors* would be considered ludicrous. This example illustrates the entrenchment of the division between 'public' work and 'private' responsibilities in current understandings of the nature of work. Joan Acker (1989: 220–1) describes how reforms like pay equity which target wage setting assume a concept of 'a job' which is gendered because it 'already contains the sex-based division of labor and the separation between the public and private domains and assumes a particular organization of domestic life and social production'.

Alternatives to Pay Equity: Wage Solidarity Approaches

Wage solidarity schemes attempt to bypass the regressive effects attendant on schemes that involve job evaluation. As noted at the outset, wage solidarity approaches target 'women's poverty' as the problem. They see this poverty as due to women's location in poor paying jobs. To alleviate this poverty, reforms propose ways to raise the wages of those at the bottom of the wage hierarchy. Debra Lewis (1988: 113–27) produces a list of the schemes developed by Canadian wage solidarity reformers, including campaigning for a higher minimum wage, equal base rates, flat rate increases and the elimination of increment steps. She emphasizes that these schemes were designed in ways which refused job comparison as the basis of evaluation. In so doing, the declared purpose is to challenge both the notion that wages should be attached to certain kinds of jobs, and the presumption that employers should be the ones assigning value to jobs. The goal moreover is to try to flatten rather than to entrench job hierarchies.

According to Rosemary Warskett (1990: 58), a wage solidarity proponent, '[T]here is a dualism running through the literature on women's low pay and the wage gap':

> [O]ne position is that the skill of women's work is undervalued as compared to the work men traditionally do and, as a consequence, women are paid at a lower rate. In this case equal value is the prescribed strategy to raise women's pay. The other approach documents how women have been drawn into the most subordinate and degraded positions in the work

place with limited bargaining power, low pay and little opportunity for promotion into higher skilled jobs. Wage solidarity strategies which seek to raise the wages of the lowest paid and decrease the differentials between low and high paid workers are prescribed to address this problem.

Warskett (1993: 261) quotes from the LO, the union congress of blue-collar workers in Sweden, to explain the grounds for a wage solidarity strategy:

> [W]ork organisation in the firm must be developed so that it can adjust to the growing knowledge and experience of all workers, not via 'careerism' but through the development of work itself, a development that increases one's knowledge, broadens and deepens the range of tasks performed, and increases one's responsibility and authority (from Mahon, 1991: 309).

Warskett (1990: 59, 62) accepts Braverman's (1974) argument that 'capital, in striving to increase the appropriation of surplus value, had degraded and deskilled labor by separating conception and planning from the execution of tasks'. From this she accepts that 'skilled tasks are those needing control over self and/or over others' and that women 'are found in the most subordinate and controlled positions in the office'. She concludes that large numbers of women workers who 'perform "unskilled" work in the sense of being controlled and having little control over the tasks they perform . . . will not benefit from equal value'.

Warskett (1990: 63, 68) is keenly aware that 'defining tasks as skilled, semi-skilled and unskilled involves processes of power and struggle', and she admits that many men workers have been successful at maintaining an 'image of skill'. Women, she notes, will be found at the bottom of the wage hierarchy 'no matter how skilled or deskilled the job content may be in terms of self control'. She also accepts that women's jobs tend to demand more interpersonal or human relations 'skills' than men's jobs. On the other side, some pay equity advocates (see Acker, 1989: 103) are willing to talk about some women's work as 'unskilled'. For example, Acker claims that '[S]ome clerical work is certainly unskilled and deskilled; other clerical work is not.' On this last point, she notes 'the dispersion of supervisory tasks to lower levels' and the lack of recognition of these tasks. Anne Phillips and Barbara Taylor (1986: 55) also accept that '[O]bviously it is true that there are jobs which require training, and it is also true that women workers (as well as some men workers, especially Blacks or Asians) have generally been refused access to this training, ensuring their exclusion from areas of work requiring more knowledge and initiative.' Phillips and Taylor (1986: 59) acknowledge the relevance of Braverman (1974) and his 'deskilling' thesis.

So, to draw a sharp line between two distinct problem representations – one stressing women's location in 'unskilled jobs' and the
other emphasizing the undervaluing of 'women's skills' – misses
the overlap in the approaches. It also misses an important shared
assumption, that things called 'skills' exist. References to the desirability of 'increasing one's knowledge' (the quote above from LO)
and to some areas of work 'requiring more knowledge and initiative'
(Phillips and Taylor above) assume that, at some level, jobs and value
are attached to these criteria. And, it follows, workers would be wise
to pursue and acquire these criteria. We have seen already how pay
equity advocates work with a notion of 'skill' which in the end holds
workers responsible for proving their worth. Here we see that wage
solidarity claims also rest upon an assumption that there are things
called 'skills' which need to be acquired. All the problems discussed
earlier in connection to skills discourse in pay equity proposals,
hence, are applicable equally to wage solidarity approaches. I would
like to propose that the recognition that 'value is primarily determined by power, not by job content' (Armstrong and Armstrong,
1990: 124) means, of necessity, challenging both the suggestion that
jobs have intrinsic worth and that people are 'rewarded' for recognized 'skills'.

It is also difficult to address the relationship between paid work
and family responsibilities within wage solidarity approaches. Those
intent upon flattening the wage hierarchy through raising the wages
of the lowest paid generally pay little attention to the problems many
women face with simply getting that work done, due to the demands
placed upon them by family and other caring commitments. The
experience of Swedish feminists here is exemplary. Feminists there
have consistently attempted to reduce the working day, only to be
countered by men unionists who prefer the idea of a longer weekend.
Gender issues have difficulty working their way onto a wage
solidarity agenda (Bacchi, 1996: Chapter 6).

Conclusion

What sorts of conclusions are we to draw from this kind of analysis?
The point of the exercise – applying a What's the Problem? approach
to reform proposals in the area of wages and work – has been to bring
to the surface a consideration of the effects of different problem
representations. So, I have highlighted how equal pay for equal work
proposals assume a limited understanding of discrimination and
are unlikely to touch the underpayment of women's work. I have
also suggested that pay equity proposals necessarily employ job
evaluation as a means of comparing jobs, with all sorts of problematic

consequences. Wage solidarity proposals are also seen to accept conventional notions of job worth and the constructed separation between paid and unpaid work.

Some might suggest that an analysis like this paralyses reformers with the realization that everything they do buys into framings which minimize change. In contrast, I would like to suggest that the kind of scrutiny provided here assists in pinpointing what it is about particular proposals which disturbs us. In this chapter we have seen as examples: the way in which the acceptance of 'market forces' in determinations of equal pay excludes consideration of the discrimination operative in the market; how the targeting of separate institutions within pay equity legislation limits the impact of the legislation; how silences in Ontario's 1987 Pay Equity Act, regarding the right to strike and allowing employers to divert wage increases to make up pay equity adjustments, created the conditions for worker in-fighting. The same kind of analysis encourages reformers to make proposals which reduce or obviate some of the regressive effects which have been identified in some problem representations. I have mentioned the way in which a wage line approach reduces reliance on job evaluation and lessens friction among workers. I also described the way in which the careful framing by Burton et al. (1987: 90–4) broadens the category 'Human Relations skill' by challenging the value placed on hierarchy instead of appealing to a notion of 'caring skills'. For many women it will be enough of a victory that some women receive more money, and I do not wish to diminish the importance of this achievement.[3] My point rather is that teasing out the implications of different problem representations sharpens an awareness of the effects of the frameworks we adopt and encourages us to try to find proposals that diminish effects we want to discourage.

At the same time, the exercise highlights the need for a sensitivity to context. What works in one place at one time may not work elsewhere. Joan Acker (1989: 196) concludes, for example, that, in Oregon in the 1980s, constructing the problem as poverty relief served to accomplish more than equity agreements which set worker against worker. We mentioned earlier the context, the swing to the right politically, within which Swedish feminists are turning to pay equity (see Acker, 1991). The recognition that feminists are constrained by institutional and political factors should reduce the tendency to generalize about the appropriateness of particular reform approaches, which leaves the impression that feminists simply cannot agree about how to proceed (see Bacchi, 1990). The critical question, I would suggest, is not 'choosing' between reform instruments, say between campaigning for a higher minimum wage or a pay equity act, which is seldom an option, but working carefully within constraints to frame problems in ways that maximize gains and minimize losses.

Asking What's the Problem (represented to be)? also highlights the limitations in approaches that create separate 'social problems' and assign them to particular branches of the bureaucracy. Separate legislative instruments isolate 'problems' in problematic ways, for example separating race and gender issues in the formulation of pay equity. Along related lines, Patricia McDermott (1992) describes the limitations imposed by the separate targeting of pay equity and employment equity, the term used for affirmative action in Canada (Bacchi, 1996: Chapter 4). Such a separation allows employers to move women into job categories which have been constructed as higher without allocating them higher wages. The meaning of success in employment equity becomes highly dubious in this case. A What's the Problem? analysis helps to identify the effects of creating pay inequity and employment inequity as separate problems and, hence, provides arguments for challenging their separation.

A What's the Problem? approach therefore reveals the way in which single-policy 'solutions' oversimplify and misrepresent 'social problems'. Consistently, feminists have been at pains to show that pay equity is part of a package, including most of the reforms addressed in this book (Armstrong and Cornish, 1997: 73; Evans and Nelson, 1991: 242; Fudge and McDermott, 1991: 4–5). And yet this is not how the problem gets produced. Rather, we are left with the impression that pay equity will solve *all* of women's problems, and all *women's* problems. By highlighting the effects of meaning construction in problem representation, a What's the Problem? approach assists in challenging this impression. Producing employer inconsistency of one form or another as the problem, which is what current pay equity legislation does, encourages the view that single-policy 'solutions' are adequate – all we have to do is make employers consistent. In contrast, identifying the problem as the ways in which 'skill' and 'the job' are considered to be the 'measure of man' points to the need for a multi-pronged agenda addressed to challenging these assumptions.

Notes

1 It should be noted that Cuneo made this comment in 1991. In 1995 the Mike Harris Conservative Party came to power, removing Employment Equity legislation and amending pay equity in ways which seriously undermine its effectiveness (Armstrong and Cornish, 1997).

2 Wendy Bastalich is currently writing her PhD thesis at the University of Adelaide and is jointly enrolled in Politics and Women's Studies. She has presented a number of seminars outlining her argument but is, as yet, unpublished. I am currently

co-supervising her PhD thesis and would like to acknowledge her influence on the ideas on skill discourses contained in this chapter.

3 On this point, I ought to mention the recent ruling by the Canadian Human Rights Tribunal that the federal government has underpaid almost 200,000 current and former employees for the past 13 years. One estimate (*The Globe and Mail*, 30 July 1998, p. 1) is that workers, most of whom are women clerks and secretaries, will receive $15,000 each.

5

DISCRIMINATION: WHO IS RESPONSIBLE?

In Chapter 2, I spoke about the importance, within a What's the Problem? approach, of paying heed to the *effects* of discourse, amongst which I included the discursive constitution of subjectivities. The goal in this chapter is to illustrate what this means and how to produce an understanding of the process. As with the other chapters in this part of the book, its purpose is to provide a guide to method through the application of a What's the Problem? approach to a particular issue. Methodologically we need to find ways to uncover the implicit (and sometimes explicit) characterizations of policy 'targets' and to reflect upon the implications of those characterizations, particularly for members of these 'target' groups. In this chapter I will offer reflections upon the discursive positioning of those targeted as 'victims' of discrimination in antidiscrimination, affirmative action and managing diversity policies, and in the 'counter-discourse' offered in the 1995 Regents' decision at the University of California. Although the chapter concentrates upon the meanings ascribed to 'women' in antidiscrimination discourses, many of the observations are applicable equally to other 'target' groups.

The idea of a human rights policy, and the antidiscrimination ethic it produced, emerged after the Second World War, stimulated by the international struggle against fascism and the 'surge of egalitarian idealism which the war had generated' (Howe, 1991: 787). The economic prosperity of the period was propitious. It was a good time to be generous. Patricia Williams (1991) has drawn attention to the symbolic importance of these moves for groups on the periphery of power. This I do not wish to dispute. Rather, I want to trace the trajectory of developments in understandings of discrimination, to see how those wanting greater change have struggled to expand those understandings. I want also to highlight certain stumbling blocks in the ways in which the issues are being represented. A What's the Problem (represented to be)? approach helps us to achieve this goal.

Direct Discrimination

Antidiscrimination legislation is similar in form in all Western democracies. There are either specific Acts condemning kinds of

discrimination, most often racial or sexual discrimination, or omnibus
pieces of legislation with closed or open-ended lists of the kinds of
discrimination disallowed. Initially antidiscrimination laws focused
upon behaviours resulting from malice or evil motive. Attitudes were
represented to be the problem. This is commonly called direct or
'facial' discrimination and occurs, for example, when an employer
adopts a policy which treats 'certain classes of workers differently
from other classes of workers on the grounds of race, religion,
national origin, or gender' (Williams, 1981: 668). Other commonly
enumerated grounds, depending on country or jurisdiction, include
sexual preference, Aboriginality, marital status and disability. Here it
is important to note that in the United States antidiscrimination
legislation, in the form of the Civil Rights Act, was addressed directly
to the situation of Black Americans. The status of women as a group
seldom came up in the debates leading to the legislation (Bacchi,
1996: 41). The primary rationalization for change was the need to
make reparations to Blacks for the sins of slavery. Women were seen
to be responsible for their social location, through the 'choices' they
made, in ways in which Blacks were not. In this understanding
'women' become dubious 'supplicants', and Black women disappear
completely from the analysis (Bacchi, 1996: 48–9).

Antidiscrimination legislation is complaint-based, and this reveals
a good deal about the problem representation it contains. The
foundational assumption is that society's rules are generally func-
tioning fairly, but that a particular attitude produces an unfair
behaviour called 'discrimination' which requires 'intervention'.
Donald Black (1989) challenges the notion that law is primarily an
affair of rules and that discrimination is an aberration. He shows that
many factors – such as the social elevation of each party, the social
distance between them, whether they are individual or corporate
beings – influence who will win and what the punishment will be. If
discrimination is not an aberration, treating it as such necessarily
hides the way in which 'social differentials pervade law'.

When the problem is seen to be a racist or sexist *attitude*, to be
prejudice, this reduces racism and sexism to *individual* aberration
(Henriques et al., 1984), suppressing recognition of the institutional
and structural dimensions of discrimination. Moreover, the notion
plays into the dominant credo regarding the meaning of success in
industrial capitalist democracies. The argument runs that people
should not be judged by unsubstantiated generalizations, by stereotypes, but by their personal abilities. There is little awareness here of
the social structuring both of abilities and of understandings of just
what constitutes an ability. Stereotypes are indeed damaging, and
Nadine Taub's (1985) suggestion that their use be automatically
labelled discrimination is a progressive one. This strategy leaves

many problems unaddressed, however. By focusing upon the individual, this approach underestimates the structural problems which prevent people from 'measuring up' to established criteria of success. Therefore only those individuals who manage to free themselves from those structural constraints will succeed. And their success will, doubtless, leave the impression that the system is working. The types of structural constraints which affect most women, such as those associated with the sexual division of labour, cannot be addressed using this model. Nor will a challenge to stereotypes help women in situations where the stereotypes may be 'true' to an extent. The most intractable problems arise where stereotypes are so strong that they have become some women's reality (Cole, 1984: 56; Littleton, 1981: 488). We will see this model of antidiscrimination as condemnation of stereotypes appearing in the education chapter (Chapter 6) and will comment further on its limitations there.

Other consequences flow from the problematization of discrimination as attitudinal bias, or prejudice. The model seems to suggest that, since discrimination is due to a mistaken belief that people are 'different', 'differences' do not exist, making it difficult to address the 'differences' which result from social and economic causes, and biological and cultural 'differences'. The notion that fairness means simply 'treating likes alike' is in its essence assimilationist. The goal becomes some notion of equal treatment which ignores 'difference' (Bacchi, 1990, Chapter 5). There is also a shift in focus from the perpetrators to the 'objects' of prejudice, producing a preoccupation with just what it is about 'these people' which causes others to perceive them as 'different'. The model therefore casts the victims of discrimination as the problem. They are labelled 'disadvantaged', which becomes almost an explanation of their social location. As Didi Herman (1994: 45) explains, antidiscrimination law constructs a 'classification of identities', categories of person who are, in some way, 'lesser than' the unstated norm. It is not surprising then that antidiscrimination laws contribute 'to a low sense of self-worth in victims of discrimination and to the public impression of them as inferior' (Bumiller, 1988; Edelman, 1988: 26). To say this is not to suggest that we ought to do away with antidiscrimination laws, but that we need to rethink the way they work and make proposals which recast the problem representations they contain. We will examine later the reformulation of the problem in Joan Eveline's (1994a, b) call for a discursive shift from victims of discrimination as 'disadvantaged' to the advantages of those profiting from existing relations of domination.

In addition, antidiscrimination law is a workplace reform, attacking what is represented to be a workplace problem. At least initially it was offered as a means to break down barriers to workforce participation and promotion (its expansion into the area of education will be discussed in Chapter 6). As a result, unsurprisingly, it maintains a strict demarcation between public and private activities which severely constrains its usefulness. Private schools and single-sex clubs are considered outside the ambit of the legislation due to their 'private' character. Most noticeably, the family and the work performed in the family, mainly by women, are produced as invisible within this formulation of the problem (Thornton, 1991a, 1995b). Problem representations which place the public supervision of a range of activities out of bounds because of their 'private' character will also be observed in operation in our discussions of domestic violence (Chapter 9) and sexual harassment (Chapter 10). With this limited problematization, attempts by feminists and other reformers to expand understandings of discrimination are not surprising.

Indirect Discrimination

Some authors draw attention to a fundamental ambiguity in anti-discrimination discourse. Kimberle Crenshaw (1988: 1335) for one feels that it 'can accommodate conservative as well as liberal views of race and equality'. In her opinion, it is not clear whether the goal of the American Civil Rights Act is a 'mere rejection of white supremacy as a normative vision' or whether the goal may be expanded to include 'a societal commitment to the eradication of the substantive conditions of Black subordination'. This tension between what Crenshaw calls a 'restrictive' and an 'expansive' view is clearer when one looks at the way in which affirmative action is 'allowed', but only through an exemption from the antidiscrimination provision, about which more will be said later.

The discursive and ideological openings identified by Crenshaw and others (Howe, 1991; McCann, 1994; McCrudden et al., 1991; Taylor, 1991) create a space for making particular kinds of political claims. The notion of indirect discrimination made its way onto the political agenda through these openings. The idea of indirect discrimination is one important outgrowth of experience with the inadequacy of the direct discrimination model. It can be seen as an attempt to shift the problem representation in antidiscrimination law from individual aberration to structural inadequacies. Indirect discrimination can be claimed if it can be shown that an apparently neutral rule, such as a height or weight requirement not necessary for job performance, has a disproportionate adverse impact on one of the groups enumerated in antidiscrimination legislation. This adverse impact can, at least theoretically, be demonstrated statistically (Wilenski, 1977: 180). In fact, the means of proving indirect discrimination has become a political battleground, hinting at its subversive potential. In the United States the pendulum has swung away from the possibility of using a statistical discrepancy to prove the discriminatory impact of a particular rule. In *Wards Cove* (1989; see Francis, 1993 for details) the US Supreme Court held that 'disparate impact' plaintiffs cannot rely solely on statistics to establish a *prima facie* case of discrimination. Without invoking statistics, it is difficult to see how indirect discrimination can be proved.

As Chris Ronalds (1987: 99) describes, using the example of Australia's Sex Discrimination Act, the definition of indirect discrimination 'considerably widens the impact of the legislation by recognising that discrimination occurs beyond an individual's behaviour or actions'.[1] Hence, it purportedly recognizes that '[D]iscriminatory decisions are often based on policies and practices which form the structures and patterns of an organisation in particular, and society as a whole.' This recognition of what has been called structural or systemic discrimination opens the door to examining a wide range of work practices. Feminist reformers see its potential in drawing attention to the ways in which the world of work disadvantages many women. For example, it may be possible to argue that a short-leave or no-leave maternity policy has a disproportionate adverse impact on women and hence is indirect discrimination. The possibilities of the approach are suggested by an important British case in which the Employment Appeal Tribunal upheld the complaint of Ms Price against the Civil Service Commission that the upper age limit of 28 years for new applicants had a disproportionately adverse impact on women, 'as fewer women could comply with such a requirement than men, since many in their twenties were otherwise engaged in bearing or bringing up children' (Equal Opportunity Commission, 1982: 63).

This very victory, however, indicates the limitations of an approach which, like direct discrimination, focuses primarily on getting women into the labour force (see Price case above), or on 'allowing' them time out to give birth (see maternity leave example above). It takes a step in the right direction by recognizing that women's traditional domestic obligations have an effect on their workforce participation, but it does little to address the tensions and stresses created by trying to combine child rearing with paid labour. Even if the reform were used to win parental leave policies, there is still a presumption that when parents, read mothers, return to work, the children disappear. Moreover, if parental leave policies provide only for unpaid leave, they address the needs of only those women who can afford to take unpaid leave. Here, it is interesting to note that, even in countries with generous paid leave, such as Sweden, presumptions regarding men as full-time career workers mean that few men take leave (Bacchi, 1996: 107).

Indirect discrimination, then, even in its most subversive and expansive form, remains tied to the dictates of the market. This is illustrated most tellingly in the fact that in Britain the employer needs only to advance 'good grounds' 'acceptable to right thinking people' to justify policies which, it is claimed, are justified by business necessity – whether or not any particular group suffers disproportionately an adverse impact. B. A. Hepple (1983: 82–5; see also Gregory, 1987: 45–6) is convinced that the 'business necessity' test is not rigorous enough in an area where decisions will clearly have a dramatic impact on employment practices. Hepple in fact concludes that the structure of the judicial process is not suited to the kind of 'purposive social engineering' implied in discrimination cases of this sort, and that perhaps there is a need for 'new forms of public arbitration'.

And, while the notion of structural discrimination clearly draws attention to the size of the obstacles blocking members of particular groups from 'equal' participation in the labour force, it remains wedded to the notion that removing such obstacles will create a truly equal society. The impression is left that the problem can be isolated and dealt with. Moreover, by making everything structural, it becomes difficult to find someone to hold responsible for the discrimination (see Thornton, 1995a: 218). The power relations which install and maintain inequitable organizational systems become difficult to discern. Finally, it is but a short step from 'structural discrimination' to the suggestion that organizations are themselves best placed to 'sort out' this kind of problem. The argument here is that, since the practices at issue are parts of an organization's systems of operation, good personnel practices are all that is required to 'update' administrative procedures. Regulation is described as unnecessary and intrusive. It is just this argument which was advanced by business advocates in their initial opposition to affirmative action, and in the attempts to replace affirmative action with managing diversity programmes, topics to which we now turn.

Affirmative Action

Notionally, affirmative action was introduced because of identified limitations in complaint-based approaches to structural discrimination. The argument was put that companies and large public organizations needed to confront *proactively* the systemic barriers in their rules and practices which effectively barred 'women' and other groups from access and promotion (Bacchi, 1996: 20). It appears as several models (Bacchi, 1990: 166). In the United States in the 1960s Presidents Kennedy and Johnson issued Executive Orders which obliged government departments and firms holding government contracts to produce written affirmative action plans under threat of contract cancellation. Under these orders institutions conduct an analysis of their workforce and set targets for increasing the representation of Blacks or women. Federal courts have at times imposed mandatory targets or quotas upon employers found guilty of discrimination (Sawer, 1985: 6). British sex discrimination legislation contains some modest positive action provisions which permit training schemes to be targeted at underrepresented groups. Jeanne Gregory (1987: 52–3) calls the provisions 'little more than a goodwill gesture . . . within which people and organisations already committed to the fight against discrimination can develop programmes for action'. In 1986 the Australian Parliament passed the Affirmative Action (Equal Employment Opportunity for Women) Act which required all higher education institutions and all private sector employers with 100 or more employees to produce affirmative action programmes. Separate legislation requires government departments and statutory authorities to introduce equal opportunity programmes. These programmes follow an eight-step model, including the requirement to analyse the institution's employment profile, to consult with unions and employees, and to set objectives and forward estimates (Ronalds, 1987: 28–9). Employment equity is the phrase used to describe affirmative action programmes in Canada (Bacchi, 1996: Chapter 5).

Because antidiscrimination legislation is couched in race- and sex-neutral language, it has been possible to argue that legislation like affirmative action which targets 'women' or 'Blacks' is a *kind of* discrimination, *albeit* 'reverse discrimination'. This has necessitated including, within antidiscrimination law, an exemption allowing affirmative action.[2] In European law, for example, an exemption 'permits' Member States to adopt 'measures to promote equal opportunity for men and women, in particular by removing existing inequalities which affect women's opportunities' (Docksey, 1987: 17). Antidiscrimination laws generally have a number of exemptions. Most, for example Australia's federal *Sex Discrimination Act* (1984; see Ronalds, 1987), exempt what is referred to as 'special treatment' for pregnancy. Zillah Eisenstein (1988) notes that such an exemption reveals the implicit male norm structuring the legislation. Similarly, the way in which affirmative action is 'allowed' in antidiscrimination legislation highlights the conceptual limitations surrounding it. By being located as an exemption, affirmative action programmes are placed on the defensive and need to argue for exemption status. This happened in Australia in the Proudfoot case (1992) in which women's health services came under attack as discrimination against 'men' (Bacchi, 1996: 22).

The character of the programmes also comes under intense scrutiny. So, those which are deemed to have moved 'too far' from conventional understandings of equality as 'treating likes alike', themselves fall victim to the charge of discrimination. A case in point, the 1995 ruling by the European Court of Justice condemning a Bremen law which required city agencies to hire female candidates over male candidates with the same qualifications for posts where women were underrepresented, indicates that a narrow definition of 'equality' is being upheld. The Court ruled that the Bremen law constituted sex discrimination (Case C-450/93 *Kalanke* v. *Freie Hansestadt Bremen* [1995] ECR I-3051). A more recent, and undeniably more liberal ruling in *Marschall* v. *Land Nordrhein-Westfalen* (Case C-409/95; 11 November 1997) granted an exemption for a hiring policy which allowed a woman candidate to be selected over a man when the two were held to be equally qualified only because there was a 'saving clause' which specified that 'women are not to be given priority in promotion if reasons specific to an individual male candidate tilt the balance in his favour'. In addition, this ruling diagnosed the problem as 'prejudices and stereotypes concerning the role and capacities of women in working life and the fear, for example, that women will interrupt their careers more frequently . . . or that they will be absent from work more frequently because of pregnancy, childbirth and breastfeeding'. As I suggest in *Same Difference* (1990: 127), to move beyond this work-centred understanding of discrimination would mean that a company would be 'charged with discrimination, not because it applied a stereotype which might *not* be accurate in this particular case, but because it should accept that the applicant might indeed need specific social supports'.

In effect, the location of affirmative action as an exemption to antidiscrimination confirms and strengthens the dominant view that affirmative action is in opposition to and incompatible with equal opportunity. This has led some proponents to reshape its content, softening reform proposals and repositioning affirmative action targets as the 'problem'. This produces the dominant current understanding of affirmative action, even among many supporters of the reform, as 'preferential' treatment to assist 'disadvantaged' people to move into 'better' jobs. As Margaret Radin (1991: 134–6) says, 'the dominant ordinary language view is that affirmative action gives benefits to people who are less qualified or less deserving than white men or indeed are wholly unqualified or undeserving'. Within this understanding, notions of merit go unscrutinized. It also accepts a broad vision of society as open to opportunities, except in a few instances. A focus on expanding opportunities in this way in effect disaggregates social categories into competing individuals. The impression is left that we are dealing with barriers to individual achievement rather than unequal power relations between and among groups.

Those who 'need' more are automatically labelled as 'wanting' in some way. The targets become the 'problem', because of their presumed lack of expertise or initiative. Attempts to alter their status become 'handouts', to be severely restricted given their 'exceptional' nature and their 'contravention' of a basic equal treatment rule. The *Marschall* v. *Land Nordrhein-Westfalen* (Case C-409/95; 11 November 1997) decision, mentioned above, is significant here because of the way in which the hiring policy became the rule, with individual men having to press their individual case to have it rescinded. None the less, the ruling used the language of 'prejudices and stereotypes' to explain women's 'disadvantage', and described the disputed hiring policy as 'treating [women] preferentially' and giving 'a specific advantage to women'. This continual framing of affirmative action as 'preferential treatment' readily produces the conclusion that its targets are receiving 'preference' beyond need and, hence, paradoxically are 'advantaged' (Radin, 1991). All these terms suggest that otherwise 'undeserving' recipients are being 'privileged'. There is no way within these terms to question the standards which were applied to those currently holding positions of power and authority, or which continue to be used in hiring and promotion. This representation of the problem explains the revulsion against quotas which are described as anathema to any *genuinely* equal opportunity programme. Quotas or 'equal results' are set in opposition to equal opportunity. Quotas are represented as going 'too far', as contravening the equal treatment rule, and hence as themselves discriminatory.

To the charge that 'equal results' mean 'quotas', and 'quotas' mean hiring people regardless of their 'qualifications', some feminists have replied that only 'qualified' women would be hired. Others, however, have gone further and suggested the need to question the standards by which people are assessed (Game, 1984). In a pamphlet published early in the life of the Affirmative Action Agency, set up by the Australian government to monitor compliance with the Affirmative Action Act, Clare Burton (1988), for example, called for a 'redefinition' of 'merit'. At one level drawing attention to the meaning of 'merit' means ensuring only that unfair stereotypes are not imported into supposedly objective assessment. We have already hinted at the limitations in this problematization. Some reformers tar this approach as acquiescence to traditional standards of assessment and hence as assimilationist. Others, however, argue that putting 'merit' on the agenda for discussion opens the door to all sorts of questions about desert in job selection and status in hierarchies. Clare Burton makes this case:

[W]hen we refer to equitable organisational arrangements, we are not restricting our view to 'narrow, distributive concerns of equity' (Pateman,

1981: 36) which address who has which job, or to the formal rules governing the allocation process, but to the exercise of power at the work place, how jobs are organised and practised and the fundamental pre-conditions for the development of alternative arrangements. (Burton, 1987: 432)

Dominant understandings of affirmative action stop short of this kind of analysis. As with understandings of antidiscrimination, the focus is on *barriers* to achievement and to an extent those barriers are seen to inhere in outgroups. Though groups form the basis of policy design, such an interpretation effectively constitutes recipients as competing *individuals*.

At the same time members of targeted groups are impelled to select an attachment, an identity, from a restricted list of offerings. As with rights struggles (Williams, 1990: 758–9), making use of affirmative action legislation requires taking up the identity categories made available. This means working with discrete categories that pay little attention to the fact that lives are not lived in neat packages as 'women', 'Blacks', and so on. It also means emphasizing common-alities and downplaying differences within these categories. Mean-while, outgroups are constituted as 'interest groups' and are set in competition with each other. Cynthia Chertos (1983: 240) talks about the way in which a 'zero-sum mentality' is created which suggests that 'there is a finite number of opportunities for "others" and, if a member of one group obtains a position, it is at the expense of another group'. This creates problems both for groups facing multiple forms of oppression, and for reformers trying to make meaningful change.

In all this, little attention is directed to those doing the categorizing, those defining just what the 'problem' is. Nitya Iyer (1993: 185) describes how being in the speaker's position, being the categorizer or comparison maker, is to occupy a position of power: '[A]s categorizer, I can make myself absent from the process. I can create one side of the comparison as "a difference", while constituting my particular con-stellation of attributes as the invisible background norm.' Importantly, categorizers are also in charge of offering 'solutions'. Richard Delgado makes this point convincingly:

[A] 'we–they' analysis . . . justifies a disadvantage that we (the majority) want to impose on ourselves to favor them (the minority). This type of thinking, however, leaves the choice of remedy and the time frame for that remedy in the hands of the majority; it converts affirmative action into a benefit, not a right. (1984: 570–1)

The point I am adding to this insight is simply that the solutions, the 'benefits' if you will, depend upon a representation of the 'recipients' as 'the problem'. The categorizers do not just have control over 'solutions'. This control means they also create the 'problems' which need to be 'solved'. Delgado implies as much. How these are created determines the dynamics which regulate the degree of challenge or acquiescence to the status quo.

Affirmative action, moreover, as it is presently conceived, goes no further than either direct or indirect discrimination legislation in resolving the conflict between paid work and family (defined broadly) responsibilities. Despite its obvious importance, it has the same blind spot as antidiscrimination legislation since it does not address directly the impact of living arrangements on workers' lives. The suggestion here is not that the legislation will not work, but that it will work only for a few, those who are best able to approximate the male profile or, more precisely, the profile of white, middle-class, able-bodied males. As Margaret Thornton (1995a: 223) says, '[I]t is only if individual women comport as closely as possible with the male model in the public sphere that they will be "let in" and possibly even rewarded for being "good"'. Margaret Wallace (1985: 28–9) describes affirmative action as fitting comfortably into the liberal 'rat-race' model for society. It only 'takes some notice of the condition of the "runners" and of the "track"'. Frances Olsen (1983: 1555) offers an even more stinging condemnation in her suggestion that affirmative action hurts rather than helps women, since it creates 'another reason for women to blame themselves when they fail in the marketplace'.

Managing Diversity

The way in which current understandings of affirmative action disaggregate targeted categories into numbers of competing individuals has been a first step in the integration of affirmative action into management practices. Initially, when the reform was proposed, there was a great deal of hostility among employers, on the grounds that the government ought not to intervene in business matters (in the United States, Australia, Canada), or in business and union matters (Sweden, Norway, the Netherlands). In the 1980s, however, it was easy to find positive endorsement from business leaders. The fact that business spokespeople in the United States undercut President Reagan's attempts to *end* affirmative action is only the most obvious example of this (*Harvard Law Review*, 1989). This turnabout can be attributed to the ways in which affirmative action programmes have become a management prerogative. I noted above how descriptions of structural discrimination could be used to locate the problem in management and organizational systems, and how this could lead to business demanding control over these processes. In effect, this interpretation has provided the leverage which has led to the absorption of affirmative action into human resource planning. The identification of structural discrimination as a 'human resource' problem, moreover, has allowed companies to reduce union participation in what is represented to be a company 'problem' (Bacchi, 1996: 60, 85).

Despite this taming of affirmative action through its institutionalization, it is apparent that business representatives would prefer to have *no* government regulation of their management of workforce composition and hiring policy. Managing diversity programmes offer one way for employers to increase control in this area. A number of companies in Canada are offering the introduction of managing diversity programmes as evidence of compliance with employment equity legislation (Bacchi, 1996: 77 fn 4). Managing diversity programmes, according to their defenders, confirm moreover that what we are talking about is 'just good business sense', a part of normal personnel practices, and not something that should be subject to government regulation.

While there is some managing diversity literature which recognizes group inequality and positions itself as part of a social justice agenda (Miller, 1994), the public face of managing diversity, and much of the influential literature, focuses on individual differences and individual enablement. In contrast to the explicit targeting of groups in affirmative action policy, the emphasis in managing diversity is upon expanding diversity to 'multiple diversities' (Thomas Jr, 1991: 81). In managing diversity our 'differences' are such that efforts at change bypass the group and look to the individual. According to R. Roosevelt Thomas Jr (1990: 112), the executive director of the American Institute for Managing Diversity at Atlanta's Morehouse College, managing diversity 'is a vision which sidesteps the questions of equality, ignores the tensions of co-existence, plays down the uncomfortable realities of differences and focuses instead on individual enablement'. Clare Burton (1992) highlights the dangers in this analysis: 'it hides structural inequality which becomes invisible when the problem is individualised and broadly dispersed in this way, to cover all differences'. Put more tersely, '[S]ex and race-based power relations and control strategies are denied.' In effect, the managing diversity proponents studied here undermine the starting premise of antidiscrimination law, that groups like 'women', 'Blacks', and those with disabilities, among others, are the targets of discriminatory practices and hence ought to be the targets of reform. I noted earlier in this chapter the limitations of a 'disadvantage' discourse and the problems with targeting homogeneous target groups. However, here we see that attempts to smooth over categorical distinctions can also be regressive. The lesson in all this is to examine how *particular* problem representations position these groups rather than simply condemning or endorsing identity politics as a general strategy. In

other words, attention needs to be paid to how groups are constituted within *particular* discursive constructions of the problem.

Managing diversity programmes build upon developments in
'valuing diversity' approaches to discrimination. And, despite
disclaimers, they offer a similar problem representation, a representation similar, in effect, to that we identified in direct discrimination
legislation. The problem in essence is seen to be prejudice, unfair
stereotyping and a fear of the unknown (Harvey and Blakely, 1996: 76,
178; Henderson, 1994: 223). There is a premise that increased sensitivity to people's differences will remove hostility. The problem is
cast in psychological terms and in individual terms. The problem
becomes prejudiced individuals and the goal, to move them beyond
their prejudice. There is an implication in much of the literature that
talking about differences will reduce racial, sexual and other kinds
of hostility and discrimination. This can be seen in some of the
products available as part of the new multi-million dollar managing
diversity industry.[3] Such products suggest that we are involved in
a consciousness-raising campaign to draw attention to the shared
humanity of the 'objects' of prejudice and the rest of 'us'. Chandra
Mohanty (1990: 201) identifies the problem representation in
'prejudice-reduction workshops' as cultural misunderstanding or
lack of information about other cultures (see also Baker, 1996: 155;
Cavanaugh, 1997: 40). She castigates this 'individualized discourse of
harmony and civility that is the hallmark of cultural pluralism', while
admitting some benefits for the practice – 'for instance, the introduction of new cultural models can cause a deeper evaluation of
existing structures, and clearly such consultancies could set a positive
tone for social change.' Still, as she says, the baseline is 'maintaining the status quo' – 'diversity is always and can only be added on.'
The goal becomes recognizing the 'competencies' of those who are
designated different and encouraging them to develop their 'skills'
(Thomas and Ely, 1996). Using the insights of governmentality
scholars and recalling the effects of a skills discourse in Chapter 4, the
result is the production of a discourse which, in the end, holds
individuals responsible for their own success or lack of success.

The focus on cultural diversity as 'understanding' can also have
dangerous implications for women. In much managing diversity
literature 'diversity' is about racial or ethnic diversity. 'Women' is, if
anything, an embarrassment, since it is assumed that different cultures have different attitudes to 'women' and their role, and these
attitudes must be accommodated. 'Attitudes to women' then becomes
one of the 'differences' that can be talked about and sorted out
(Bacchi, 1996: 54). The emphasis on cultural differences transforms
gender inequality into issues where on which simply have different
points of view which need to be discussed or accommodated.

On the other side, in an attempt to distance managing diversity from affirmative action, proponents emphasize that all individuals, including white males, will be encouraged and enabled to give their best to the company. Thomas Jr (1990: 108) specifies that the goal is 'creating a work setting geared to the upward mobility of all kinds of people, including white males'. In a 1992 conference on managing diversity, sponsored by the Alberta Multiculturalist Commission, John Cleghorn, the President and Chief Operating Officer, Royal Bank of Canada, gave the keynote address. Here he emphasized:

> [T]he important thing for business to understand is that diversity includes everyone: it is not something that is defined by race or gender. It encompasses age, background, education and personality. It even includes, if I may say so, that popular Canadian pejorative phrase, 'white men in suits'. In my experience they are as diverse as their colleagues. So a commitment to managing diversity is a commitment to all employees. There's nothing exclusionary about it. (Cleghorn, 1992)

This explicit targeting of white men in effect denies injustice in their domination of positions of influence. They become victims along with the rest of the population.

The language of economic rationalism frames managing diversity proposals. The argument runs that 'deregulation' will enhance competitiveness and this will generate commercial incentives to 'reward merit regardless of other factors' (Niland and Champion, 1990: 5). The underlying assumption is, as Thomas Jr (1990: 108) says, that 'prejudice is almost gone'. Productivity, we are told, is the employers' primary concern and hence they will grasp the logic of 'creating a work setting geared to the upward mobility of all kinds of people, including white males'. The underlying goal, as in much human resource management, is creating conditions to get 'satisfactory performance' from the new diverse workforce. Thomas Jr (1990: 112) is blunt: '[I]t means getting from employees, first, everything we have a right to expect, and second – if we do it well – everything they have to give.' Paul du Gay's (1997: 286) insights into the development of concern with organizational culture are apt here. He emphasizes the attempt to get all individuals to see their lives in terms of an organization's goals to 'enable them to make the right and necessary contribution to its success'. In this discourse, the subject of enterprise becomes 'an entrepreneur of the self'.

Given the emphasis on 'getting everything employees have to give', it is not surprising that there is little attention to domestic responsibilities in much managing diversity literature. When the subject is raised it is within the framework that something should be done to 'assist' women with 'their' domestic obligations. 'Women' and the pull of the domestic continue to be represented as 'problems', while men's relationship to home and family, and the value of nonmarket activities go unanalysed.

The Truly Disadvantaged and the Regents' Decision

Given the limitations of current understandings of affirmative action, it is not surprising that many on the left are disillusioned. Common criticisms are that it benefits only some women and some Blacks, those who need 'help' least, and that it is assimilationist, compelling outgroups to adopt the standards of ingroups. Marilyn Frye (1992: 787) describes it as 'a quite selective strategy of assimilation, co-optation, and tokenism'. In reaction, Frye finds the language of 'diversity' appealing, that '"[M]ulticulturalism" has a sweeter sound . . . than affirmative action.' Others, like Paul Starr (1992), are turning to class. According to Starr, due to the fallout accompanying affirmative action, 'Americans concerned about reducing racial inequalites' ought to shift their focus to 'the reconstruction of civil society in minority communities' and 'broad policies for economic opportunity and security that benefit low- and middle-income Americans, black and white alike'. This position, particularly the argument that affirmative action is overinclusive, is popular among those who align themselves with conservative politics (Edwards, 1987; Lynch, 1989). It is also commonly linked to an analysis which insists that poverty is the 'real' cause of 'disadvantage'. To quote William Julius Wilson (1987: 110), 'the race-specific policies emanating from the civil rights revolution, although beneficial to more advantaged blacks . . . do little for those who are truly disadvantaged'.

On the turn to 'class', Barbara Ehrenreich (1989) makes the point that at particular junctures in American history a focus on poverty as the problem has been considered safer than a focus on race. We are living through one such juncture. This project is safer because analysts create the 'poor' to suit their analysis, as in the recent invention of the 'underclass'. We can detect here undertones of the ways in which direct discrimination discourses constitute their targets. The underclass becomes a distinct population, a group *with* 'problems' which, though these may derive from their poverty, require attention directed *to them*. They require for example initiatives to 'improve themselves', counselling to attend to their feelings of insecurity and failure. They become in effect the problem. Ruth Levitas (1996: 17, 8) notes, in her deconstruction of the term 'social exclusion' in key European Commission White Papers on social and economic policy issued in 1994, that the identification of an 'underclass' construes the problem as the 'fissure between the bottom 30 percent and everyone else'. This in her view constitutes this group as 'marginalised, insecure and vulnerable', excluded from 'the cycle of opportunity'. The cause of exclusion then becomes 'not the fundamental nature of capitalism (which never gets discussed)' but 'contemporary economic and social conditions'. What remains unproblematized is 'the fissure between the top 1 percent or 10 percent and the rest'. Levitas adds that the focus on employment as the key to 'inclusion' collapses civil society into the market, and ignores the fact that 'social labour takes place outside the market, most notably as unpaid work by women'.

The way in which attention to 'class' plays itself out in affirmative action debates is nowhere clearer than in the decision on 20 July 1995 of the Board of Regents of the University of California to end affirmative action. The Regents resolved that 'effective January 1, 1997, the University of California shall not use race, religion, sex, color, ethnicity, or national origin as criteria for admission to the University or to any program of study', resurrecting the old ideal of a sex-blind, and race-blind polity (Post, 1996: 10 fn 1). And yet there is acknowledgement in the decision that environmental factors can affect prospects of academic success. Section four sets out the kinds of adverse social circumstances which might well be 'rectified' through 'special considerations'. In this section, consideration of minority status is replaced with consideration of 'economic disadvantage' and 'unwholesome' family and neighbourhood environments (Butler, 1996: 79). The admissibility of these characteristics, however, depends upon the candidate demonstrating 'sufficient character and determination in overcoming obstacles to warrant confidence that the applicant can pursue a course of study to successful completion'. The way in which the victims of environmental fallout are constructed in this vision as supplicants, and as needing assistance corresponds, unsurprisingly, to the negative constitution of the victims of discrimination as I have already described it. Here, however, there is an explicit reversion to the discourse of the deserving and the undeserving poor which characterized nineteenth century British Poor Law. Only those who manage to pull themselves out of the mire of poverty will be 'rewarded'.

Paralleling Ruth Levitas' (1996) insights into the discourse of social exclusion, Judith Butler (1996: 79) notes that the category 'economic disadvantage' resonates with 'class', but is also clearly distinguished from it, 'characterizing contingent and local economic environments and, hence, having none of the systemic or institutionalized status usually associated with class'. Rather, the problem becomes 'abusive and dysfunctional families and neighborhoods'. As Butler clearly states, in this proposal, 'the problem of discrimination is localized, apparently stripped of its racial, ethnic, and sexual dimensions and of any reference to the broader national context of its operation or the systemic ways within which it proceeds.' In effect, Butler goes on, 'the policy does not oppose a view of discrimination as victimization but redescribes the field of relevant social injustice such that the "breakdown" of families and the decline of neighborhoods are what truly victimize promising young students.' We are left with 'a certain production of individual autobiography in ways that localize every victimization and individualize every solution'. Insightfully, Butler (1996: 82) asks: '[H]as this kind of narrative taken the place of the discourse of discrimination, or does the narrative of abuse, victimization, and individual solutions constitute the contemporary devolution of antidiscrimination discourse (mirroring the turn to "self-esteem" and abuse narrative that predominates within certain circles of diluted political leftism?).' Her point here is that, within antidiscrimination discourse, there lodge assumptions about the causes of the 'problem' which resonate with the Regents' decision. These include the individualizing of the problem, the creation of the victim as 'disadvantaged', the denial of the power relations which keep oppressed groups oppressed. In effect, we are dealing with more of a continuum, rather than a dramatic deviation, in representations of the problem.

Conclusion

In this chapter we have traced a discursive battle over meanings of discrimination. We have seen attempts to take and use a discourse which created 'discrimination' as an attitudinal problem to effect broader challenges to the status quo. Notions of structural discrimination and affirmative action indicate such attempts. At the same time, we have noted that in each case it has been difficult to shift responsibility from the victims of unjust practices to those perpetrating them. The ways in which groups have been constituted within affirmative action, managing diversity and class discourses continues to create those who are poor and oppressed as the problem.

The effects of this discursive positioning are deeply troubling. A number of women and members of other targeted groups oppose affirmative action because they dislike the implication that affirmative action recipients are 'less qualified' than those they may replace, and that they have been 'assisted' to surmount 'their' 'disadvantages'. Not all affirmative action recipients feel this way, of course, and it is important not to allow this argument to itself become a justification for ending affirmative action programmes. Still, it seems more than coincidence that some of the most articulate defenders of managing diversity programmes are Black men. Both R. Roosevelt Thomas Jr (1990, 1991) and George Henderson (1994), for example, see valuing diversity and managing diversity as likely to produce happier outcomes for Black Americans than affirmative action. Their concerns are primarily the stigma attached to affirmative action recipients, the perception that these groups were 'assisted', given 'help' they did not deserve, got jobs that should have gone to 'better-qualified' people. Instead of challenging this characterization of the problem (which I feel is essential and which I initiate in this chapter), they accept it. Thomas Jr (1991: 105, 168), for example, describes affirmative action as 'special assistance or preferential treatment', and stipulates that 'managing diversity is not about leveling the playing field to give minorities and women an extra advantage'. The language here indicates the discursive power of equal opportunity rhetoric.

The analysis of managing diversity programmes in this chapter suggests, however, that these programmes will accomplish little, given the emphasis upon prejudice as the problem and upon cultural understanding as the solution. Rather, I suggest that a way has to be found to draw attention to the systemic character of the problem. Joan Eveline (1994a) recommends, as a means to this end, a shift from a discourse of disadvantage to a discourse of advantage. In her view this shift would bring attention back to the holders of power and influence, and would disrupt a version of the problem which in the end holds those who are oppressed responsible for their oppression. In *The Politics of Affirmative Action* (1996; see also Bacchi, 1993), I too emphasize the need to make visible the invisible norms structuring reform responses, how, in particular, the representation of affirmative action as 'preference' fails to address the power and influence of ingroups, leaving them in place as the ones responsible for identifying who is 'needy', just what they 'need', and when they 'need' it. In this chapter I have argued that a What's the Problem? approach provides a tool which uncovers some of these dynamics.

Notes

1 It should be noted that different countries have added indirect discrimination to their legislation at different times. The addition has been most recent in Sweden (Nielsen and Halvorsen, 1992: 9).

2 Notably, Sweden's 1980 Equality Act (see Dahlberg, 1984) created a separate directive for positive action, not tying it to antidiscrimination in the ways other countries have done. However, elsewhere (Bacchi, 1996: 110–11) I explain that this has had minimal impact on the effectiveness of the legislation.

3 I offer as examples here the games advertised in a 1993 training catalogue from the management studies publishers, Pfeiffer & Company, *Diversophy: Understanding the Human Race*, and *Diversity Bingo: An Experiential Learning Event*. The former is described as a means to 'address the sensitive issue of diversity in a nonthreatening way. This involving game encourages awareness of traits, customs, and common misconceptions of all types of groups' (Pfeiffer & Company, 1993: 75).

6

EDUCATION POLICY: ACCESS OR TRANSFORMATION?

Policy debates in the area of education provide useful examples of the nesting of problem representations mentioned in the Introduction. For example, competing approaches to reform in the area of girls and education are grounded in different views of both the 'problem' of 'women's inequality' and of the nature of education more generally. Even when there is agreement about either of these issues, disagreements surface over possible causes and meanings of girls' unequal education, and hence over desirable 'solutions'. Applying What's the Problem (represented to be)? to education policy allows us to probe all these levels of problem representation. The point is to recognize that expressed views on what is desirable for girls often will and usually do reflect other reform agendas. This chapter explores this insight through an examination of the history of 'responses' to the 'problem' of girls' education, culminating in the shift to a focus on the 'success' of girls and the 'underperformance' of boys.

It is important to indicate here that applying a What's the Problem? approach can appear on occasion to oversimplify positions, to suggest sharp distinctions between positions when in effect boundaries between them are blurred. The purpose of the approach, however, justifies oversimplification as a strategy. The goal is not to categorize people but to provide a tool for thinking about the effects of problem representations, including our own, as has been illustrated in preceding chapters (Chapter 4 and 5).

Will Education Free Us?

Lyn Yates (1993a: 90) notes that current curriculum theories in the field of girls and education 'are differentiated according to different beliefs about the nature of schooling and education'. She outlines three positions and these provide a useful guide to debates in the area. Yates identifies some (her examples are Jane Martin, 1985, and Jean Blackburn, 1982) who 'assume it is appropriate and possible to build enlightenment for students on the basis of a renovated liberal education'. Yates's second grouping, which includes Weiler (1988), Arnot (1985), Weiner (Weiner and Arnot, 1987), and Kenway and Modra (1989), suggests that the teacher has a duty to be more directly concerned with the development of political consciousness. The third group, including Valerie Walkerdine (1990) and Bronwyn Davies[1] (1989), in Yates's account, suggests that 'schooling is basically going to be regulatory and oppressive whatever curriculum framework is adopted, and what is achievable at best is some ongoing counter-critique'.

Yates's categories reflect a longstanding tension among reformers about the nature and purpose of education. Some see education as the great equalizer, the key to promoting social mobility (Codd, 1988: 237); for others, it performs the function of socializer into existing norms. For the former, education holds out the promise of smoothing over social distinctions, allowing the poor to 'do well' and to 'make good'. For the latter, an education dominated by the elite will serve that elite by producing well-disciplined and law-abiding citizens who believe, mistakenly, that they will indeed 'make good'. For the former, education promises liberation; for the latter, it mystifies the reality of domination. For those who see education as equalizer, the problem is lack of access or inadequate access. All those who have campaigned for free and universal education, at any and every level, have this as their agenda. For those who see education as oppressor, the problem becomes elucidating its role, challenging the mystification which keeps people from recognizing its oppressive character. One approach here, reflected in Yates's second category, is undermining the system from within by encouraging critical reflection upon, among other things, the education process. Others are more sceptical of this project. Valerie Walkerdine (1992: 16) cogently puts these concerns, warning against any position which portrays education as liberation:

> [T]he emergence first of popular and then compulsory schooling related specifically to the problems of crime and poverty understood as characteristics of the population: criminality and pauperism. Schooling was seen as one way to ensure the development of 'good habits' which would therefore alleviate these twin problems.

For Walkerdine, the spectre of the always regulated child means that, rather than progressivism freeing working-class children from 'harsh authoritarianism', it makes 'powerlessness, the product of oppression, invisible'. Some of these concerns about the purpose and effects of education provide important links with the discussion of early childhood development in the next chapter.

Tension between critical pedagogists, Yates's second category, and sceptics like Walkerdine, appears today in disagreements about whether any form of education can claim an ability to 'liberate' its subjects or, more appropriately, in the language of the sceptics, its objects. Some suggest that even critical pedagogy, which makes claims to wish to alter the curriculum and to create a space for students to challenge the dynamic which places them as 'receivers' of knowledge, is itself trapped within a model that creates critical pedagogists as leaders and students as followers. Feminist poststructuralists are playing a leading role in making this challenge (see Luke and Gore, 1992). As Julie McLeod (1993: 114) notes, however, while these authors 'all share a strong scepticism about these grand claims of critical pedagogy, there are ambivalent and mixed attitudes to the dreams of emancipation and transformation'. Some seem to feel that teachers can indeed 'assist' students to develop a critical consciousness. Many focus specifically upon developing critical consciousness of the production of gender. More will be said about this approach below. In contrast, McLeod (1993), who typifies the sceptics, takes exception to any dream of 'transcendence and emancipation' and cautions feminists to 'concede that feminist educational practices involve processes of emancipation *and* of regulation'. She points out that the 'ambition to free students from, for example, stereotypical gender identities . . . is usually represented as a matter of doing away with constraints and the negative effects of patriarchy, but not as also a matter of instituting other (feminist) forms of regulation and self-management.' This concern with the types of subjects or subjectivities feminism creates is relatively recent and is linked directly with the governmentality literature introduced in Chapter 2.

The critique of progressive education stands outside mainstream approaches to reform in the area of girls and education, as we will see in a moment. Critiques of feminist strategies as themselves means of regulation, like McLeod's, are also marginal to mainstream feminist discourses. There is a suggestion by those wary of this theory that the approach is too abstract and has little to say about what we decide to teach. In the words of Lyn Yates (1994: 432), '[A]ll that seems to matter in this account, is an endless quest to uncover regimes of truth' instead of 'what students might learn differently'. Yates (1993c: 184) is concerned that much feminist theory writes off 'institutionalized schooling as a field for feminist practice', neglecting to acknowledge that this education may have contributed to these feminists' own 'ability to criticize or "see through" the sexist forms of contemporary society.' For our purposes, this debate suggests what is at stake in competing problem representations. For people like Walkerdine, education itself is the problem; for Yates, by contrast, the problem is what is taught. Some, like Davies, tread an uncomfortable middle ground, recommending significant curriculum reforms especially in the area of gender relations.

Competing visions of women's inequality exist alongside competing visions of education as either repression or liberation. Those who view education as liberation generally see women's inequality as due to lack of access to dominant social structures, including educational institutions. There is usually but not always a connection between a focus on lack of access to education and lack of access to the labour market. That is, those who have pressed for the 'equalizing' of girls' educational opportunities often express the view that this is necessary for them to receive adequate compensation in the labour market. By contrast, those who view education as oppression unsurprisingly are highly critical of a model of reform which focuses almost exclusively upon incorporation of girls into existing educational and market structures.

Equal Access in Education

The dominant problematization of girls' inequality in education in Anglo-Saxon countries has been an access, and hence an education as liberation, model. Girls as an educational category, in fact, first appeared when they were discovered not to exist in equal numbers to boys in educational institutions. Canada's 1967 Royal Commission on the Status of Women (Pierson, 1995: 166) directed attention to girls' underrepresentation in educational institutions. In Australia, initially the 1970s era of Labor-led educational reform focused on class and socioeconomic disadvantage. Then, in the climate of International Women's Year (1975) and with the prompting of Elizabeth Ried, Women's Adviser to the Prime Minister, an enquiry into girls' education was established. This resulted in the 1975 report to the Schools Commission, *Girls, Schools and Society* (Australia, 1975) which emphasized that at every level girls received less education than did boys, and that subject choices in secondary schools perpetuated sex divisions in the labour market. In the new era of equal opportunity, there was increasing attention to gender segregation of educational areas, noted in universities where girls tended to select humanities and arts subjects, while boys tended to dominate science and mathematics. Again, there was a focus on how this translated into women's unequal opportunities in the labour market which led to an emphasis upon getting girls into nontraditional study areas. Once the numbers of girls in educational facilities and their retention rates began to improve, the focus on the ways in which their studies failed to translate into post-educational (meaning job) opportunities became paramount. It needs to be mentioned that the emphasis on 'restrictive' post-school options remains the dominant focus in *current* policy documents, as do attempts to move girls into nontraditional study areas. However, while the underrepresentation of girls in science and technology studies continues to be represented as a concern, the causes are now described, at least by some, very differently, as we will see below.

Without underestimating the importance of integrating girls into nontraditional study areas, it is useful to identify the presumptions underlying this project. First, this agenda fits exactly an understanding of the 'problem' of 'women's inequality' as lack of access to the labour market with all its attendant limitations (see Preamble to Part Two). Second, there is a privileging in this agenda of study and work areas where men dominate. The suggestion that the problem might be the other way around, that boys are not choosing to study the arts, for example, finds few supporters. And, third, the emphasis upon encouraging girls to study science and technology fits an economistic discourse which emphasizes technological innovation as the key to international competitiveness.

It is important not to paint all supporters of equal access models as simply assimilationist. The Australian education reformer Jean Blackburn (1984: 10, 15), for example, illustrates that it is entirely possible to start one's assessment from an observation of girls' unequal representation and move onto a critique of educational institutions and what they offer. As long ago as 1984, Blackburn warned against uncritically underwriting existing curricular content which might well only make girls more competitive and aggressive. 'Asserting that the care of dependents is more valuable than missile building,' she says, 'is a prior issue.' Unsurprisingly, given Blackburn's leadership role in the Schools Commission Report, 'one thrust' of the *Girls, Schools and Society* curriculum concerns was that of teaching boys 'to see the obligations of parenthood as a serious aspect of their lives' (in Yates, 1993a: 14). This reminds us of Marion Maddox's (1997) point that committee reports often can and do house more than one problem representation. Importantly, however, this was a thrust that was not pursued. Along lines reminiscent of Blackburn, the American educational philosopher Jane Martin (1991: 12) objects to women's education being designed 'to develop traits genderized in favor of males'.

Blackburn and Martin, however, are exceptions. The dominant problem representation (the concern) among most equal access advocates is that girls are underrepresented in particular kinds and levels of education and this is described as an impediment to their liberation. This linkage between reform in the education area and a belief that liberation involves labour market participation is certainly prominent in the academic and policy literature produced in the early period of reform efforts. Lise Julien (1987: 5) found that in Canada in the period up to 1987 over 50 per cent of listed resources had as their focus the broadening of career goals. Lyn Yates's survey (1993b) of the field found that, in Australia, the 1975 to 1985 decade was dominated by 'the issue of job choices by girls and the contributions of schooling to this'.

It is not surprising then that debates about girls' education map directly onto debates about discrimination. Access to education was presumed by many to be the key to access to good remuneration in paid labour, and discrimination was considered to be the major obstacle blocking this path. So in 1972 in the United States, Title IX of the Education Amendments was signed into law uncontroversially, outlawing sex discrimination in elementary, secondary, as well as post-secondary education (Gelb and Palley, 1987). Having observed this connection, it becomes necessary to rehearse the kind of problem 'discrimination' is represented to be in different contexts. As we saw in the previous chapter, antidiscrimination discourse suggests that there are obstacles, primarily discriminatory attitudes or institutional biases, hindering individual achievement. It presumes the benefits of incorporation and assimiliation. Translated into the educational domain, a concern with ending discrimination produced a focus on the need to counter 'restrictive' stereotypes and to offer a wider range of role models for girls. The argument, put simply, was that girls were being 'held back' because of societal expectations that they fill traditional domestic roles and that all that was required, for girls to 'achieve', was to challenge these expectations. The problem in this view is that girls are 'socialized' into 'limited' roles.

Socialization, Stereotypes and Sex Roles

It is important here to think about the relationship between feminist theories of oppression and dominant discourses of oppression. Feminists, no less than other groups, operate within dominant discourses. They also, of course, attempt to challenge those they identify as oppressive of women. Their theoretical forays are both shaped by and shapers of ongoing cultural developments. This is clear in the education field. In the 1970s, 'the sex role approach provided the theoretical ideas that underpinned liberal feminism' (Connell, 1987: 33). Hence, reforms in this period included attempts to counter 'demeaning' stereotypes and to broaden sex roles. 'Sexism' served as a shorthand for attitudes which constrained girls' options. Reforms called for the need to eliminate 'sexism' and to increase 'opportunities'.

The list of early (to 1980) government initiatives in this area confirms this focus. All of the titles of Australian policy initiatives in this period indicated either a need to counter sexism or to expand opportunities, or to do both. A 1980 policy statement issued by the Victorian Ministry of Education typically called for *Equal Opportunity and Elimination of Sexism* (Gilbert, 1996: Appendix I). The concrete work of addressing stereotypes and eliminating sexism targeted the content of teaching texts (Julien, 1987: 4). Attention was drawn to the paucity of women and girls featuring in these texts, and to their appearance in traditional roles when they did feature. There was also a questioning of the common character portrayals of girls and women as caring and passive, and of boys and men as active and aggressive. The goal became to alter these images primarily by offering examples of women in leadership roles and in a wider array of activities, including especially occupations outside the home. In the language of the 1967 Canadian Royal Commission on the Status of Women (cited in Gaskell, 1992: 18):

> a woman's creative and intellectual potential is either underplayed or ignored in the education of children from their earliest years. The sex roles described in these textbooks provide few challenging models for young girls, and they fail to create a sense of community between men and women as fellow human beings.

In proposals like these, the problem of women's inequality is attributed to 'stereotyped customary expectations, both held by men and internalized by women' (Connell, 1987: 33). What is needed for reform then is 'a change of women's identity and expectations'. The focus is on changing women and on changing attitudes. The presumption is that other change will follow. Men are seen to suffer equally from the limitations of confining sex roles. For example, a 1978 Ontario Ministry of Education Report entitled *Sex-role Stereotyping and Women's Studies* (Ontario, 1978: 2) notes that '[B]oth males and females are confined by their respective stereotypes.' Notably, however, few recommended showing men and boys in uncharacteristic behaviours or occupations, nursing the child or taking in the wash, for example.

This representation of the problem contains important silences. Among other things, as Connell (1987: 33) notes, this approach 'missed the significance of power in gender relations'. Confirming the point made in the last chapter, it also says little about the importance of the domestic and child-rearing tasks for which women continue to assume major responsibility. And for some Black feminists (Bryan et al., 1985), to demand their daughters' right 'to do motor mechanics or play football, when our sons could aspire to nothing else, would be a denial of reality'. One wonders also just what is achieved by portraying women *as if* they were widely represented in a broad array of occupations when women and girls continue to face constraints in entering these occupations. Does the portrayal in any way guarantee the outcome? The presumption here seems to be that girls need to be encouraged to 'broaden their horizons' and that this indeed will be accomplished by *seeing* women and girls in nontraditional occupations in teaching texts. The same motivation lies behind pro-grammes which invite women in nontraditional occupations in the community to come into schools to address girls. Girls and their attitudes become the problem and the reform target. There is an implication that girls are 'in deficit', lacking either self-esteem or motivation or abilities to undertake subjects which will lead to good pay and 'fulfilling' work. Gaskell et al. (1989: 11–12) point out how a similar interpretation (or problem representation) has been used to explain the 'poor' performance of economically 'underprivileged' children:

> [T]hey came to school with a 'deficit' that needed to be diagnosed and then remedied with good teaching. The deficit was usually traced to their home backgrounds. It might be wrong attitudes and values or inadequate skills and language. It might be lack of confidence or underdeveloped cognitive skills. The trick was to spot the real trouble, and then intervene at school or preferably even earlier at daycare to make up the deficit.

This interpretation is relevant here because of the way in which many feminists and other reformers began to look for the 'deficit' in girls. In its application to issues of class, it becomes directly relevant in the next chapter. This deficit model has become the focus of attack in more recent feminist educational analyses (see Foster, 1996; Gaskell et al. 1989; Kenway, 1990; Pierson, 1995: 171). For example, it is pointed out that such interpretations pay insufficient attention to other obstacles girls face when trying to enter these occupations. Moreover, they presume that indeed entry to these occupations is a desirable goal. The focus on girls as the problem directs attention away from these other issues.

Developments in feminist poststructuralist education theory con-stitute a serious challenge to socialization as explanation of oppression. Bronwyn Davies (1994: 76) makes the important point that such explanations portray teachers as the problem (see discussion below). The teacher becomes the socializer, 'shaping the "internal" beings of his [sic] students'. Rather, Davies says, we need to recognize that both teachers and students are 'caught up in multiple discourses, positioned in multiple ways'. She (1994: 75) describes a shift from the humanist concept of socialization to the poststructuralist concept of subjectifica-tion in the following way: 'this then is a challenge to the humanist vision of one who essentially is, rather than being positioned as one who can or cannot speak in this way or that.' Davies offers strategies to help both students and teachers 'see how we ourselves are constituted through discourse, coerced by it, and yet made into speaking subjects who can begin to disrupt and move beyond coercive patterns we do not want'. The two strategies she recommends are collective biography, 'in which students examine their own biographical texts', and the examination of popular texts written/produced by others. Her central goal (1994: 100) is 'to examine the multiple possible readings of any text and how they are arrived at' in order to 'make visible' that which 'is usually taken for granted'.

And yet it is possible to detect a lack of theoretical clarity in some poststructuralist analyses of subjectification, and a position closer to socialization theory than these theorists would wish. For example, Davies (1994: 100–1) uses collective biography to discover the place of menstrual taboos in girls' attitudes to their bodies. She concludes that '[I]ndividual men need do little to oppress individual women once they have taken on, as their own, the discourses about their own body which make it something to be secretive and shameful about. The oppression exists in the bodies as they are discursively constituted in this way.' The key focus for Davies then is girls' subjectivity and we will see below the reasons for feminists' increasing preoccupation with this topic. At this point, I wish only to suggest that Davies' statement seems to let men off the hook for their oppressive behaviours. Men too in this account are simply products of discourses, as we will see in the recent return to gender and gender equity among some poststructuralist feminists. If it is possible to disrupt discourses, I want to ask, can men be held accountable for failing to make this effort? Is it not also possible that current discursive constructions are seen as useful by some men? And, how are suggestions that women and girls are constrained and oppressed by their views about themselves any different from theory which talks about the need to challenge stereotypes, here the stereotype of women as 'polluted'? Is collective biography any different from consciousness raising, which suggested that women needed to get together to 'free themselves' from collective myths which constrained them? As Julie McLeod (1993: 110) elaborates, '[U]ltimately, Davies' resolution is not unlike that suggested by the sex-gender problematic, or by socialisation accounts which place great faith in the possibilities for changing social messages (read discursive forms and practices) through rationally instituting alternative messages.'

Poststructuralist analyses have, none the less, proved useful in rethinking the relationship between language and oppression as this was expressed in 1970s reform efforts. At that time, the attention to teaching texts produced a preoccupation with sexist language and with the need to remove it. There is no doubt that removing sexist language is a useful reform, but it is important to think about the theory and the inadequacies of the theory promoting this change. Language in this approach is treated as something we can stand outside of and alter. The implication is that language is a tool which can be used for repression or liberation. Poststructuralist theories of language challenge this assumption. In poststructuralist analysis (Black and Coward, 1990: 123), language is 'not inherently sexist or "man-made"'; rather linguistic systems 'serve as the basis for the production and interpretation of sets of related utterances – discourses – which effect and sustain the different categorization and positions of women and men'.

A simple illustration from a government publication addressed to nonsexist language allows us to pinpoint the different implications of these two approaches. A 1974 Ontario Status of Women Council publication entitled *About Face: Towards a More Positive Image of Women in Textbooks*, recommended challenging stereotypes 'by changing a few words'. One recommendation was to alter the aphorism 'boys will be boys' to read 'children will be children'. It is, of course, quite clear that a simple exchange of terminology does not capture the layers of meaning in the phrase 'boys will be boys'. Rather, the phrase neatly encapsulates a plethora of cultural codes regarding what boys are like and what they are allowed to do because of this. The task in approaching such usage can never be simple substitution of gender-neutral terms, but rather working 'to understand the cultural codes of the already-said' and their effects (Black and Coward, 1990: 125).

Making Girls Comfortable

The early 1970s emphasis in much feminist theory on women's *exclusion* from male domains was countered in the 1980s with new attention to the positive aspects of women's roles and character (Bacchi, 1990: Chapter 4). This new positive evaluation of women and their nature took many forms but in general the point was made that women did not want to become 'like men'; rather, they had positive contributions to make to considerations of social values and social change. In some versions this shift in emphasis produced writings which tended to characterize oversimply something they called 'women's culture'. Other feminists, in particular Black feminists, took these analyses to task for their essentializing tendencies and drew attention to important differences among women. Feminist theory in the 1980s as a result paid more attention to the content of the category 'women'. This had important effects on the foci and recommendations for change in the educational domain.

In education theory this shift in emphasis appeared in increased attention to girls' educational experiences. Lyn Yates (1992: 98) describes the change from a 'framework of reform' of 'women's inequality' to a framework of 'Girls Comfort in Schools'. Gaskell et al. (1989: 39) talk about 'Reformulating the Problem: Giving a Voice to

Women'. Government documents reflected this change, with the word 'girls' now featuring prominently, replacing words like 'sexism' and 'equal opportunity'. Pam Gilbert (1996: 2) draws attention to this shift in nomenclature. Another way to think about the change is as a shift from a concern with creating a nonsexist environment, one in which gender would not matter, to an antisexist environment, paying particular attention to the impact of sexist practices on girls. There was an emphasis on encouraging gender awareness, instead of gender neutrality. The new focus on girls' experiences and the implications of this focus can best be understood by examining five interrelated themes: teacher behaviour, boys' harassment of girls, nontraditional study areas, girls' resistance to feminism, and differences among girls.

Theories which emphasized the role of teachers as socializers (see above) brought attention to bear on teacher behaviour. Dale Spender and others (Spender and Sarah, 1980) produced useful studies showing that teachers, male and female, gave more attention to boys than girls. Disturbingly, this was the case even when teachers consciously attempted the reverse, that is, to pay more attention to girls. One response to this discovery, the most obvious response, is to include some study of gender issues in teacher training. While this was proposed, little in fact has been done (Julien, 1987: see also Dagenais, 1996). The discovery that even teachers who were sensitive to gender issues found it difficult to treat boys and girls equally, moreover, suggested that improving teacher education would not necessarily solve the problem. Rather, this insight into the intractability of gender bias strengthened analyses which stressed that teachers did not and could not stand outside the production of gender. Poststructuralist analyses of subjectification (see above) seemed more useful then than socialization theory.

The chief new discovery about problems in girls' experience of schooling was the discovery of harassment. Here it was found that girls experienced great discomfort because of a range of behaviours by boy students. At times these behaviours were called sexual harassment but, as Pam Gilbert (1996: 18–20) shows, many felt that it seemed odd to call behaviours amongst elementary school children 'sexual'; and yet girls were certainly being harassed. More general terms, 'sexist harassment', 'sex-based harassment', 'gender harassment' were coined to describe these behaviours. Lyn Yates (1993b: 5, 8) is doubtless correct to suggest that the explicit addressing of these behaviours in policy marks an important shift in problematizing from girls' to boys' behaviours. She notes approvingly the appearance in the 1987 *National Policy for the Education of Girls in Australian Schools* (Commonwealth Schools Commission, 1987) of 'sexual harassment' as 'a key issue for schools to confront'. And yet, as with any policy area, it is important to apply What's the Problem (represented to be)? to sexual harassment policy. We need to ask, for example, to what extent the 'problem' is represented to be systemic in contrast to being a matter of individual deviancy. We will be taking a closer look at the problem representations in portrayals of violence and sexual harassment in Chapters 9 and 10.

The discovery that the gender politics of the classroom harmed girls' educational experience led some educators to endorse single-sex education, either for schools or for some particular classes, such as mathematics. This suggestion has not gone unchallenged. Some feminists have questioned the claim that girls perform better in single-sex situations, drawing attention to the fact that most single-sex educational experiences tend, in Australia at any rate, to be in private schools (compare Weiner et al., 1998: 100). So, the problem may be not the presence of boys but the character of the education. Some also question whether segregation is a desirable way to solve the 'problem' which Eileen Byrne (1992: 190) for one describes as a 'discipline problem'. She wants to institute a reform agenda which highlights the need for boys to alter their antisocial behaviours: '[O]ur argument is to deal with the real problems head on, and not by (yet again) asking girls to take evasive action, leaving boys to remain unsocialised with impunity.'

It was noted earlier that a concern with the underrepresentation of girls in science and technology studies has been constant from the early 1970s, but that some later studies offer new explanations of or reasons for the problem. Some feminists (see Acker and Oatley, 1993) began to question the assumption that the problem was girls' social-ization, or their lack of skill or unwillingness to take on the challenge. The new analysis looked at the science and mathematics curriculum and criticized its conceptual base, suggesting that girls respond better to studies that seem to have some community relevance. The problem then was the whole way in which these subjects were taught. Other feminists (Kenway, 1990) are confronting head-on the presumption that it is indeed desirable for girls to follow nontraditional pathways.

Part of this willingness to question the assumption that girls ought to be the ones to change and that such change would do them good comes from a greater willingness to learn from girls' schooling experiences and their experiences of feminism (Kenway, 1993). The discovery of a lack of responsiveness to or even active hostility on the part of girls to feminism has produced the conclusion that 'unidimensional, essentialist, quick fix, one-off approaches to gender reform will not work for them; that different feminisms will be appropriate for different circumstances'. This research also emphasizes that 'any pedagogies which imply a deficit view of girls or of femaleness and which position them as passive should not be employed' (Kenway, 1993: 75). Drawing upon poststructuralist insights into the constitution of subjectivities, the advice is to work through pleasure instead of being relentlessly critical of girls' fantasies. The focus on girls' and women's agency means allowing them the space to think through and play with the roles they have been assigned. The point here is that behaviours which would at an earlier stage in feminist theorizing have been called 'false consciousness', now appear as reasonable behaviours given the ways in which women are constrained to live their lives (Manicom, 1992: 373). These behaviours, from applying heavy makeup to reading romance, become strategies for dealing with oppression, not signs of that oppression. Along similar lines, Victoria Foster (1996) insists that, given the heavy penalties imposed on those who openly associate with feminism, the aversion of many girls is readily understandable.

Attention to girls' educational experience also reflected the new emphasis in feminist theory on differences among women and girls. As noted in passing above, many feminists have become attuned to the need not to generalize or homogenize women's experience, how doing so not only excludes the experiences of some women, but also misrepresents the problem for some women. For example, it is now commonly accepted that Betty Friedan's (1965) description of life in suburbia as the 'problem with no name', really described the experience of white, middle-class women. Black feminists pointed out that Black women often have a completely different experience of family life which, for many, provides a genuine haven in a racist world (Bacchi, 1990: Chapter 4). The way in which attention is directed to differences among girls is not unproblematic, however. Georgina Tsolidis (1993) notes the tendency to see 'other' girls as themselves the problem, transferring the deficit model from all girls to marked groups of girls. A focus on differences among women can also be used to challenge the political usefulness of a category 'women', undermining reforms which target this category (Bacchi, 1996: 76). In addition, Lyn Yates (1992: 103) is critical of the ways in which references to girls' 'differences' and 'differences among girls' have been incorporated into the *National Policy for the Education of Girls* Commonwealth Schools Commission, 1987). She finds that critique has been replaced by the 'language of embracement'. From this example, Yates draws attention to the ways in which the language of feminist politics is taken up but transformed and contained when it is made policy. In her view, the way in which difference was taken up in the *National Policy* was very different from the way feminists spoke about it; it became a matter simply for addition rather than seeing it as a way of 'contesting what is to count as the problem'. Girls', she concludes, continue to be 'those to be done to' (Yates, 1992: 105). Here we gain an insight into the politics of problem representation, making it necessary to attend closely to problem representations to tease out their implications. The politics of problem representation is nowhere clearer than in the recent discussion of boys in education.

Girls are Beating Boys – What's the Problem?

In many countries a new education discourse has appeared, one which insists that equal opportunity for girls has achieved its purpose, and that boys are now the ones who need 'help'. Headlines in Australian newspapers declare 'Boys left behind at school' (*The Adelaide Advertiser*, 23 July 1996) and 'Put to the test, girls are smarter' (*The Adelaide Advertiser*, 15 July 1996). Along similar lines, Montreal's *le Devoir* (31 October 1995) asked: '*Les garçons: victimes du système?*' *The Times Education Supplement* (Evans, 1996: 20) bemoaned the 'Perils of ignoring our lost boys', while the *Guardian* (11 July 1996, p. 9) noted 'Schools urged to focus on low achieving boys'. Victoria Foster (1995) highlights how girls' achievements in mathematics and science are being represented as proof that girls have achieved equality. This 'presumptive equality', in her view, sets the ground for current efforts to redirect funding, which previously targeted 'girls' inequality', to the 'needs of boys'.

The representation of boys as disadvantaged fits a new discursive representation of men as the victims of reforms benefiting women (see Bacchi, 1996: 157). 'Men' and 'boys' are portrayed as 'losing out' because of the attention paid to 'women' and 'girls'. The assumption is that the battle for 'girls' has been won, that 'girls' have had their day, and now it is time to turn attention and resources to 'boys'. So, we are told that 'girls' at school are now achieving better than 'boys', though it is sometimes admitted that the scholastic success does not carry over into postgraduate study. Other 'problems', like boys' violence and suicide rates, are explained as due to an educational experience which pays insufficient attention to boys' self-esteem (Foster, 1995: 8). A 1994 enquiry into boys' education, chaired by New South Wales MP Stephen O'Doherty, was followed by announcements that initiatives would soon be taken to improve boys' 'level of self-esteem and participation in a wide range of academic and associated activities' (*The Australian*, 2 February, 1995 in Bacchi, 1996: 97).

The focus on boys' self-esteem ignores social context (Foster, 1995: 8; Weiner et al., 1998: 104). Complex problems, such as stress due to unemployment and lack of resources, are reduced to psychological diagnoses. With such a problem representation, the 'solution' becomes therapy rather than social change. The focus on 'boys' educational disadvantage' also tends to present the situation as a win–lose scenario, so that for boys' needs to be tended to, attention to girls needs to cease or be reduced. Such a representation serves as a rationale for redirecting resources away from programmes targeting girls (see Foster, 1995). Studies highlighting the scholastic success of some girls also pay little or no attention to the *content* of the school curriculum. As Alison Jones (1993: 19) points out, in general, 'girls' are achieving an understanding of an 'alienated curriculum' – '[T]hey are learning that boys' and men's perspectives and achievements are better, more worth listening to, more authoritative. They are learning to undervalue women's work and authority and contribution to school knowledge.' They are offered an understanding of 'woman' as 'she' is currently positioned by men's discourses in our society. Supplementing this insight, Victoria Foster (1996: 49) points out that the 'problem' is being represented as one of 'girls beating boys' and beating them in their own areas, mathematics and science. She wonders if any attention would be paid to girls beating boys in home economics.

Foster (1995: 7) draws attention to the resurfacing of the language of 'restrictive stereotypes' in the 1994 New South Wales Draft Report on the Inquiry into Boys' Education and some of the problems with this: 'it is assumed that while girls have one lot of problems (which have largely been ameliorated), boys have another complementary lot'. Foster notes appropriately, '[T]his discursive content avoids altogether any challenge to the fundamental asymmetry of gender relations in society and in schooling. The preference is rather to view men's place in gender relations as roughly equivalent to women's place in gender relations, and of the same order of oppression.' We noted earlier the way in which socialization theory which grounds a focus on stereotypes has produced analyses which see men as equally 'disadvantaged' by the gender order, ignoring the benefits men accrue from current social arrangements.

Having drawn attention to some limitations in the current casting of 'boys' as 'disadvantaged', it is important to note that attention to boys and their education is coming simultaneously from a completely different direction and is a result of the poststructuralist interest in subjectification and in the production (or social construction) of gender. The concern, as expressed in writers like Bronwyn Davies (1994), is the way in which boys and girls get locked into construc-tions of masculinity and femininity which narrow their visions of the world and which can have some very negative consequences especially, but not solely, for girls. Davies is particularly attentive to the negative effects of hegemonic masculinity. For poststruc-turalists the way to undo these effects is for students to reflect upon the discourses which operate to so construct their subjectivities. We mentioned before the strategies of collective biography and the deconstruction of popular texts. The ultimate goal, in Davies' words, is the production of multiple I's and the freeing of men and women from the restrictive male/female binary. As Lyn Yates (1993a: 52) describes, the goal for writers like Davies is 'an eventual stage where gender ceases to be important, where we do not conceive masculinity and femininity as organising frameworks.'

This analysis offers a very different agenda from the 'boys as disadvantaged' position described above. For the latter the problem is simply lack of attention to boys which can be met by reducing attention to girls; for poststructuralists the problem is hegemonic masculinity which requires a rethinking of the curriculum for boys and girls. Pam Gilbert (1996: 14) notes how the use of 'gender' in educational discourses can serve very different purposes. While on the one hand it represents 'a strategic policy of being regarded as "even-handed" in the consideration of girls and boys', on the other it indicates 'a theoretical commitment to working with issues affecting girls within a framework of gender relations and the social construction of gender'. These different representations of the problem have very different effects: the former suggests nothing other than 'equal attention', which could be translated as equal resources; the latter wants significant revision of the curriculum to direct attention to the social construction of gender. These very different problem representations need to be emphasized because of the ease with which they could be represented, for political purposes, as one and the same agenda.

Here it becomes important to ensure that the theoretical grounding of the poststructuralist analysis be sound. As I suggested earlier, I feel there are theoretical lacunae which need to be filled. In a sense the proposal that gender cease to be important sounds a little like 1970s feminist hopes for an androgynous future. Attention to the negative effects of gender constructions then is certainly not new, though the emphasis on hegemonic masculinity is greater in the poststructuralist literature, and the use of discourse to understand the processes certainly is new. But, as Julie McLeod (1993: 112) points out, in some accounts, discursive construction 'might just as well be described as "socialization"'. Yates (1993a: 70) is also justifiably concerned that such a project could produce a new limiting stereotype of girls as uninterested in mathematics, making invisible the many girls who enjoy the subject.

In order to ensure that feminist interpretations of the nature of a gender agenda not be co-opted, a number of feminists have conceded the need to retain the education discourse which focuses upon girls and their negative experiences in particular educational settings. Pam Gilbert (1996: 16) identifies the two agendas as the 'education of girls' programme which 'places its emphasis more on the impact of schooling on girls' lives: on the education of girls', and a 'construction of femininity in relation to masculinity' programme, 'working to improve the lot of girls (and of boys) by breaking down the dualistic gendered order of gender or "sexist" stereotypes'. In her view, discourses about gender and education need to 'draw from both agendas'.

Conclusion

In this chapter we have seen the need to ask repeatedly What's the Problem (represented to be)? in order to uncover the layers or nesting of problem representations and the stakes they involve. For example, it is difficult to compare approaches to girls' education without considering more general attitudes towards the function of education. Those who are optimistic about the role education can play as social equalizer tend to represent educational reform as the key to ending 'women's inequality'. Others who see education as a lead player in the mystification of oppression are less sanguine about reform in this domain. It is no coincidence here that groups commonly excluded from the cultural frameworks shaping educational institutions are highly suspicious of an approach which advocates simply 'joining in'. Roxana Ng (1993), for example, notes that such an agenda underplays the social relations *outside* the school which shape what happens *in* schools.

In this chapter, asking What's the Problem (represented to be)? allowed us to draw out distinctions between 'equal access' and poststructuralist approaches to education, while identifying ambiguities in positions, and indeed some common ground. For equal access advocates, the dominant emphasis is upon gaining entry to existing educational opportunities. Poststructuralist scholars are sceptical about the benefits of this enterprise, but many none the less want equal access to an altered curriculum. We have also gained insights into important differences in current concerns with boys' education. Here a focus on proposals revealed two very different problem representations. Recommendations to shift resources from girls to boys construct the problem to be excessive attention to girls and inadequate attention to boys. By contrast, demands for changes to the curriculum to create space to reflect on the socially constructed nature of masculinity and femininity construct the problem to be the power of the gender binary in our lives. By clarifying problem representations, a What's the Problem? approach clarifies contending political agendas.

Note

1 I would place Davies in the second category. As seen below, she offers concrete strategies which she believes develop critical consciousness.

7

CHILD CARE POLICY: WHO GAINS?

A What's the Problem? approach recommends examining policy proposals, including policy instruments, as a way to uncover problem representations. Currently, the central debates about child care concern how the service is to be provided and paid for. Proposals often intersect with general debates about funding of public services, and the place of 'private' enterprise in providing public services. Within these proposals, at least three problem representations emerge: first, child care as necessary to facilitate women's workforce participation; second, child care as welfare; and third, child care as early childhood education. Some things can usefully be said, as we will see, about each of these representations separately. But more useful is to examine the ways in which they combine to shape the possiblities for the provision of child care. In the process of analysing this shaping of child care, it is important to keep in mind the positions of those who oppose child care in almost any form, and their reasons for opposition. However, the main purpose of a What's the Problem? approach is to examine how *endorsements* of a reform carry problem representations which have particular effects. And in the assessment of these effects, it is always crucial to ask what is not problematized in this or these representations.

Child Care and Women's Inequality: 'Letting' Women Work

In this part of the book we are examining the theme of 'women's inequality' and the kinds of reforms promoted by governments to deal with it. To date we have looked at pay equity (Chapter 4), equal opportunity and affirmative action (Chapter 5) and education reform (Chapter 6). In a number of countries, including Australia, Canada and the United States, child care is increasingly being put forward as *the* solution to women's inequality.

Feminists active in these countries in the 1970s put the issue on their wish-lists early in the piece. The American National Organization for Women, for example, included it on their first agenda (Bacchi, 1990: 80). And Canada's Royal Commission on the Status of Women (1970: 270) made it a key demand. Rosalie Abella's 1984 Report on Equality in Employment in Canada (Abella, 1984: 178, cited in Friendly, 1994: 34) described child care as 'the ramp that provides equal access to the workforce for mothers'. Child care provision in this interpretation provides the necessary support to facilitate women's access to the labour market which, it is assumed, will improve their social status and their material living conditions.

In Canada the prominence of the representation of the problem as 'women's lack of access to the workforce' is clear in the fact that the computing of need for child care is based upon the numbers of 'working' mothers (Friendly, 1994: 43). A tax deduction for child care expenses was introduced in 1971 (Mahon, 1997: 400), tying the 'problem' of child care to women's employment. In Australia in 1994 (Brennan, 1994: 210), under Prime Minister Paul Keating, a child care cash rebate was introduced, amongst the beneficiaries of which were again 'working' women. Feminists in other countries have had less success in winning recognition of child care as a business expense, and some feminists are reluctant to go down this path. Among the latter, there is a recognition that such a policy benefits only some women at the expense of others and misrepresents the kind of reform child care needs to be. Audrey Macklin (1992: 498) puts the case that '[W]hile such an analysis may operate to the taxpayer's advantage in the particular case, it ultimately harms women by assisting the least needy and legitimating the inequality of the most disadvantaged.' In most countries in Western Europe, according to Martha Friendly (1994: 42), 'child care supply is considered in relation to *all* children, not just children whose mothers are in the labour force [original emphasis]'. Her example is Sweden. And yet, even in Sweden, which is reputed to lead the way in the provision of publicly funded child care services, 'working' mothers are given priority in access to child care.

There is a nesting of problem representations here which needs to be untangled. In the Preamble to Part Two we touched briefly on some of the limitations in an interpretation which equates women's 'equality' with labour force participation. Such an analysis ignores the fact that many women have been participants in the workforce for some time and this has not produced their liberation. A class dimension is sadly lacking in this analysis. In addition, such an analysis equates workforce participation with success and self-actualization, implying denigration of homemaking and child rearing as fulfilling tasks. Some feminists associated with equal rights feminism in the United States and elsewhere encouraged this understanding. Listen for example to the written submission from the Commission on the Status of Women, Iowa State House, to the Equal Rights Amendment Senate hearings: '[I]f women were meant to be maternity machines, they would not have been given minds' (Bacchi, 1990: 80). To note this is not to paint feminism simplistically as anti-maternity nor to suggest that governments ought to encourage women to be full-time homemakers, but simply to draw attention to the underexamined assumption that paid labour is necessarily challenging and rewarding while mothering is not. For many women, paid labour means long hours on assembly lines. For some women mothering offers a kind of personal fulfilment unavailable in the market. Most women confront the dilemma of trying to meet the obligations of both domains. A focus on access to paid labour as liberation also collapses all the many difficulties women face, in the realm of personal harassment and violence, to a common base of economic dependence.

In addition, Simon Duncan (1996: 415) found, in his analysis of the underlying cause of gender inequality in the European Union, that child care is not the determining variable in women's employment levels and status. Nor does child care on its own 'address the gendered division of labour in the home' (Teghtsoonian, 1995: 425 fn 41). Despite the continued efforts of feminists worldwide to direct attention to the unequal division of domestic responsibilities, this subject has attracted less attention than a narrative which talks about 'releasing' women to 'work'. Even in those countries, like Sweden and Norway, where child care is considered a community need, women continue to struggle to achieve meaningful change in the domestic division of labour within the home. Susan Prentice (1988: 61) agrees that

> [W]hile expanded childcare services will improve many women's lives and make their paid labour more possible, it leaves gender relations within nuclear families unchanged, does not challenge the social definition of woman as mother, and does nothing to reorganize the seemingly unbridgeable chasm of 'public' and 'private' realms and responsibilities.

Tying the need for child care to women's workforce participation also has some dangers. There is an unexpressed assumption here that women are 'permitted' to 'work' when the economy requires their presence. In the United States, the National Governors' Association argued that government support for affordable child care services was necessary, in part, because 'tightening of the U.S. labor markets in the 1990s means that in order for our country to remain economically competitive, we will need to further encourage the participation of women, poor, and minorities in the labor force' (US Senate Committee on Labor and Human Resources, 1988: 224, cited in Teghtsoonian, 1996: 135). The flipside, of course, is the ease with which removal of 'support' could be justified in less favourable economic conditions. In the 1994 Canadian budget the priority placed upon economic need was confirmed by the fact that the federal funds allocated for increasing the number of regulated child care spaces during the 1990s would not be spent 'if Canada's economic growth is less than three percent annually' (Teghtsoonian, 1995: 439 fn 72). In these scenarios, women's labour force participation is only contingently acceptable (Teghtsoonian, 1996: 134).

Moreover, as Allison Tom (1992/3) points out, there is, in the easy assumption that child care will free women, inadequate attention to the providers of that care. These providers will almost invariably be women who are paid inadequately. In many instances, migrant women will provide the care so that white, middle-class women can 'go to work'. Finally, in the equation of child care and 'freedom' to 'work', there is an assumption that women who do not engage in paid labour have full and sole responsibility for child nurture, and that this is appropriate, even natural. As a result, it has been very difficult to get the issue of child care for 'non-working' mothers seriously addressed. Deborah Brennan (1992: 73) points out that Australia has been more successful here at achieving some 'respite' care for 'non-working' mothers, but the assumption remains that in general the task of family nurture is theirs. Even some articulate promoters of child care express ambivalence when it comes to the subject of child care provision for 'stay-at-home mothers'. Listen, for example, to Martha Friendly (1994: 254), a long-time campaigner for child care in Canada: 'whether the private care of one's own children should be paid for by public funds is a separate question.' Here there is a clear need to analyse and break down the care/work dichotomy and the conception of child nurture as a private task which structures some of this discussion.

Many of the *opponents* of public provisioning of child care describe child rearing as a 'private' issue and hence as an inappropriate arena for government intervention in any form, even for 'working' mothers. Under Thatcher in Britain, the view that child care is a 'private matter' was explicit: '[I]n 1985, Chris Patten, the minister with responsibility for child care matters, stated that "day care will continue to be primarily a matter for private arrangement between parents and private and voluntary resources, except where there are special needs" ' (Brennan, 1992: 75; see also Morris and Nott, 1995: 72). We will be saying more about 'special needs' shortly. For people who express this view, the care of children is not a problem since it is clear who should be doing it and where – mothers at home. Here we have a clear and forceful instance of the evocation of the public/private dichotomy to contain agendas, to prevent certain issues from gaining recognition as appropriate topics for political consideration. This provides a striking example of a fundamental premise of a What's the Problem? approach – the ways in which the discursive construction of a problem limits what can be talked about (see Chapter 2).

The operation of the public/private dichotomy in political debate has attracted a good deal of theoretical attention, from feminists and others (Kennedy, 1982; Okin, 1991; Pateman, 1983; Thornton, 1991b). The term 'private' is most commonly applied in discussions of 'private' enterprise and in descriptions of family life. The commonality in the invocation of the term in these instances is to suggest that different treatment is appropriate in these 'different spheres' or, more specifically, to serve as a rationale for distinguishing degrees of justifiable 'public' intervention into the several 'parts' of our social existence. The 'private' part of the dichotomy, be it the family or 'private' enterprise, is represented to be solely of 'personal' interest and hence closed to 'public' supervision. And yet the application of this rule is inconsistent. For example, conceptions of the family as the socialiser of the next generation are used to justify 'public' intervention when families are deemed to be inadequate to the task. This was the rationale for removing Aboriginal children in Australia from their families and mothers. So, it seems, some families are more 'private' than others, and this distinction is based upon judgements about quality of family life, judgements which are necessarily normative. A central task of a What's the Problem? approach is to examine linkages in arguments, expose inconsistencies and tease out their implications. The implied distinction between 'quality' and 'unwholesome' family life in the creating of some families as more 'private' than others provides the background to the development in child care debates which postulates the need for child care for 'children at risk' in 'problem families' (see below).

Frances Olsen (1985) adds the important insight that the intervention/non-intervention dichotomy, which acts as a supporting narrative in the public/private distinction, is highly mystifying since in reality the government is intervening all the time in the shaping of our lives, when it legislates and when it fails to legislate. Not funding child care, for example, is a form of intervention in our intimate lives since the availability or lack of availability of child care will affect how we live those lives. This is especially so for women who, it is assumed, fill the role of child carer naturally. Here we have a central insight produced by asking What's the Problem (represented to be)? – the way in which declaring certain areas outside the bounds of justifiable intervention mystifies the ways in which government activities constitute relations within those areas. We can see then the central importance of drawing attention to the way in which a whole range of issues is located in a space labelled 'non-political'. The feminist claim that the personal is political, in one interpretation, is a direct challenge to this labelling. In Roberta Hamilton's (1996: 171) words, '[F]eminists led the way in transforming every woman's private trouble into a public policy issue.' Increased availability of child care on its own does not overthrow the public/private distinction, however. As we saw above, availability of child care does not necessarily touch the domestic division of labour and is only one step to the kind of rearrangements of working conditions which would allow a successful blending of market and domestic responsibilities.

Here it is important to remember that, from the outset, there was a clear administrative agenda behind the introduction of child care policy. In a What's the Problem? approach, it is always useful to consider when and why an issue comes onto the agenda. Rianne Mahon (1997: 397) notes that the first federal peace time subsidies for child care (included in the Canada Assistance Plan of 1966) were largely the 'product of bureaucratic initiatives', and that, as in Sweden, this beginning of the break with the male breadwinner model commenced when 'labour markets were tight, job growth was increasingly concentrated in the service sector and women's labour force participation was on the rise'. In Australia, the first Child Care Act was introduced by a Liberal government in 1972. As Deborah Brennan (1994: 111) points out, the Act was framed 'with reference to the needs of the workforce'. This same emphasis on child care as a prerequisite to women's labour force participation is clear, more recently, in the 1995 Joint Hearing on Child Care and Child Welfare (US Committee on Ways and Means and US Committee on Economic and Educational Opportunities, 1995: 10), when the Assistant Secretary for Children and Families, US Department of Health and Human Services, Mary Jo Bane declared: '[F]or working parents and for those who are seeking to establish a foothold in the labour force, child care is an essential service.'

The ageing of the population and the need for a tax-paying labour force to fund welfare provision of the aged and those of poor health has meant that women's labour force participation becomes an attractive prospect. A 1990 Occasional Paper produced for the OECD (Very, 1990: 9, 17) describes child care policy as a 'subsidy to child-bearing' which might assist with the ageing population problem. The same report pointed out that the tax governments glean from working mothers covers the costs of child care provision. The other social change prompting the encouragement of female labour force participation and hence child care has been the liberalization of divorce laws and the number of divorced women on public 'assistance'. In many countries women form the majority of those on social benefits and many of these are divorced women. In the Netherlands, for example, Wiebrens (1988: 133) records a rise from 46.3 divorces per 10,000 married males in 1971 to 83 per 10,000 in 1981. In 1990, one out of every ten women, between the ages of 28 and 44, depended on minimum social benefits in the Netherlands. Here, as in all the Western democracies serving as examples in this study, there have been overt attempts to get these 'single' women who are often mothers 'back to work'. In the Netherlands it was proposed in 1993 that even women with children under the age of 12 ought to be required to pursue a job if they were to be entitled to government support (Bacchi, 1996: 128). Deborah Brennan (1994: 199) confirms that the expansion in child care services in Australia is due to the fact 'that the Labor government has become increasingly receptive to the argument that expenditure on child care is not simply a drain on the economy but, if linked to workforce participation, can lead to increased taxation revenues and reductions in certain kinds of welfare expenditures such as sole parents pensions and family payments' (see discussion below).

We could see child care here as reflecting a more general shift in welfare policy which Sheila Shaver (1993) describes as a shift from 'difference' towards 'equality' in the treatment of women. What Shaver calls 'equality', however, is more appropriately described as *equal treatment* and is premised on the desire to increase self-sufficiency. Listen, for example, to the stated intention of the Dutch Ministry of Social Affairs and Employment in its 1985 Equal Rights Plan – 'adults will usually be expected to maintain themselves by working' (Bacchi, 1996: 129). As Ann Orloff (1993: 326) points out, in many countries the majority opinion is coming to favour all women working for pay. Where this leaves the unpaid responsibilities of rearing children and caring for others who require care is unaddressed in this vision.

The goal in encouraging women's workforce participation is not, however, necessarily *women's* economic independence. Rather, women's earning capacity has been identified as making an import-ant contribution to the capacity of *families* to remain economically independent. The Australian Council of Social Services (ACOSS), the peak organization representing welfare agencies in Australia, stated that '[C]hild care services make a considerable contribution to the capacity of families to remain economically independent' (ACOSS, 1988, cited in Brennan, 1992: 72). The problem representation in this vision of child care is *family dependence*, not women's inequality. And the solution becomes the two income family. Child care has long been seen as necessary to *family* self-sufficiency in the Nordic coun-tries. In Sweden, for example, where an economic boom necessitated the involvement of women in paid labour and where there was an equal concern about a declining birthrate, it was decided to facilitate women's workforce participation through the public provision of child care. Though this caused more concern than parental leave because, as Joan Eveline (1994a: 318) points out, it allowed women to *leave* their homes to work, the intent was more to make family life for 'working mothers' feasible than to undermine it. As I note in *The Politics of Affirmative Action* (1996: 154), child care can be seen 'as a means of facilitating the sharing of paid labour *between* spouses, with the woman working part-time, not necessarily increasing *"women's"* full-time labour force participation.'

The mainstreaming of child care in political discourse therefore has no necessary connection with an agenda of improving women's lives, despite its labelling as a 'women's issue'. This rubric is commonly applied to all the topics examined in this part of the book. Labelling a policy domain a 'women's issue' can be used to highlight the fact that women are disproportionately the ones affected by these policies; however, the labelling is often a way of marginalizing the topic. 'Women's issues' are also considered part of 'social policy', producing a dual denigration given the priority placed on economic policy (Saunders, 1994). And, in some accounts, the equating of child care with women as carers marks them as 'different', justifying a range of policies which instantiate the status quo (Bacchi, 1990: Chapter 10 and *passim*).

Child Care as Welfare: 'Letting' Poor Women Work

Child care subsidies, where they exist, target the 'needy'. In Canada, for example, alongside the tax rebate, federal support for child care came 'as part of the larger package of social assistance reforms', the Canada Assistance Plan (CAP) of 1966 (Mahon, 1997: 399). CAP provided assistance for those 'in need, or likely to become in need' in the form of means-tested day care subsidies for low income-parents who met the 'need' criteria set by provincial and sometimes local governments. Britain's Children Act 1989 also 'institutes a public duty to provide "day care" services, but only for children defined by welfare authorities as "in need"' (Moss and Penn, 1996: 36). This form of funding constitutes child care a 'welfare problem' and not a general right of parents, as different in other words from public education. It also of necessity makes debates about child care cross over what Nancy Fraser (1989: Chapter 8) has described as 'needs discourses'. Despite the apparent transparency of the language of need, deciding on the nature of and level of need is a normative and hence political activity. In Britain, under Margaret Thatcher, the category of those 'in need' was seriously narrowed. As Peter Moss, Convenor of the European Community Child Care Network in 1984, describes:

> [P]ublic day care . . . is only available where parents are deemed to be not coping or children are thought to be at risk: children will not be considered for a place in publicly-funded care because their parents are employed, unless the parent is a lone mother or father. In recent years even children of employed lone parents have been less likely to get a place, as Social Services Departments have increasingly used publicly-funded services for children thought to be 'at risk' – especially of physical or sexual abuse. (Moss, 1991: 125, cited in Brennan, 1992: 75)

I will say more about the notion of being 'at risk' below.

Where targeting of families in 'need' takes place, the declared goal is creating these families as self-sufficient, reducing the welfare 'burden'. A report commissioned by the Australian Labour government and published by the Department of Community Services and Health (Anstie et al., 1988, cited in Brennan, 1994: 197) emphasized that women's participation in the labour force was one of the chief ways for low-income *families* to avoid poverty, relieving governments of the burden of their support. The testimony of Rep. Randy Cunningham, Chairman [*sic*], Subcommittee on Early Childhood, Youth and Families to the Joint Hearing on Child Care and Child Welfare, illustrates the continuing power of this argument for child care: '[A] mother on welfare cannot go to work unless she can get care for her child' (US Committee on Ways and Means, and Committee on Economic and Educational Opportunities, 1995: 6). In supporting evidence, Cunningham elaborated the claim that gaps in child care services limited 'the ability of low-income families to achieve self-sufficiency'. The need for better child care services was explicitly linked to the need to rethink the policies of the Great Society, in particular a system of welfare which, in Cunningham's words, 'has laid families low': '[I]t encourages births out of wedlock. It separates families. It entraps men and women into a horrible cycle of welfare dependency – or, more accurately, welfare slavery.'

A particular concern is single mothers. In Canada, child care was included under CAP 'as a by-product of inter-governmental negotiations over other matters'. As the federal government had assumed some responsibility for single mothers on welfare, Rianne Mahon (1997: 399) points out, it was prepared to learn from the US war on poverty, 'which included an attempt to get single mothers off the dole and into the labour force by making federal funds available to states that were prepared to establish the appropriate programmes'. Nancy Fraser and Linda Gordon (1994: 323, 311) note the tendency to enshrine the 'poor solo mother' as the 'quintessential welfare dependent', and how this labelling tends to create the hazards of their existence as individual problems, 'as much moral or psychological as economic'.

It is impossible to consider the implications of constituting child care a 'welfare problem' outside of consideration of the ways in which welfare itself is constituted. Again, we have an example of the nesting of problem representations which requires analysis. Fraser and Gordon's (1994) genealogy of 'dependence' provides some useful pointers. They note the general agreement among 'policy experts' that welfare dependency is 'bad for people', that 'it undermines their motivation to support themselves'. In this representation, welfare recipients are constituted the problem, lacking character and drive. A good deal of policy analysis, as we have already seen, constructs 'victims' as 'problems'. Douglas Torgerson (1996: 278) draws attention to policy discourse which constructs and perpetuates stigmatized identities through 'individuous distinctions' such as self-sufficiency/ dependency, deserving/undeserving, responsible/promiscuous. He offers an example useful for our purposes here: '[T]he troubles of poor women with children are thus perpetuated by a discursive practice that helps to construct female-headed, single-parent families as a marginal "other" suited for inferior benefits and punitive therapeutic practices.' Problem representations in policy texts play a crucial role in the way in which groups are assigned position and value within policy discourse. Unless we recognize and discuss this, there is a tendency to accept these designations as accurate reflections of some outside reality.

There have been moves in Australia and Canada to replace targeted child care subsidies to poor families with a child care benefit paid directly to 'families'. The conservative parties in Sweden have advanced a similar agenda (Bacchi, 1996: 117). In 1995 in Britain John Major's Conservative government piloted a programme in which families were given vouchers of £1100 for pre-school education for 4-year-olds (Moss and Penn, 1996: viii). In these proposals the 'problem' of child care is represented to be a matter of 'women's choices' and, more often, a matter of 'family choice'. We are told that families ought to be provided with the funds directly so that they can 'choose' the kind of care they 'want' for their children. Defending the nation-wide expansion of the voucher scheme in Britain, Education Secretary Gillian Shephard claimed '[N]ursery vouchers give parents a real choice by placing purchasing power squarely in their hands' ('*PA*' *News*, 1 April 1997). A 1996 Australian Task Force (Economic Planning Advisory Commission, 1996: 47), endorsing the paying of a credit directly to parents, heralded the way in which families would be 'empowered'. It was argued that direct payments 'may help to foster desirable cultural and attitudinal changes in both families and providers'. These 'desirable' changes are not elaborated, but the impression is that this reallocation of decision making to parents will encourage such things as independent thinking which in turn produces, it is hoped in this interpretation, self-sufficiency. Here we have an excellent example of the role of policy in constituting particular types of subjectivity.

Feminists have spent some time examining the language of choice and its uses in politics. The theme was touched on in Chapter 4 on pay equity and comes up again in the next chapter on abortion. The rhetorical framing of the problem of child care as a matter of choice plays to the power of this ideograph (see Condit, 1990: 227), while neglecting the conditions which facilitate genuine choice. People can use public child care facilities, for example, only if these exist and, if public funding of infrastructure is denied, this is unlikely to be the case. As Peter Moss and Helen Penn (1996: 144) explain, by themselves, vouchers (or similar subsidies) 'provide no new places'. The language of choice in this case also suggests a minimal role for government in 'private' lives, neglecting the way in which this kind of policy creates the conditions which will *shape* people's lives (see above). Moreover, the targeting of 'families' ignores the operation of power *within* families, power over resources for example. Feminists have insisted upon the need to reconsider the common assumption in policy making that families are harmonious units.

References to the importance of family life are more commonly associated with *opponents* of child care. Here it is interesting to see how a continuing effort to defend the traditional family form is reconciled with a desire to get more women into the labour force, recognized by many as an economic necessity and as a way to reduce the welfare 'burden'. Katherine Teghtsoonian (1995: 418–20) describes how class is used to mediate this tension. In the political discourse of Canada's conservatives, for example, it is clear that the goal is to increase labour force participation for *working-class* women, while encouraging *middle-class* women to retain an 'appropriate' maternal presence at home. Similarly in the United States, conservatives 'seek to reinstate the male breadwinner/female homemaker for the middle class, while demanding that single mothers work' (Fraser, 1994: 592). Conservatives who opposed the Better Child Care Services Bill (see Teghtsoonian, 1996: 126) proposed in its place tax assistance to all families with young children, whether or not they had child care expenses. They argued that any other approach penalized women who 'chose' to remain home with their children. However, this tax credit was to be made available 'only to families in which at least one adult was employed in paid labor'. This requirement, as Teghtsoonian (1996: 139) argues, imposes 'a particular definition of the family structure within which women's decision to mother full-time would be deemed worthy of public support: those in which mothers are married to employed men'. She continues:

> [D]espite the rhetoric about the importance of full-time parental care for children's well-being, single mothers receiving welfare benefits were presented as being best served through support for child care services that would permit them to undertake paid employment.

In all the countries considered in this analysis, there has been debate about the size and role of private child care facilities. The swing to neoliberalism and 'market friendly' policy in Canada, the United States, Britain and Australia has meant an ever increasing role for private facilities. Katherine Teghtsoonian (1993: 121) remarks that federal subsidies to private facilities became more of a contested topic in Canada than in the United States where free market assumptions have a more secure heritage. In a 1996 Australian Task Force on child care (Economic Planning Advisory Commission, 1996: 36) the decision to encourage private facilities to operate, by allowing families to spend their benefit where they 'chose', was explicitly linked with a 'market friendly' policy direction. The same is true in Britian where one of the main attractions of the vouchers scheme was that 'it supports the development of a free market in services and empowers parents to participate fully in that market' (Moss and Penn, 1996: 144). Allowing private companies to 'sell' child care produces child care as a 'commodity'. What are the limitations in this problem representation? Markets sell what makes a profit. Even where there are provisions for standards, these will be difficult to enforce given this premise. Quality is seldom cheap. Some groups will also be underserviced. Private facilities are less likely to be available for the high-demand and hence high-cost infants and toddlers.

A shift towards the 'privatization' of care is also implicit in the increasing appearance of 'family friendly' policies as part of employment packages. Employers are left free to construct policies to suit economic circumstances. Those who make family friendly moves, meanwhile, score affirmative action points in countries which have such programmes for women (Bacchi, 1996: 133). This reinscribes the measures as 'for women', entrenching the allocation of child caring responsibilites to women. In addition, given the dominant construction of affirmative action as 'handouts to the needy', this locating of the policy brands it as 'a favour' rather than an obligation. The priority throughout, as Ruth Levitas points out, quoting from a 1994 European Commission White Paper on social and economic policy, is 'reconciling professional and family life' to facilitate the 'full integration of women into the labour market' (European Commission, 1994: 31, cited in Levitas, 1996: 8). In addition, the reframing of the issue as an 'employer responsibility' reduces the pressure on governments to provide publicly funded services. Clare Ungerson (1990, cited in Brennan, 1994: 209) makes just this point about the trend in Britain under Thatcher.

Some feminists, clearly opposed to the privatizing of child care, also express concerns about the *form* of *public* provision. For Susan Prentice (1988: 62) and Deborah Brennan (1994), the institutionalization of child care is a problem. Prentice talks about the focus on quantity rather than quality, and is insistent that the child care movement 'extend its demands beyond the call for universal access to include the transformative possibilities of non-commodified care'. Some of the firmest opposition to the 1996 Australian Task Force (Economic Planning Advisory Commission, 1996: 6) on child care came from the National Association of Community Based Children's Services and some feminist academics who objected to the emphasis in the report on market-driven choice, overlooking the special benefits of community-based care – 'promoting parental involvement and generating a greater sense of community'. Similarly, Peter Moss and Helen Penn (1996: 144) place a high value on 'social cohesion', to be accomplished through the provision of 'community-based, multifunctional and flexible' services. Concern about the institutionalization of child care intersects with the fear expressed in the preceding chapter about institutionalized education as regulator and normalizer of behaviour. Just as state education is a problem for people with such concerns, *state* child care is also a problem. This is so particularly when child care is represented as child development for children 'at risk'.

Child Care as Early Childhood Development: 'Rescuing' Poor Children

The third problem representation found in child care policies is the need for governments to participate in early child development. The reasons for this commitment are expressed differently in different places. In the United States the 1990 Act for Better Child Care Services stated as its goal to provide 'young children with a sound early childhood development experience' (in Berry, 1993: 176). This is in line with the National Education Goal established in 1990 that '[B]y the year 2000 all children in America will start school ready to learn' (in OECD, 1993: 1). A 1993 OECD Report, *Why Child Care Matters*, explained the context for this commitment: '[B]usiness and the economy as a whole gain a more productive work force when employees feel confident that their children are secure and learning. And society as a whole benefits when more families are self-sufficient . . .'. This emphasis on 'family' self-sufficiency appears repeatedly in the American child care literature. The view that education is a positive experience, even for the very young, however, has been expressed in many European countries for many years (see Friendly, 1994: 42, 55). In the United States it is clearly a particular group of children who are considered 'at risk' and in need of 'educating'. The OCED (1993: 1) report just mentioned emphasized 'the need to focus on the development and education of all children, *particularly* those who start life disadvantaged by such factors as poverty, racial discrimination, lack of English-language skills, and family and community breakdown [emphasis added].' However, it is not unusual to find a pedagogic discourse among social democrats in Sweden, for example, endorsing education and public day care as a way of erasing the 'disadvantages' arising out of working-class origins (Mahon, 1997: 390). When we look at particular proposals, however, different problem representations appear and with them different implications for the groups targeted.

A 1972 Brookings Institute report (Schultze et al., 1972, cited in Rainwater, 1974a: 269) identified three reasons for the growing pressure for public provision or subsidization of day care: first, concern with reducing welfare rolls by enabling welfare recipients to work; second, concern with the children of working mothers generally; and third, concern with early childhood development, especially for low income children. The expressed 'hope' was that 'early intervention could reduce the handicaps of the poor and might increase the capabilities of all children'. In the end the report rejected direct funding of child care as too costly and declared that the childhood development goals could be accomplished more cheaply through television programming, visiting nurses and 'teachers', and special education for mothers (in Rainwater, 1974a: 277). As to the argument that 'the only way to achieve real equality for women is for society to take over the financing of child care for those who want to work outside the home', the authors of this report declared this proposal 'too costly'.

By the 1995 Joint Hearing on Child Care and Child Welfare (US Committee on Ways and Means, and Committee on Economic and Educational Opportunities, 1995), the consensus seemed to be that the kind of indirect measures endorsed by the 1972 Brookings Institute study were not producing the citizens desired. The primary concern in this Joint Hearing, as we saw earlier, is to provide child care to allow the poor to work, reducing demands on the welfare system. In addition, however, there is an emphasis on the desirability of ensuring that children are in 'healthy, safe and nurturing settings', and to meet the needs of 'society's most troubled families'. The 1993 OECD (1993: 6) study, *Why Child Care Matters*, also emphasized that 'not all parents have either the skills or resources to provide adequate nurturing'. To relieve any doubt about which parents these might be, the report elaborates: '[P]oor children or those otherwise at risk educationally may need programs that combine comprehensive healthier and educational services, etc etc.' Confirming a point made earlier, the implication is that working-class children are more 'in need' of out-of-home care than middle-class children who, it follows, can afford to be left to their stay-at-home mothers (OECD, 1993: 32): '[I]n their first five years, disadvantaged children are most in need of an environment that addresses both their developmental and their educational needs because they are less likely than middle-class children to get adequate nurturing at home', and '[T]he data on the long-term benefits of high-quality child care for non-disadvantaged children are considerably less conclusive.' Explicit links are drawn here with Head Start, America's educational programme for the 'disadvantaged'. The children of the poor are the targets, with the intent both of reducing budget deficits and shaping 'good' citizens. The report (1993: 7–8) states explicitly that the potential costs of not investing in child care for 'disadvantaged' children include 'social disintegration and crime, physical decay, and heavier tax burdens for social services'. Britain's 1993 National Commission on Education struck a similar tone:

> [W]e are persuaded that the gains made by children who receive high quality pre-school education will reduce the need for remedial education at a later stage, help to ensure that we do not waste talent, and perhaps also reduce the social costs which arise from youth unemployment and juvenile crime. (National Commission on Education, 1993: 137, cited in Moss and Penn, 1996: 58)

We are dealing with children 'at risk' in families 'at risk'.

Some of this language should be familiar. Recall how the reframing of equal opportunity in the California Regents' policy identified 'worthy' recipients of 'aid' as those who managed to overcome the 'culture of poverty' (see Chapter 5). As we have noted elsewhere, in this problem representation, the oppressed become responsible for their oppression. The 'problem' of crime and social unrest is individualized and sheeted home to those involved in the unrest. As Colin Gordon (1991: 38) asserts, most commonly social analysis paints the problem as 'sick people' rather than a 'sick society'. There is no way in this problem representation to challenge the *conditions* producing the unrest. The creation of 'at risk' families produces this silence.

As with the 1972 Brookings Institute report, there is a continuing emphasis in the 1993 OECD report on cost-effectiveness. It is unambiguously economic factors which drive the analysis. And here again, in the end, child care is found to be too costly, or at least the report postulates the existence of a cheaper alternative for some women (1993: 43): '[G]iven the uncertainty about the effects of non-maternal infant care, the special importance to infants of high-quality care, and the much higher costs of caring for infants compared with older children, parental leave appears a socially cost-effective alternative to out-of-home infant care for families who find this feasible.' The implications for women are unanalysed, neither the assumption that middle-class women will assume this nurturing responsibility, nor the assumption that working-class women will be unlikely to find this 'cost-effective' alternative feasible, since the parental leave on offer will be unpaid.

In the identifying of 'unwholesome' families, single mothers have attracted an undue share of attention, as we have already seen. A submission to the Joint Hearing on Child Care and Child Welfare from the National Fatherhood Initiative (US Committee on Ways and Means, and Committee on Economic and Educational Opportunities, 1995: 98–102) identified an unsurprising link between 'father absence and welfare dependency'. I say 'unsurprising' here because of the commonly drawn link between single motherhood and poverty, a phenomenon some feminists have called the 'feminization of poverty' (Bacchi, 1990: 182). Wade F. Horn, the Director of the Initiative, called, not for increased welfare spending to relieve the poverty of these women and children, however, nor even for measures to encourage women into the workforce, but for 'family preservation services'. The problem here is represented to be neither working mothers nor undereducated children, but fatherless families. The assumption is that family preservation will eradicate all these 'ills'. Fathers, it should be noted, are not much discussed in child care policy debates. Katherine Teghtsoonian (1996: 133) talks about a 'deafening silence around the question of men's participation in child rearing' in Canada and the United States. It is significant that when they do appear it is not as parents or husbands or as members of the working poor, but as patriarchs.

Some social conservatives oppose all funding for child care, even for children 'at risk'. Phyllis Schlafly, a leading critic of feminism and a defender of the nuclear family, suggested that '[the ABC] bill is the first step of the long-range plan to bring all children under government control' (US House of Representatives, 1988: 169, cited in Teghtsoonian, 1993: 112). A private child care provider, who we might expect to have an agenda quite different from Schlafly's, paradoxically, put a not dissimilar argument: '[W]ith programs all the same, the caregivers all trained the same, in centers where no philosophical differences could be expressed . . . What kind of citizens would be produced? Would these children all think alike or be capable of stimulating debate?' (US House of Representatives, 1988: 215, cited in Teghtsoonian, 1993: 112). Donna Varga's (1997) concerns regarding the way in which child care is increasingly focused on the moral development of the child sounds similar. She (1997: 14) talks about the way in which day care provision in Canada has, in her view, moved away from a primary concern with the needs of mothers to 'a concern for the developmental supervision and management of children'. And yet Varga is certainly not endorsing doing away with child care facilities. She is even aware that her critique of the 'normative curriculum' could be used by those who wish to cut back on services.

Applying a What's the Problem? approach facilitates sorting through the paradoxes in these positions. As in the case of the boys' education debate (see Chapter 6), in order to clarify the problem representations at work, we need to look to proposals. For Schlafly the goal is to encourage women to stay at home and hence she would offer no inducements to set up child care facilities. In contrast, private child care providers would use the argument about government control and institutionalization to defend the privatization of care. On the other hand those, like Varga, who object to a normative curriculum, propose 'a form of care allowing greater spontaneity of children'. They do not recommend curtailing child care facilities. Apparent similarities in the arguments disappear when we look to concrete proposals which indicate very different problem representations.

This leads us back to the existence, particularly in Europe, of a social democratic pedagogic discourse recommending the positive effects of education to reduce the disadvantages of the working class. Peter Moss (1997: 28) elaborates how this discourse differs from the problematizations we have considered so far, which he labels the 'child care for working parents' discourse, the 'nursery education (or kindergarten) for over 3s discourse', and the 'day care for children in need' discourse. Moss adds a fourth framing discourse, a discourse of 'early childhood services' which calls for the public funding of child care for all children because of the social nature of childrearing. In Moss's words, this fourth discourse 'rejects the concept of services as businesses supplying a product to a consumer or as a means to deliver an intervention to a targeted group'. Rather the 'early childhood services' discourse 'conceptualises these services as institutions of cultural, social and economic significance, community resources that should be multi-functional to meet a variety of needs including care, education, socialization, health and family support, and that should be available to all children and families irrespective of parents' employment status'.

That being said, Moss (1997: 30) is well aware that, '[U]nderlying the Swedish policy is a belief that parents should be in the labour market, apart from a year or so after each birth when there is the opportunity to take paid parental leave.' This objective, as we have seen, is expressed though a priority given to 'working' mothers in access to child care. Some other voices are expressing misgivings about this assumption, expressing the view that a shorter working day is necessary to achieve an appropriate balance between paid work commitments and the lives we lead outside of paid work (Bacchi et al., 1992: 16). A proposal such as this contains a problem representation which challenges the dominant assumption in child care policy in the United States, Canada, Australia, and Sweden for that matter, that the market should set the terms for the way we live our intimate lives. Of course, this proposal is facing considerable opposition wherever it is voiced. The point here is simply to bring to the surface the very different social vision which lodges within it.

Conclusion

In the child care debate, we can tease out the problem representations framing the issue from specific policy proposals. Where funding is tied to labour market participation, the assumption is that independence and self-sufficiency are both desirable and attainable. As Ruth Levitas (1996: 9) maintains, in this position 'the overwhelming emphasis is on paid work as the mechanism of [social] integration', a discourse which operates 'both to devalue unpaid work and to obscure the inequalities between paid workers'. Where subsidies are means-tested, the problem is generally represented to be the need to get poor single women and poor women generally off welfare and into the labour force, while rescuing children 'at risk'. A commitment to reduce the budget lies behind this framing. A social control agenda is also evident. It is assumed that 'stable families are and must be economically independent, and that families needing "outside help" to support children could not be stable in the long run' (Gordon, 1988: 114). In the process working-class women are created as 'welfare drones' and 'inadequate mothers'. Katherine Teghtsoonian (1996: 138) notes a '(generally unspoken) identification of "single mothers on welfare" with women of color' in the United States, producing 'a devaluation of their work as mothers'. Middle-class women who engage in paid labour meanwhile are caught between discursive constructions of the 'good mother' and a model of self-actualization based on paid labour. The reconciliation of this tension depends in part upon the exploitation of other, usually poor and non-Anglo Saxon, women.

8

ABORTION: WHOSE RIGHT?

I have noted several times in this part of the book that it is important to consider how an issue achieves 'social problem' status. This provides the opportunity to reflect upon the fact that an issue can achieve 'social problem' status differently in different places, or at different times, or not at all. Discovering this makes it possible to question the taken-for-granted status of some problem representations which are securely anchored in our own time and culture. Recognizing the context-dependent and time-dependent nature of 'social problems' creates them as social rather than as natural phenomena. Abortion provides an excellent example for this kind of reflection. As we will be seeing, abortion was not always considered to be a 'social problem' in Western democracies, nor does it carry the same opprobrium in some non-Western countries today. These insights suggest that, despite the common framing of abortion as an obvious moral problem in the United States, Canada, Britain and Australia, history and context have more to do with its status than a foundationalist morality (Dean, 1992: 223).

In Chapter 2 the connection between a What's the Problem (represented to be)? approach and genealogy as a method of social investigation was touched upon briefly. There I mentioned Mitchell Dean's (1992: 216–17) characterization of genealogy as 'the methodical problematization of the given, of the taken-for-granted'. One way of doing this, as Dean elaborates, is 'by constituting lineages' of 'assemblages', like madness, sexuality, the economic, 'of which we are all too familiar'. For Dean, genealogy involves the history of regimes of truth, and hence puts 'into question all values'. A genealogy of the 'truth' of abortion achieves exactly this purpose.

Early History

For a large part of the nineteenth century in Britain and the United States abortion was a common method of fertility control (Gordon, 1977: 35–6, 415), and this continued into the twentieth century. Working-class women shared information about how 'to bring on a period'. There were many folk remedies to assist them. Women felt no compunction about this before what they described as 'quickening', their perception of a distinct movement and hence development in the status of the foetus. Given the unreliability of forms of contraception, *coitus interruptus* being the most common, abortion and contraception were fused in the popular mind in the single category of birth control. It should be added that women in this period were more or less compelled to turn to induced abortion as a method of controlling family size since the medical profession supported the ban on giving advice about contraception.

The ban on contraceptive advice was linked to a governmental interest in population, including numbers and calibre. A startling decline in the birth rate, from around 1860, attracted the attention of all Western governments. Added to this were concerns about 'the differential birthrate', the fact that the lower classes tended to outbreed middle and upper classes, and the proliferation of the 'feeble-minded' (Bacchi, 1980). The period is commonly characterized by the phrase 'race suicide scare', indicating that the concern was primarily with the dwindling numbers of *particular* populations, specifically the Anglo-Saxon population.

Michel Foucault sees the concern with population as indicative of a new form of governance, one focusing upon the control of the conduct of the populace rather than upon a preoccupation with territorial boundaries. Population marked out the new territory, as it were, for government to manage (Foucault, 1978, cited in Burchell et al., 1991: 100). Foucault, moreover, examines the trend away from direct disciplinary supervision to the inculcation of proper behaviour through self-government or self-regulation (Sibeon, 1996: 114–16). Here it is important to remember Pat O'Malley's (1992: 255) point that Foucault does not suggest the *replacement* of disciplinary with regulatory technologies of power; rather he recognizes 'discipline and regulation as "two poles of development linked together by a whole intermediary cluster of relations", characterized by "overlappings, interactions and echoes"' (Foucault, 1984: 149, cited in O'Malley, 1992: 255).

The physiological facts of pregnancy and childbirth produce women and their bodies as the focus of surveillance when population is the concern (see Flax, 1990: 212; Gordon, 1977). Policy proposals on abortion reflect this conflation of national/racial interest and biological imperative. James Mohr (1978: 167) points out that, in the United States, one concern in the mid-nineteenth century was that Anglo-Saxon Protestant women were practising abortion and consequently were being outbred by migrating Catholic Southern Europeans who did not practise it. Similarly in Canada, at this time, prolific French-Canadian Catholics threatened to outbreed English-Canadian Protestants, because of different abortion practices. These were some of the pressures leading to criminalization of abortion in the latter half of the nineteenth century. In Britain it was not a crime for a woman to abort herself until the 1861 Offences against the Person Act, which became the model for Canadian and Australian legislation. From that time a variety of actions to procure a miscarriage was declared unlawful whether carried out by a pregnant woman or by another person (Albury, 1993: 51).

The medical profession played a paramount role in producing abortion as a criminal problem. Both James Mohr (1978) and Barbara Brookes (1988) emphasize the pressure exerted by the medical profession in the United States and in Britain respectively to have abortion made illegal in order to stop unregulated practitioners from operating in this area. This was the same period in which the medical profession waged and won its battle to eliminate midwives from medical practice in the childbirth field. Rebecca Albury (1993: 51) sees these moves as 'part of the more general campaign by the "scientific", university educated medical profession to gain unquestioned authority in the provision of health services'. As Albury says, the main effect of laws criminalizing abortion was to 'hand the regulation of abortion over to doctors'.

The role of the medical profession in the criminalizing of abortion returns us to the governmentality literature introduced in Chapter 2. There we identified a liberal mode of government which 'extends the boundaries of rule by placing limits on the action of the state' (Dean, 1992: 218). This extension takes place in large part through the cordoning off and handing over of areas of supervision to groups of professionals who retain a special relationship with the state. In the case of the medical profession this relationship is recognized in the state licensing of medical practitioners. With the passing of legislation criminalizing the act of abortion, the 'problem' of abortion is produced as a legal problem, with women and those assisting them in the procurement of abortion becoming criminals. Despite the role of the medical profession in the production of abortion as crime, for the next hundred odd years, doctors remain backgrounded in the genealogy of abortion. Criminalizing of abortion, meanwhile, created the conditions for the ascendancy of a moral framework for abortion. While I am not suggesting a simple confluence of moral principles and the law, the creation of a category of criminal behaviour supported a moral judge-ment about wrongness of behaviour which reshaped the popular discourse about abortion.

Both Brookes (1988: 52) and McLaren (1978: 334) describe how doctors had a difficult time convincing women that abortion was illegal. While this may be so, the criminalization of abortion made the earlier fusion in the popular mind of contraception and abortion more difficult to maintain. This was so particularly with the increasing acceptance of certain methods of contraception as not only legal but also as socially responsible. Linda Gordon (1977) describes how medical and eugenic professionals took over control of both contraceptive knowledge and access to abortion. In the first case, it seems that, given the persistence with which some groups of middle-class women used birth control while working-class women eschewed it, the strategy of governance shifted from controlling access to birth control information to targeting birth control information at the 'lower' classes (Bacchi, 1980). By the 1930s, moreover, birth control was being discussed as an appropriate complement to a fulfilled and fulfilling marital relationship (Bacchi, 1988). In addition, the criminalization of abortion was not achieving the desired effects. Abortions continued to be performed and often by doctors. This situation created the conditions for the reform of abortion laws in the 1960s and 1970s. Forecasting the argument to follow, in this later period, legal and medical discourses surrounding abortion shifted from criminalization to medicalization, all the while retaining a close relationship between the state and the medical profession in the production of the problem.

The Period of Reform

The onset of liberalization in abortion laws owed a great deal to changes in the position of the medical profession on the issue. According to Brookes (1988: 155), a key factor leading to England's 1967 Law Reform Bill was that the medical profession was now secure enough not to need a restrictive law against its competitors (unregistered practitioners), and saw that a law shaped by them could give them more control. As Sally Sheldon (1995: 107) notes, the Act allowed terminations late into the course of a pregnancy but resisted 'any challenge to medical control on the basis of claims of female reproductive autonomy'. This 1967 law became the model for Canada's 1969 legislation and also for South Australia's 1969 legislation. In Canada, prior to the 1969 reform legislation, an 'informal abortion system had evolved within some Canadian hospitals where abortions were performed on a daily basis' (Collins, 1982: 2, cited in Kellough, 1996: 77). Gail Kellough (1996: 77) notes how this informal committee system 'diffused personal responsibility from individual doctors while retaining the profession's right to act as a moral gatekeeper'. The 1969 amendments to the Criminal Code of Canada did little more than to bring the law almost up to what was then the standard practice in a handful of hospitals. It was designed as a compromise and adopted the Canadian Medical Association's 1966 resolution *verbatim*. It was a fairly restrictive law and allowed abortion only when continuation of pregnancy was a threat to the pregnant woman's health. It also permitted abortions only in approved hospitals, where TACs (Therapeutic Abortion Committees) of three doctors would rule on each case regarding the health threat. Janine

Brodie et al. (1992: 11) capture concisely the impact of the reform: '[I]n effect, this reform of the law replaced judicial control after the fact for medical control before the fact.'

One of the main pressures for reform in the United States was also the desire by doctors to legitimize what for many of them had become common practice (Tatalovich, 1996: 6). In 1970 the American Medical Association adopted a resolution calling for legalization of abortion while making clear the continuing role of the doctor as decision maker in the process. The resolution stated that abortion policy should be based on 'sound clinical judgment' and 'the best interest of the patient', rather than 'mere acquiescence to the patient's demand' (in Joffe, 1995: 46; see also Schambelan, 1992: 29). Carole Joffe (1995: 46) describes a tension between the medical establishment and the growing women's health movement due to the perception by some in the medical profession that legal abortion 'had the potential to subvert the traditional relationship of physician and patient, rendering the former into a mere "technician" who would do the patient's bidding'. At a 1970 AMA convention where feminist groups supporting legal abortion picketed outside the convention hall, one doctor complained: '[L]egal abortion makes the patient truly the physician: she makes the diagnosis and establishes the therapy.' The endorsement of the legalization of abortion in the AMA resolution above reflected the desire on the part of the medical establishment to keep clear the roles of patient and physician. The change in law, then, was 'a response less to feminist concerns than to the legally vulnerable position of the medical establishment' (Kellough, 1996: 77). To say this is not to deny the importance of feminist campaigns around the issue, nor to deny a connection between abortion and the problem of 'women's equality', about which more will be said in the next section. It is to indicate yet again that reforms commonly associated with the women's movement for liberation had important links with other agendas, links which proved crucial to the ways in which the reforms were framed.

Abortion: a Medical Problem?

The production of abortion as a medical problem is clearest in the landmark case in American abortion history, *Roe* v. *Wade* (1973). There have been numerous interpretations of the Supreme Court decision, a standard view being that it created, at least in the first trimester, a woman's constitutional right to abortion. Celeste Condit (1990: 112) makes this case:

> [I]t [the decision] did not specify what purposes for abortion would be acceptable nor place control of abortions in outside committees as other Western countries had done; instead, it reflected the liberal American

tradition, recognizing women as individuals with rights that could not be violated for 'the good of the community' except in extreme cases.

Myra Marx Ferree and William A. Gamson (1996: 9) also stress the achievement with *Roe* v. *Wade* that 'there is a constitutional right for women limiting the state's ability to regulate her abortion decision in some (as yet not fully determined) manner'.

The majority decision, delivered by Justice Blackmun, did indeed make a case for women's privacy rights in the need to access abortion services. The case is limited, however, by trimester, with the state's interest in the pregnancy increasing in the second and third trimesters. The state's interests, identified here (Schambelan, 1992: 35, 40–1) as 'protection of health, medical standards, and prenatal life', are held to be dominant in the later stages of pregnancy. The case for the state's 'compelling interest' in the second and third trimesters hinged upon 'the now-established medical fact . . . that until the end of the first trimester mortality in abortion may be less than mortality in normal childbirth'. The state's interest in the health of its citizens then permitted regulation of the abortion procedure in the later, more 'dangerous' trimesters 'to the extent that the regulation reasonably relates to the preservation and protection of maternal health.' Blackmun clarifed the exact forms of this permissible regulation: 'requirements as to the qualifications of the person who is to perform the abortion; as to the licensure of that person; as to the facility in which the procedure is to be performed, that is, whether it must be a hospital or may be a clinic or some other place of less-than-hospital status; as to the licensing of the facility; and the like.'

The presumption of state interest in shaping national health goals for its citizenry stands as a backdrop to the decision. In other contexts it is just this presumption which is used to justify curtailing access to abortion for pronatalist purposes (De Sève, 1996) or facilitating access to abortion services in order to curb 'overpopulation'. Carole Joffe (1995: 44–5) describes how some of the pressure for abortion reform came from the interest in the 1950s and 1960s in 'population control' issues in the 'developing world on the part of both the US government and numerous private organizations':

> [W]hile the primary aim of population organizations in that period was to disseminate birth control methods, there were also attempts to make available to Third World health care providers the euphemistically named 'menstrual extraction kits' – which provided early abortions.

This linking between abortion and 'overpopulation' in 'developing' countries indicates a nesting of problem representations which requires addressing. Rashmi Luthra (1995: 202, 198) points out that a solution that seeks to reduce the 'numbers of the absolute poor' produces the problem as simply *numbers* 'rather than addressing the structural underpinnings of poverty'. She also shows how an analysis that produces abortion as a solution to overpopulation creates the problem as one due to 'internal constraints rather than colonial legacy or the world economic system', providing the grounds at the very same time for intervention and supervision.

Returning to *Roe* v. *Wade*, in the early stages of pregnancy, decision making regarding an abortion rested with 'a physician and his [*sic*] pregnant patient'. As Justice Blackmun explained, the freedom from state interference granted the pregnant woman in the first trimester is tied to her relationship with her physician:

> for the period of pregnancy prior to this 'compelling' point, the attending physician, in consultation with his [*sic*] patient, is free to determine, without regulation by the state, that, in his [*sic*] medical judgment, the patient's pregnancy should be terminated. If that decision is reached, the judgment may be effectuated by an abortion free of interference by the State.

Lest there be any confusion as to where decision-making responsibility lies, Blackmun repeated (Schambelan, 1992: 42): '[F]or the stage prior to approximately the end of the first trimester, the abortion decision and its effectuation must be left to the medical judgment of *the pregnant woman's attending physician* [emphasis added]'. He made clear that it was the Court's judgment that, up to the point of compelling state interests, 'the abortion decision in all its aspects is inherently, and primarily, a *medical decision*, and basic responsibility for it must rest *with the physician* [emphasis added]'.

In the companion case of *Doe* v. *Bolton* (1973), the majority opinion, also put by Justice Blackmun, clarified that the concern of the court was not a woman's right to privacy *per se*, but her right to doctor–patient privacy (Schambelan, 1992: 75, 62, 65). This decision ruled against hospital committees intervening in abortion cases on the grounds that

> [W]ith regard to the protection of potential life, the medical judgment is already completed prior to the committee stage, and review by a committee once removed from diagnosis is basically redundant. . . . The woman's right to receive medical care in accordance with her licensed physician's best judgment and the physician's right to administer it are substantially limited by this statutorily imposed overview.

On similar grounds, the Court disallowed demands for two-doctor concurrence in abortion cases:

> [I]f a physician is licensed by the State, he [*sic*] is recognized by the State as capable of exercising acceptable clinical judgment. If he [*sic*] fails in this, professional censure and deprivation of his [*sic*] license are available

remedies. Required acquiescence by co-practitioners has no rational connection with a patient's needs and unduly infringes on the physician's right to practice.

It seems clear from these extracts that these classic abortion cases were more concerned with sorting out the relationship between the state and the medical profession than with a woman's 'right' to abortion. As Gail Kellough (1996: 72) states, the 'primary concern was the intrusion of the state on physician's autonomy'. Nowhere is a woman granted a final decision-making power, not even in the first trimester. The medical profession managed to protect effectively the practitioner's autonomy and to prevent the reduction of 'his' role to 'mere technician'. The most the pregnant woman is granted is the right to find a physician who might sympathize with her point of view. Women, in this case, remain dependent upon the benevolence of a doctor.

At the same time, doctors are granted the right to refuse treatment. The majority judgment in *Doe* v. *Bolton* (Schambelan, 1992: 63) stated explicitly that 'the hospital is free not to admit a patient for an abortion . . . Further, a physician or any other employee has the right to refrain, for *moral* or *religious* reasons, from participating in the abortion procedure [emphasis added]'. Similary in Canada, in the 1969 legislation, physicians could refuse to sit on TACs for moral, financial, or political reasons, 'circumventing any legal guarantee of abortion services as a "reproductive right"' (Currie, 1992: 95). Gail Kellough (1996: 72) states pointedly that '[T]he pattern which emerges is one in which medical agents are not to be restricted in the practice of their craft and yet are free to withhold their services.'

The appearance of the language of morality in what we are told is a purely medical decision looks odd, and indicates that the framing of abortion as a moral problem has achieved a separate status by this time. To an extent the medicalization of abortion appears to challenge the moral framing of abortion. And indeed some churches and their representatives objected to *Roe* v. *Wade* on the grounds that it put discretion over abortion as a 'moral' issue in the hands of individual physicians (Albury, 1993: 55). But the framing of abortion as a moral dilemma clearly remains in both *Roe* v. *Wade* and in the Canadian abortion legislation in the provision allowing doctors to refuse to provide abortions for moral reasons.

Moral language to frame abortion appears also in other public jurisdictions. For example, in political debate, abortion is often characterized as a moral problem. In the 1968 debate surrounding the Canadian Liberal Party's omnibus Bill C-195 dealing with lotteries, passports, firearms, bail reform, homosexuality and abortion, the then prime minister, Pierre Trudeau, justified the legislation in just these terms: 'morality is a matter of private conscience. Criminal law should reflect the public order only.' On these grounds Trudeau saw no reason for a free or conscience vote (Currie, 1992: 80). Interestingly, this same argument, that morals are a matter of individual conscience, is often used in other jurisdictions to *justify* conscience votes on a range of issues called 'moral', including abortion, prostitution and homosexuality. Here moral seems to be a code word for sexual (Albury, 1993: 52). Declaring the issue 'moral' allows a yielding of responsibility away from the party leadership. Similarly, allowing doctors the right of discretion in abortion cases makes the matter one of individual judgement rather than social responsibility. In addition, it creates abortion as an exceptional medical intervention, one associated with complicated 'moral' debates.

This is the background which has meant that in the United States (see Joffe, 1995) and elsewhere (see Albury, 1993; Currie, 1992) abortion services are inadequate. In the language of What's the Problem?, one effect of the framing of abortion as a moral problem is inadequate provision. Carol Joffe (1995: x, 151–3) notes that many doctors shy away from association with the practice due to the 'isolation and stigmatization' associated with abortion within the medical community. The stigma is due to two things: the feeling that abortion, like contraception, requires no great skill, and the continuing connection with 'backyard abortionists', a legacy of the period of criminalization. As one doctor in Joffe's study put it, '"Abortionist" carries a still unpleasant connotation. It carries the connotation of a sleaze.' The lingering moral condemnation associated with what was once an illegal practice means that, even where women have been a given a 'right' to abortion, there is no guarantee that they will be able to find a provider of the service.

On 'allowable' grounds for abortion, the *Roe* v. *Wade* decision is remarkably liberal, compared to Canada's 1969 legislation. Whereas the latter (Currie, 1992: 82) restricted access to abortion to cases where 'the continuation of the pregnancy would or would be likely to endanger [the] life or health of the woman', Blackmun (Schambelan, 1992: 34) specified a range of circumstances which could be taken into consideration:

[S]pecific and direct harm medically diagnosable even in early pregnancy may be involved. Psychological harm may be imminent. Mental and physical health may be taxed by child care. There is also the distress, for all concerned, associated with the unwanted child, and there is the problem of bringing a child into a family already unable, psychologically and otherwise, to care for it. In other cases, as in this one, the additional difficulties and continuing stigma of unwed motherhood may be involved.

Several points need to be made here. First, within this 'generous' framing, medicalization of the problem remains paramount: '[A]ll

these are factors the woman and her responsible physician necessarily will consider in consultation.' The framing also creates abortion
as acceptable only in certain kinds of cases. The cases which can be
made for abortion, which Celeste Condit (1990: 35) calls 'socially
justifiable excuses', position women in awkward and degrading
ways: 'abortion is "allowed" when women are seen to be too poor,
too young, too physically or mentally incompetent, or some foetuses
too defective.' Whether before a hospital committee, as in Canada, or
an individual doctor, as in the United States, women have to plead
their individual cases, forced in many instances to present themselves
as psychologically unstable persons. Gail Kellough (1996: 206) comments on the effects of this individualizing of the problem: '[A]s
inequality comes to be popularly perceived as the result of individual
inadequacy or an unfortunate aberration, psychological and legal
solutions are preferred, and political dissent is diffused.'

Probing deeper, Gail Kellough (1996: 123) points out that 'the idea
of foetal rights is inherent in a law which "allows" its removal only
in "exceptional" circumstances'. Although *Roe* v. *Wade* (Schambelan,
1992: 38, 40) declares an inability to decide that 'difficult question of
when life begins', Blackmun asserted the state's 'compelling' interest
in 'protecting the potentiality of human life'. The point at which
this legitimate interest takes effect is 'viability': '[T]his is so because
the fetus then presumably has the capability of meaningful life
outside the mother's womb.' Given the decision held that the
state's compelling interest takes effect *after the first trimester*, there
seems an odd mismatch in this statement. Even with recent developments in technology, no 3-month fetus is capable of independent
life. Be that as it may, Blackmun concluded: '[I]f the State is interested in protecting fetal life after viability, it may go so far as to
proscribe abortion during that period, except when it is necessary to
preserve the life or health of the mother.' Despite the disclaimer then
that the court could not rule on when life begins, the judgment
effectively gives the protection available to a living person to the
'viable' fetus. Hence, it is not surprising that subsequent debates
around abortion have come to focus more and more on the status of
the fetus.

As early as 1973, Joel Feinberg (1973/84: 3), in an edited collection
of philosophical essays entitled *The Problem of Abortion*, declared: 'the
"problem of abortion" has become "the problem of the status of the
fetus"'. Fifteen years later a Canadian Law Reform Commission
Report (1986: 6) agreed that 'apparently the humanity or personhood
of the fetus is *the* central issue in abortion'. This report, prepared by
the Fetal Status Working Group, proposed a comprehensive legal
policy offering, 'as far as is reasonably possible, similar standards of
treatment for the variety of assaults upon the fetus', including '*the*

assaults inherent in abortion, fetal experimentation, fetal surgery, or indeed common assaults on pregnant women leading to harm to the fetus [emphasis added]'. The status of the foetus as equal actor in abortion cases is upheld in the landmark Canadian Supreme Court's judgment in the 1988 *Morgentaler* case, which struck down the abortion provision in section 251 of the Criminal Code as an unjustified limitation of a woman's right to security of the person, guaranteed in section 7 of the Canadian Charter of Rights and Freedoms. The same decision defended the right of parliament to pass laws to protect the foetus and to balance the rights of the foetus against the rights of the mother, creating mother and foetus as equals in opposition (McCallum, 1989: 310).

Gail Kellough (1996: 126, 89) finds in the focus on the foetus and in the portrayal of abortion as unnatural, an assumption that it is natural for women to nurture. After all, as she says, 'fetuses require something more than noninterference if they are to achieve the independence of moral legal subjects'. So, in discussions about abortion, the decision 'not to nurture becomes the problem'. In all this there is a startling silence about the cause of the 'problem'. It is as if women become pregnant all by themselves. Celeste Condit (1990: 33) notes how, in abortion debates, women are 'generally held responsible for their pregnancies'. Men manage to absent themselves as objects of the analysis; all the while they remain in the vast majority the producers of the analysis.

The medical framing of abortion continues in contemporary medical discourse where abortion is generally described as an option when contraception fails. As Lyndall Ryan et al. (1994: 193) suggest, in this understanding, contraception becomes the 'good', against which abortion is cast as 'bad'. So abortion becomes permissible if contraception 'fails', and the woman who is perceived to be using abortion as contraception stands condemned. Ryan et al. note the way in which contraception here is equated with modernity and involves 'the rational surveillance and self-control of bodies and desires'. The equating of contraception with modernity produces what they (1994: 193) call an 'ethnocentric variant', the implied characterization of countries and cultures 'in which abortion is common and an integral strategy in women's fertility control' as 'less "humane" or less "developed" or less "civilised" than countries and cultures where contraception is distinguished from and valorised over abortion'. Portraying abortion as a less civilized 'solution' to the problem can then provide a rationale for denying funding to those countries which use abortion regularly (see Luthra, 1995: 198). At the same time, it is precisely 'India's developmental program, which has included a program of population control, that has made the right of abortion much less controversial within the Indian context' (Cornell, 1995: 84).

Abortion, it seems, achieves social problem status only when it appears to contradict desired national goals.

Feminist Voices

A What's the Problem? approach provides a tool to assist in the identification of discursive frames, within feminists' arguments as well as within the arguments of those who challenge feminists' views.[1] From the first stirrings of the revived women's movement, 'the demand for universal abortion services has been central to almost all factions of the Women's Movement' (Currie, 1992: 86). The argument developed that, in order to gain access to and compete with men on equal terms in public life, women needed to gain control of reproduction. Access to abortion on demand symbolized the kind of control over women's bodies which appeared to be necessary to achieve this liberation and which became expressed in campaigns for 'reproductive rights' and 'a woman's right to choose'. For some, the political aim was to separate sexuality and procreation, a separation believed necessary to secure sexual liberation for women (Currie, 1992: 87). The language of privacy, rights and choice framed the demand. As Celeste Condit describes (see above), this liberal terminology proved useful in achieving the *Roe* v. *Wade* decision, though I would argue that the pregnant woman's right to privacy or to choice was always constrained by the need to gain the support of her physician. None the less, the decision marked an important change from the preceding period of criminalization.

A number of feminist authors have pointed to problems with framing abortion as a right, especially as a right to privacy. Catharine MacKinnon (1983) argues that the privacy framing of abortion facilitated arguments for removing public funding for abortion in the United States, on the grounds that a *private* right did not call for *public* funding. The decision in *Harris* v. *McRae* (1981 in Kellough, 1996: 73) was explicit: 'although government may not place obstacles in the path of a woman's exercise of her freedom of choice, it need not remove those not of its own creation. Indigency falls in the latter category.' We have examined elsewhere the operation of the public/private dichotomy in mystifying the impact of government decisions on intimate lives. Nowhere is this clearer than in the removal of public funding for abortion which means necessarily that women without adequate funds will have to seek illegal and cheap abortions, or cope with unwanted children. The *McRae* judgment that indigency owes nothing to government policy indicates links here with the discursive construction of poverty as personal responsibility.

Margaret McCallum (1989: 308) argues that 'defending a right to privacy is not the best strategy for gaining recognition of women's rights'. Her point, like MacKinnon's, is that the language of choice and privacy suggests that social context is irrelevant. According to McCallum, for choice to have any meaning, the conditions have to exist for women to be able to choose to have children as well as to choose not to have them. For women to be able to choose to have children means that it should be possible to have supports and services necessary to raise children (child care, parental leave, etc.). Dawn Currie (1992) develops this argument to suggest that feminists who use the discourse of 'abortion as a woman's right' are in fact privatizing the issue and hence reinforcing the status quo. Rather she says they should be insisting on the creation of a social context where pregnancy and child rearing would be less problematic. Currie's (1988: 248) study of women's responses to the abortion decision highlights the ways in which the language of choice creates problems for women who internalize its framing of the problem, and hence feel guilt about their abortions instead of recognizing the structural factors shaping and constricting their 'choices'. Here again we have an example of a problem representation which individualizes the causes of problems, denies structural constraints, and produces subjects who internalize this understanding. The result is self-monitoring and inadequate critique of social structural arrangements. Drucilla Cornell (1995: 84) offers the example of female foeticide, specifically the aborting of female foetuses in India, to highlight the inadequacy of a 'choice' framing of the abortion decision.

Other authors (see Kingdom, 1991: Chapter 3) emphasize that claiming a 'right' to abortion opens up the possibility of counter-claims by foetuses and by husbands. The Canadian 1988 Supreme Court decision that parliament has the right to 'balance the rights' between the foetus and the mother implicitly accepts foetuses as potential claims-makers (see above). The notion of 'foetal rights' is being used increasingly to achieve other political ends, for example to deny women access to certain kinds of jobs, or to facilitate monitoring and control of pregnant women's lives (Bacchi, 1990: Chapter 6). In these debates, foetuses are produced as equal moral agents, often in dispute with pregnant women.

Rights in liberal democracies are generally constituted negatively, as the right for example to be *free from* state intervention, the right to be left alone. And, as Cornell (1995: 33) insists, the right to abortion is clearly not a right to privacy, 'if that right is understood as a right to be left alone', picking up that point from Kellough (see above) that more than noninterference is required in the development of a foetus to child. Any decision to invoke the rhetoric of rights needs, therefore, to attend to the dominant discursive construction of rights in the community in which this decision is made. Both Gail Kellough (1996: 252–3) and Lyndall Ryan et al. (1994: 193–4) show that feminists who invoke the language of rights often endorse a broader, more positive interpretation of the concept. The problem they face is the intractability of dominant understandings of rights. In Kellough's (1996: 15) words, 'the language in which the victory was sought reaffirmed the existing legal paradigm.' The lesson here is the need to pay more heed to these dominant discourses and to confront them directly. Kellough (1996: 298) concludes and I agree that '[W]hat was needed was a strategy that would not only respond to the practical problems of individual women but would address problems of abortion discourse as well.' As Nancy Fraser (1989: Chapter 8) explains with regards to 'needs' discourses, we are involved necessarily in political debates about the meanings of concepts and the connection of those meanings to desired outcomes. More will be said about the strategic implications of this kind of analysis in the Conclusion.

A useful counterpoint to the framing of abortion as a privacy right is found in Germany. There, as Ferree and Gamson (1996: 12, 28–9) point out, the 'operative concept is the definition of the fetus as "human life" that has to be respected by criminalizing abortion'. This has meant that those who advocate abortion rights in Germany adopt a discursive strategy which focuses upon efforts to 'define what policies do or do not "respect human life"'. Hence, more is accomplished in Germany by concentrating upon the health risks to women in illegal abortions. Women are again defined as 'objects' of policy, but this time as those who should be 'helped not punished'. As Ferree and Gamson argue, the American discourse of women with rights, of women as powerful individuals, leaves women 'whose economic need or social vulnerability makes them less autonomous in practice "outside" the dominant "pro-choice" discourse'. This in turn has made these women ready to be 'claimed' by anti-abortion advocates as 'victims of abortion' along with the foetus. In contrast, the specific gendering of German discourse 'places the woman as "victim of abortion" argument on the pro-liberalization side'. This example highlights a point made by Gail Kellough and one which runs throughout the argument in this book – that is, the need to attend to context both in identifying dominant frames and in determining what can be done about them. In Kellough's (1996: 205) words, 'prescriptions for change , including evaluations of any particular reform strategy, cannot be abstractly considered from a point outside the change process'. Michael McCann (1994: 11) agrees that 'legal tactics should identify those contextual variables most and least favourable to movement success'.

Kellough (1996: 5 and *passim*) identifies what she believes to be the major structuring assumption in both anti-abortion claims and much pro-choice argumentation, and that is an accepted dichotomization of liberty and need, or of self-interest and responsibility. She (1996: 8) argues that this dichotomy, which lodges deep within Western legal and philosophical traditions, produces a 'hegemonic mind-set' that 'reduces its conceptualization of reproduction to a biological event'. This conceptualization (1996: 32) buys into a 'social code' which accepts autonomy as the 'hallmark of maturity' and denies the active commitment involved in caring work. This argument is linked to Kellough's critique of the assumption that women are *natural* nurturers, an assumption which underlies the production of abortion as unnatural (see above). According to Kellough (1996: 23), a simple insistence on freedom of choice works within this hegemonic mindset and allows the construction of the woman seeking an abortion as selfish. By contrast, recognizing the active work involved in producing a child creates the option for women of *ceasing that active involvement*.

Kellough's (1996: 32) sensitivity to the impact of the autonomy/ responsibility dichotomy prompts her to criticize the way in which 'much of the liberation struggle for women has been oriented towards freeing women from their dependence on others'. The simple insistence on the right to abortion on demand can be interpreted, as Kellough has shown, as supporting an emphasis on independence. I recall in the 1960s framing of abortion as a necessary right, the way in which feminists stressed that access to abortion would 'free us' to have sex without consequences, to have sex 'like men'. But men can only have sex without consequences if they refuse to acknowledge those consequences. The problem here is not simply the *language* of rights and privacy, but a mind-set which accepts the privileging of autonomy over connectedness. The way in which we frame our reform demands hence is crucial to the effects which will follow. I will allow Kellough (1996: 18–19) the final word here:

> [C]hanges in institutional practices may, on the one hand, be considered to be real gains for oppressed groups while, on the other hand, the way that any reform is interpreted within discourse may strengthen the ideological assumptions that allow future forms of domination to reverse the gain.

Conclusion

Abortion makes a nonsense of social problem theorizing which sees social problems as the outcomes of claims by claims-makers (Spector and Kitsuse, 1987), or as forms of social movements (Mauss, 1975). The assumption in both these approaches is that an issue achieves social problem status because campaigners for a cause demand that the issue be addressed politically. This kind of thinking about social problems fits easily the issues of pay equity, antidiscrimination legislation, changes to the education agenda and access to child care, which were all demands of the revived feminist movement. We have seen how all these issues achieved social problem status for reasons additional to or other than feminist demands and how this insight gives us pause to consider the shape of these 'reforms', the problem representations they contain and their effects. But, at least, in these instances it is possible to identify 'claims-makers'.

Abortion, by contrast, became a 'social problem' in the second half of the nineteenth century because of the claims of those who *opposed* it. There was not a demand here for a new programme, but a demand to criminalize an old practice. The claims-makers who appeared in the 1960s and 1970s, including the medical establishment and many feminists, wished not to have abortion placed on the political agenda – it was already there – but to change its status. Medical practitioners wished to have it legalized in ways which protected their professional autonomy. Feminists in the main wished to have it taken off the political agenda altogether, to make it a 'non-problem'. The analysis in this chapter suggests that this demand *must be accompanied* by addressing directly the conditions under which people live, become pregnant and nurture their young.

Note

1 There is no assumption here that feminists agree on these issues. The use of the plural 'feminists' is intended to suggest the need to interrogate the variety of feminist positions, though here I am concentrating on the pro-choice position.

9

DOMESTIC VIOLENCE: BATTERED WOMEN OR VIOLENT MEN?

In Part One of the book I elaborate an understanding of policy as discourse (see Chapter 2). As described there, discourse is meant to capture the ways in which language limits what can be said. This is because existing language reflects commonly accepted ways of seeing, or frameworks for organizing social existence. Within these commonly accepted ways of seeing, I have attempted to demarcate a space for change, rejecting the view that hegemonic discourses are all-controlling. In other work (1996: 2), I have stressed the active deployment of concepts and categories for political purposes. There I build upon Tanesini's emphasis on the inferential-justificatory role of kinds of expressions. According to Tanesini (1994: 207), we need to become aware of the fact that concepts are not descriptive of any-thing, but that they are 'proposals about how we ought to proceed from here'. The purpose of concepts or categories, as Tanesini says, is 'to influence the evolution of ongoing practices'. Similarly, Derek Edwards (1991: 516) describes categorization as social practice in which 'language is primarily a medium for the accomplishment of social actions'. Because this description of language use seems to give complete discretion to language users, the notion of discourse provides a corrective or balance, drawing attention as it does to the contextual frames imposed by social codes and institutional practices.

Because concepts and categories form part of social practice, we need to focus not on abstracted category content but on situated usage. The focus on situated usage, on context, is a necessary part of a What's the Problem? approach which recommends approaching policy analysis by examining the problem representations that neces-sarily lodge within particular policy proposals. In policy proposals selected concepts and categories are deployed to produce specific problem representations. However, the same concepts could be and at times are used to defend very different agendas. So terms like 'family' and 'violence' and 'family violence' have in themselves no abstract meaning. Rather their meaning is to be understood by what they accomplish in terms of explanation within each problem representation. Any term (Bacchi, 1996: 7, 20) can be made to do any kind of political work; hence, the need to focus on exactly what is proposed rather than on the terms used to describe what is proposed.

Many different terms historically and currently are used to describe women's experience of brutal physical and psychological treatment by those with whom they share intimacy and often a place of residence. In the nineteenth century the 'problem', when it was considered to be a problem, was called 'wife battering'. By the twentieth century the label 'domestic violence' had become common. Today a cluster of phrases are used: spousal abuse, marital abuse, conjugal crime, woman battering, family violence, violence against women (see Walker, 1990: 34–5). At times different groups of feminists have intervened to try to alter the language used to frame the issue with the understanding that language matters in the construction of social problems. But the problem, as I say above, is not *just* the particular phrase which is used to describe the issue, but the ways in which a particular descriptor is deployed in a specific policy proposal to produce a particular problem representation. The point I am making here is the need to examine the ways in which terms or phrases like 'domestic violence' or 'family violence' function *as part of problem representations* rather than analysing them out of context. This will be the primary purpose of this chapter. At the same time, we will continue to reflect upon the *effects* of problem representations, including the ways in which the subjects of policy are constituted within them, and the silences some problem representations create.

Domestic violence is an area where feminists have been particularly sensitive to the repercussions of problem representation. As long ago as 1982 A. Schechter (in Walker, 1990: 85) made this perceptive comment about the shelter movement in the United States:

> [F]eminists were the first to analyse violence against women as part of the power dynamics operating between men and women in a sexist society . . . Professionals then moved in to claim violence as a mental health or criminal justice problem. The political analysis disappeared, was changed or was considered beyond the scope of professional concern.

Gillian Walker (1990) argues a similar case, emphasizing how feminists come to use the state's analytical categories, either a legal or a social work framing for example, to express their concerns. Reflecting the insights of governmentality literature, she stresses how feminist concerns about male domination become transformed, through engagement with the state, into discrete 'social problems' which are then handed over to different branches of the governmental administration. She also highlights, as do governmentality theorists, the role played by professionals, including feminist professionals, in 'social problem apparatuses'. In other chapters we have seen how complex social issues are commonly reduced to 'problems' which are then assigned to particular groups of professionals or to different departments of government, leaving the impression that the problem is being addressed. Here we are talking about both the reduction of multi-faceted programmes of change to single issues, like 'domestic violence' or 'pay equity', and the ways in which these single issues are then characterized. Two levels of analysis are involved: how complex power inequalities get produced as 'social problems', and how these social problems are then construed and with what effects.

Linda Gordon (1988; see also Breines and Gordon, 1983) provides the necessary historical background to understand how 'wife batter-ing' and 'domestic violence' achieved social problem status. She (1988: 27) argues, in line with the position developed in this book, that '[D]eviant behavior becomes a "social problem" when policy-makers perceive it as threatening to social order, and generate the widespread conviction that organized social action is necessary to control it.' This kind of explanation stands in contrast to those which describe 'social problems' as generated by claims-makers or by social movements. Gordon is emphasizing, as do I, that, if we cannot use-fully talk about a 'social problem' without reflecting upon the shape it is given, it becomes crucial to focus upon the shapes assigned by policy makers through policy proposals. This is not to dismiss the efforts of different individuals and groups to have serious social injustices addressed. Gordon (1988: 83), in fact, continuously stresses that, contrary to much social control literature, 'the clients were not merely passive recipients of help'. The point rather is to focus upon the *particular shape* given a 'problem' through policy proposals. The premise here is that the concerns of a specific period – and, though this is not Gordon's target, we can say the same is true of different cultures – produce a particular understanding of the problem. As Gordon (1988: 27–8) says, '[T]he modern history of family violence is not the story of changing responses to a constant problem but, in large part, of redefinition of the problem itself.' These meanings of the problem are political. Feminists may have played a large part in bringing attention to the issue of family violence, but (1988: 3) anti-feminists 'often dominated not only among those who would deny or ignore the problem but also among those who defined and treated it'.

Family Violence

Linda Gordon (1988: 104) develops the argument that governments become concerned enough to develop policy in the area of family violence when traditional family norms are under threat, when there is 'anxiety about gender relations'. In her words (1988: 2), 'concern with family violence has been a weather vane identifying the pre-vailing winds of anxiety about family life in general'. In fact, one of the concerns which prompted response was increasing signs of autonomy on the part of women. To quote Gordon (1988: 3) again, '[A]nxieties about family life, furthermore, have usually expressed socially conservative fears about the increasing power and autonomy of women and children, and the corresponding decline in male, sometimes rendered as fatherly, control of family members.' This link between conservative fears and problem representations of family violence produces analyses which can work against the best interests of the victims. For example, this concern is expressed at times in explanations of men's violence in which batterers are allowed 'to excuse their actions, since blame for the violence was placed on men's insecurity in the face of the challenge to traditional sex roles afforded by women's increasingly independent behaviour' (Walker, 1990: 32).

The concern in brief is expressed as 'family breakdown'. Concealed in this phrase are a number of assumptions about what 'family' and 'good family' mean, and the ways in which notions of the 'proper family' create family 'problems' (Holstein and Miller, 1989: 7). Divorce and single and lesbian parenthood, for example, are problems only if your notion of family presumes stasis, harmony and heterosexual pairing. Violence within heterosexual married couples challenges the idealized image of harmonious and continuous pairing and hence is addressed with the goal of restoring these idealized conditions. Violence is a 'problem' particularly if it threatens to break up self-sufficient pairs and to throw a number of dependent mothers on welfare support services. Given this logic, we are offered, not an analysis of the problematic dynamics of family relations, but strategies aimed at 'restoring' family harmony.

Gordon (1988: 117, 292) makes the case that, when feminists had a more active role in social work in the nineteenth century, the definition supplied for family violence had more democratic outcomes. She insists that, after the First World War, family violence was re-defined in ways that were 'disadvantageous to victims'. Specifically, definitions of child neglect from the US Progressive era (1890–1920)

tended to hold women exclusively responsible for the welfare of children; to emphasize economic deprivation but not gender domination; and, through the maintenance of a punitive approach without complementary social services, to intensify women's vulnerability to neglect allegations and to loss of their children.

Gordon notes how this analysis targeted lower-class women in particular. Part of this shift in definition Gordon attributes to the increasing domination of social work by men, and part to the 'structural imperative' for social workers 'to map the problem onto the client who was present and influenceable', who in almost all cases was the woman. Reflecting a theme from other chapters and one we will see again in the battered woman syndrome (see below), women, as the focus of analysis, become the problem, while male behaviour goes underanalysed and underproblematized.

A 1984 study by Pamela Johnston (in Walker, 1990: 78) distinguished between a psychodynamic formulation and a psychosocial formulation of the causes of the problem. In the former, the problem is represented to be one of sick individuals or relationships. The response which, in a What's the Problem? understanding, reveals exactly this problematization, calls for 'treatment', 'through counselling or psychotherapy focused on intrapyschic and behavioural patterns'. The problem is 'seen as located and maintained within the individual'. Such a focus easily becomes a form of 'victim blaming'. Martha Mahoney (1991: 27) notes that most of the early studies focused on the psychopathology of the female victims, not the aggressors.

The psychosocial formulation sees the problem 'as part of a larger system or context of family dynamics, cultural norms, and societal values that condones violence in a variety of forms' (Walker, 1990: 79). Johnston identifies three explanations for wife battering in this formulation explanations which advance socioeconomic and personal stress as causation, social learning theory and theories of how the sexist organization and traditions of society encourage wife abuse (in Walker, 1990: 79). According to Gillian Walker (1990: 80), despite the nod to sexism as a contributing factor, analysts in this tradition produce 'violence' as the problem. So, for example, a survey conducted by Straus, Gelles and Steinmetz, reported in Walker (1990: 80), to estimate the degree of violence in family relations, provided figures that indicated 'women were as or more violent than men, and that there were as many battered husbands as wives or more'. However, the survey failed to distinguish between actions taken in self-defence and failed to assess 'the severity of the injuries caused' (see also Kirkwood, 1993: 17).

In this psychosocial model, proposals to reduce violence include counselling, aimed at 'unlearning' antisocial behaviours and managing 'stress' and 'dysfunctional anger'; structural interventions aimed at eliminating 'the norms which legitimate and glorify violence in society and the family, such as physical discipline of children, the death penalty, corporal punishment, domestic firearms, media violence'; reducing violence provoking stress, 'such as underemployment, unemployment, and poverty'; integrating families 'into a network of kin and community'; and changing 'the sexist character of society and the family by eliminating sex patterned allotment of roles and tasks in the home and in the workplace' (in Walker, 1990: 81). The priority, it appears, is the need to do something about our 'culture of violence'. Violence against women, in this interpretation, becomes a subset of general societal violence and, it is presumed, will be reduced when the general level of violence is reduced. And while the acknowledgement of sex roles indicates a sensitivity to a gendered pattern in violence, explaining the lines of support between some feminists and psychosocial theory (Walker, 1990: 84), other feminists have suggested the inadequacy of sex role theory and the way it downplays the contest for power involved in male–female relations. As Johnston (in Walker 1990: 85) describes, while these models address themselves to questions of 'why men hit their partners at a particular moment', this is not the same 'as designing a theory of why men as a group direct their violence at women'. While clinical frames locate the problem in particular individuals, psychosocial theorists locate the problem in a *discrete location,* downplaying the broader patterns of gendered violence. Liz Kelly's (1988) description of sexual violence targeting women as a continuum in which '"typical" and "aberrant" male behaviour shade into one another' is a useful corrective here (see also Chapter 10).

The tendency in psychosocial analysis to see the problem as 'violence in general' or as a 'culture of violence' almost precludes violence in the response of the victim. This, of course, is the reason women appeared to be as violent as the men in the Staus, Gelles and Steinmetz survey (see above). To receive 'sympathy' in this account, the only permissible response is nonviolence or passivity. Martha Mahoney (1992: 1306) describes how '[L]aw forces upon us a discourse of victimization. Either you are on the playing field of liberal competition, in which case you require no protection, or you prove into a category as a victim who is being kept off the field.' In order to get attention you have to be pegged as 'in trouble' or as 'lesser' which also dictates the kind of 'help' you are likely to be offered. We can see a parallel here with the way in which affirmative action (Chapter 5) is constructed as assistance to the 'disadvantaged'. Mahoney emphasizes that signs of resistance can be interpreted as evidence that you can indeed function on the field. Only passivity wins you 'protection'. In this model, those presently occupying the playing field become the benefactors and the protectors while the behaviour of the 'disadvantaged' or the battered remains consistently under scrutiny. The way in which the battered woman syndrome continues to make women the focus of scrutiny indicates the difficulty of breaking out of this framework.

Battered Woman Syndrome

Battered woman syndrome has been developed as an attempt by feminist lawyers to reduce the punishment imposed on women who kill violent spouses. As Mary Ann Dutton (1993: 1197) explains, originally, 'battered woman syndrome was defined as the psychological *sequelae* to domestic violence'. This definition emphasized 'learned helplessness', 'a theory originally developed to explain why some animals fail to protect themselves in certain situations' (see Kirkwood, 1993: 9–10). More recently (Dutton, 1993: 1198), the term 'battered woman syndrome' has been used to refer to a 'particular subset of psychological reactions to violence: post-traumatic stress disorder (PTSD)'. Dutton goes on to detail the difficulties in the application of PTSD, explaining that sometimes the victim may not meet all the criteria for the 'disorder' and at other times may display reactions that result from exposure to traumatic experiences but which may be more complex than those described by PTSD. For our purposes, what is important is the way in which the victim of violence in this account is produced with 'an image of pathology, clinical disorder, or diminished capacity when this construct may not only be inaccurate, but may be the opposite of what is intended'. As we saw in the abortion chapter, in order to be heard, women often have to present themselves as unstable. If a woman displays intent, planning or foresight, she is liable not to qualify as a 'battered woman'. If she qualifies as a 'battered woman', she may well lose custody of her child or children because of the categorization which implies an 'utterly dysfunctional woman' (Mahoney, 1991: 39, 49). Mahoney is also concerned about the way in which the construction of the victim as pathological deters women from acknowledging the circumstances of their own distress. As she puts it (1992: 1310–11), '[P]eople do not identify with those they pity', and '[B]elief in one's own agency trumps identifying with victims.' Again, paralleling many women's and Black men's reluctance to be identified as affirmative action 'targets', we see how the representation of a problem can diminish awareness of it. If the options are to appear either 'disadvantaged', or 'unfairly advantaged', or 'beaten into submission', it is easy to understand why some people choose not to buy into these options, reducing awareness of the systemic injustices which form parts of their lives (see also Kelly, 1988: 145).

Mahoney offers two ways to undermine current representations of the problem. For one (1992: 1309), she challenges what she describes as the 'discourse of exit'. She notes how a common question posed to battered women in popular and legal discourse is 'Why didn't she leave?' The unexamined backdrop to this question is the assumption that all people have the resources to act independently. There is also no questioning in this analysis of the woman's desire and right to stay in her home. The question 'Why didn't she leave?', which is relevant to both domestic violence and sexual harassment cases, as we will see in the next chapter, presumes that choice is a possibility.

Hence, if the woman stays, it is assumed that she 'chose' to do so – in which case things mustn't have been so bad – or she had become so traumatized that she was incapable of choice. The power of a 'choice' discourse and the way in which it avoids consideration of the structural prerequisites for meaningful choice has been mentioned before.

To highlight the difficulties which make choice problematic for battered women, Mahoney (1991: 6) develops the notion of 'separation assault'. In her view a focus on the attacks perpetrated on women who leave or who threaten to leave highlights the 'struggle for power in the relationship'. She (1991: 29) sees this as a necessary corrective to the tendency to focus on incidents and behaviour in the battered woman syndrome. The effects of this shift in problematization are significant. In Mahoney's words (1991: 57), '[R]ecognizing the batterer's attempt at domination as the key to battering relationships allows a focus on his [since in the majority of cases it is a man] motivation rather than the psychology of the victim.' Wary of the danger of simply psychologizing male behaviour and creating 'pathological' men in the place of pathological women, Mahoney emphasizes the need to place the analysis in a larger framework of power and control in both law and culture.

Mahoney (1991: 32) draws upon feminist analyses of battering in lesbian relationships in her work on separation assault. She notes that in these analyses the focus is upon the batterer's purpose and the victim's response. Revealing the context of power and control within which the violence took place implies, in her view, little stigma for the one battered, in contradistinction to studies which focus on the pathology of the battered woman. Mahoney also notes in passing that evidence of battering in lesbian relationships raises questions about the adequacy of a gender frame. Catherine Kirkwood (1993: 30) believes that feminist theories about male violence against women 'do not yet adequately address overlapping systems of oppression such as racism and heterosexism'.

The kind of analysis offered by Mahoney is necessary and challenging. Her close examination of the framing discourses of exit and choice allow us to see why particular explanations of battered women's behaviour are more acceptable than others. Women, it seems, may be excused for acting violently against violent men if they are prepared to be branded as pathological and dysfunctional. But so long as it is women's behaviour which is represented to be the problem, the costs are significant – in terms of women's reluctance to admit to battering and in the practical consequences of being branded 'dysfunctional'. A refocusing on the batterer *and* the social relations which produce violent treatment of women promises more positive outcomes. The word 'and' here is emphasized to show the need to bring together an analysis of male batterers and the social relations which produce violence against women. A focus solely on male batterers produces the batterer either as a deviant individual or as a criminal and directs attention away from the structural aspects of the problem (see Bacchi and Jose, 1994a). None of this is meant as criticism of feminists who have worked to develop battered woman syndrome and who have used it to save some women's lives. It is to recognize the reasons why some arguments 'work' and highlights the repercussions of their working. A What's the Problem? analysis encourages this consistent re-examination of the discursive construction of feminist successes and the effects which flow from particular constructions of problems.

From Domestic Violence to Spousal Assault

Throughout the book I have noted attempts by feminists to have issues characterized as 'private' declared 'public' in order to have them addressed. As I mentioned in the Introduction, this can be seen as one of the most straightforward examples of the repercussions of problem representation, that a problem described as 'private' will be left unaddressed. Victoria Nourse (1996: 5 fn 20) puts the point this way: '[C]laims of "privacy" are really claims that we should refuse to judge, a position that inevitably affirms the status quo and, not surprisingly, avoids the crucial normative questions.' Put more forcefully: '[W]e no longer call "private" that which we have decided is wrong (e.g. racial discrimination).' The problem is not the word 'private' but the conceptual baggage associated with it in Western cultures.

Unsurprisingly, therefore, feminists have campaigned passionately to challenge the assumption that violence within the home is somehow different from 'public violence', that it is in a sense protected by its private nature. The descriptor 'domestic' has been identified as problematic because of the way it characterizes violence within the home as distinctive and, by implication, as less serious. The common police retort to calls for assistance from women assaulted in the home that 'It's just a domestic' gives credence to these suspicions (Lyon, 1995: 206). Victoria Nourse (1996: 1) notes how all the terms relating to violence against women – 'acquaintance rape', 'marital rape' and 'domestic violence' – include adjectival qualifiers which specify a relationship between the victim and assailant. Nourse condemns the framing of crimes against women through this 'veil of relationship' and recommends reframing domestic violence as a civil rights strategy in order to make violence against women of a like order to violence against men. By contrast, Martha Mahoney (1991: 6) approves of notions like 'acquaintance rape' because they move consciousness away from stereotypes of rape as assault by a stranger.

She feels it is important to *draw attention* to the *relationship* nature of the violence, illustrating the point made earlier about the different political uses of some concepts and categories.

Feminists offer evidence to support the claim that domestic violence is and has been considered a less serious offence than public violence. They have drawn on surveys which show considerable popular support for the idea that men have the right to discipline their wives (see, for example, *The Australian*, 26 April, 1990). They highlight court decisions which indicate similar assumptions (Graycar, 1995; Weeks and Gilmore, 1996: 148), harking back to the nineteenth century dictum that it was permissible to discipline one's wife so long as one used a stick no wider than one's thumb. Linda Gordon (1988: 255) makes the point that this specification of width indicates that a debate about the issue was indeed occurring and provides the first suggestion that regulations were being considered necessary. Still, the historical legacy of men's freedom to beat their wives provides powerful incentive for feminists who wish to insist that it should be made clear that this is no longer the case. The way to do this seems clearly to make the issue 'public'. Here is where engagement with the state becomes necessary, shaping the forms of 'public' recognition that are available. The most obvious option is to have domestic violence treated like common assault, to have the assailant imprisoned, indicating the seriousness of the offence and hopefully acting as a deterrent to him and to other men. Dawn Currie (1990: 84–5) describes how, in the early 1980s in Canada, many feminists endorsed stronger criminal sanctions for domestic violence. As one example, a report prepared for the Canadian Advisory Council on the Status of Women (MacLeod, 1980, cited in Currie, 1990: 84–5) advocated 'a clear, publicly advertised policy applying the same standards of non/arrest to family violence as to assault outside the family'. In the same period the Vancouver Women's Research Centre recommended, in lieu of channelling cases to a family court where the emphasis was upon reconciliation, 'mandatory response from police to all requests for intervention, arrest in certain specified cases, and mandatory minimum prison terms which range from 30 to 180 days' (cited in Currie, 1990: 85).

Two government reports produced in 1982, one Canadian – the Roy *Report on Violence in the Family: Wife Battering* (Standing Committee on Health, Welfare and Social Affairs, 1982), named after its chairperson Marcel Roy – and one American – *Under the Rule of Thumb: Battered Women and the Administration of Justice*, produced by the US Commission on Civil Rights – illustrate the extent to which the framing of violence against women as assault came into favour in this period. Both reports emphasized that domestic violence should be treated like other violence. The Roy Report (1982: 16) concluded that 'wife battery should be treated as criminal activity'. The US Commission on Civil Rights (1982: ii–iii) bemoaned the fact that 'judges often fail to take appropriate action, treating spouse abuse not as a crime against society but as a private family matter'.

These clear challenges to the framing of domestic violence as a 'private' issue indicated a certain kind of victory for the women's movement. However, other parts of these reports hint at the downside in the production of domestic violence as a criminal/legal issue. One of the major concerns of the Roy Report was that women did not always follow through with criminal charges. Hence, the Standing Committee (1982: 21) recommended that 'the victim be made a compellable witness against her husband'. This proposal removed from the woman's hand the decision about her needs. Linda MacLeod reflecting on her earlier (1980) Report for the Canadian Advisory Council on the Status of Women (CACSW), concluded (1987: 80, cited in Currie, 1990: 88) that an assault framing of the issue failed 'the test of battered women's realities'. One woman she interviewed explained why mandatory arrest was not always suitable:

> I've thought so many times about calling the police. If truth be known, I've thought about it for years – to teach him a lesson, to make him see what he's doing. But I always figured it would do more harm than good. . . . I call the police, and bang, he's out of a job, and jobs aren't so easy come by here. Then where are we at? Things'll just get worse. We'll have no money. He'll start drinking more. He'll be even more angry at me and he'll hit me more. So where's the sense calling the police?

One of the main purposes of the battered women's movement, to encourage women to feel self-confident and to take control of the situation, is clearly undermined by a proposal which forces certain options upon them, and which imprisons their partners without attending to the social supports they and their families need to survive. It goes without saying that these supports need to be provided without constituting the recipient a welfare problem!

The Roy Report (Standing Committee, 1982: 24) also recommended that schools give courses in human relations which deal generally with 'the problems of living in a family'. Along similar lines, the US Commission on Civil Rights Report (1982: 4) expressed concern that violence was 'breaking up families'. Despite the expressed challenges to the characterizing of domestic violence as a 'private' matter, the backdrop to both reports was a desire to find ways to *strengthen* families. Gordon's analysis (see above) linking concern about 'family breakdown' to initiatives to address domestic violence is relevant here. Feminist analyses, which suggest that the very nature of family relations creates the conditions for violence against women, receive no acknowledgement in either report (see Kirkwood, 1993: 21–3; Walker, 1990: 20). Rather the 'family' is to be 'saved' through legal intervention against 'batterers'.

A framing of the problem as a matter of violent men who need disciplining and passive women who need protecting fitted the agenda of the Canadian Conservative Party, headed by Brian Mulroney, who claimed the cause as his own in 1987 (Currie, 1990: 89). Sandra Burt (1996: 13) shows how, in the hands of the Conservatives, the issue was represented to be a matter of public safety, allowing a concentration of resources on society's public protection system, the police. She notes also (1988: 143) that '[T]he switch in focus from equal pay for work of equal value and affordable, accessible day care' to issues like rape and wife-beating 'reduced the pressure on federal finances and on federal–provincial renegotiation of social service funding'.

Using a What's the Problem? approach, proposals which commit resources to police (while reducing commitments to women's shelters) produce the problem of violence against women as a matter of criminal men and 'social breakdown'; the end or goal becomes tighter social control and a more disciplined population. For many feminists, as Gillian Walker (1990: 31) explains, the priority in funding should be women's shelters, run by feminists with the women themselves, to encourage self-help and confidence building. The problem representation in this proposal stands in marked contrast to the law and order framing above: '[V]iolence should be conceptualized, not as a breakdown of social order but rather as the reflection of a power struggle for the maintenance of a certain kind of social order', one in which men terrorize women. The redirection of resources from women's shelters to the police and/or to programmes for battering men (see Currie, 1990: 90) transforms an understanding of the problem as 'a critique of patriarchal power to demands for protection from male power'. In the process a movement intended originally to increase women's self-confidence and feelings of control becomes expressed as a need to protect women who are vulnerable. None of this suggests that men should not be imprisoned for beating their partners, but that proposals need to be examined closely to uncover the problem representations which lodge there and where they lead.

A similar alignment between those demanding public recognition of 'private' assault and a law and order lobby has taken place in Australia. Wendy Weeks and Mary Gilmore (1996: 152) comment on the 'downside' of this alignment: '[T]he issue is at risk of being co-opted by the "law and order" lobby, which focuses on the question of victims of all crime, looking to the fields of criminology and forensic psychology for solutions.' Weeks and Gilmore are also sensitive to the way in which this representation of the problem constitutes the subjects in instances of domestic violence: '[T]his approach again feeds into an individualising of both victim and perpetrator, thus deflecting emphasis away from gendered power relations as a central issue.' Recognizing the right wing's endorsement of a law and order agenda and punitive responses to violence offers an important corrective to the tendency in the governmentality literature to assume that liberal modes of self-regulation have *replaced* disciplinary modes of control (O'Malley, 1992: 261). For Pat O'Malley, the continuing co-existence of disciplinary and self-regulatory modes of governance means that we need to move 'from a model of technologies of power and their efficiencies toward a model of substantive political programs which deploy such technologies in ways which cannot be reduced to any simple or direct formula'.

On this point it is interesting to note the problems Swedish feminists have faced getting the issue of 'domestic' and other violence against women, including sexual harassment, onto the political agenda. In *The Politics of Affirmative Action* (1996: 115) I trace these problems in part to the defining ethic of Swedish politics as 'solidarity' across class and gender. Here solidarity acts as a discursive frame which makes it difficult to focus upon issues that highlight conflict between women and men. In Sweden the issue of 'women's inequality' is consistently referred to as 'inequality between the sexes'. At the same time the Swedes' general position on punishment and deterrence, where the desire has been to introduce shorter terms of imprisonment generally and more fines as sanctions, has meant the absence of a law and order brigade ready and eager to take up criminal sanctions against batterers. Women then, it seems, have had an easier time getting heard on the violence issue in places where and at times when there is a desire for tighter social controls of 'problem' populations. Because of this Elizabeth Sheehy (1996: 112) suggests that feminists would do well to form a coalition which includes 'racialized women and women who work with people in prison' if they wish to remain sensitive to the ease with which their analysis can become part of a law and order agenda, because these women 'are often more astute about the links between particular proposals and the law and order agenda'.

Dawn Currie (1990) offers a perceptive analysis of the ways in which 'wife battering' became a law and order issue. Her major point is that this interpretation was not *imposed* upon feminists but occurred 'through and not against feminist discourse'. Several factors were at work here. We have already mentioned the initial impetus to insist that violence at home was a serious problem which needed to stand condemned publicly and the pragmatics of framing the issue in language which would be heard. In her reflections on the 1980 CACSW Report, Linda MacLeod elaborated:

[A]nd so to take action we have simplified the problem – focussed on the physically violent act, provided support and protection to individuals. . . . Wife battering was reduced to a series of acts – violent acts of a man against a woman for which the man must take responsibility. For the purposes of action, wife battering was individualized. (1987: 6, cited in Currie, 1990: 87)

In addition, as Currie relates, feminists divided over how the issue ought to be represented; their different positions reflected 'specific locations within sometimes competing, sometimes complementary, practices of medicine, law, social science, service work and even "common sense"'. These specific locations involved feminists in distinct discursive representations of the problem. Currie (1990: 87, 92) highlights the takeover by various groups of professionals, illustrating how who 'owns' the issue 'creates or changes the definition of the problem and the services provided'. With the takeover by professionals, including feminist professionals, the issue is interpreted through a social science discourse in which 'wife battery has been incorporated into the broader and more neutral sounding topic of "family" or "domestic" violence'. The importance of examining who owns the issue and the framings they employ is powerfully illustrated in the example of gender persecution as the grounds for refugee status.

Gender Persecution

In March 1993 the Canadian Immigration and Refugee Board introduced guidelines on gender-related persecution to Canada's Immigration Act (Immigration and Refugee Board, 1993, cited in Razack, 1995: 47; hereafter referred to as *Guidelines*). As Sherene Razack (1995: 47) describes, the *Guidelines* are 'the culmination of intensive lobbying by women's groups and various Canadian and international efforts to address the issue of domestic violence as a form of persecution'. The *Guidelines* cover two types of cases: first, '[W]omen fleeing severely abusive spouses, who can show that their countries of origin are unwilling or unable to protect them', and second, 'women living in countries where they encounter severe state-sanctioned discrimination'. Razack has no hesitation in declaring the *Guidelines* a 'remarkable achievement in Canadian legal history', but she is concerned about some of the effects which flow from the way in which the problem tends to be represented.

Razack (1995: 46, 49) begins by noting that refugee hearings are always 'profoundly racialized' events, and 'the powerful are always from the First World and mostly white, while the powerless are from the Third World and nearly always racialized or ethnicized'. Beneath the 'outwardly compassionate process of granting asylum', we need to recognize how the proceedings create First World countries as benefactors, while the people of the Third World are created as 'supplicants asking to be relieved of the disorder of their world and to be admitted to the rational calm of ours'. The image of First World countries as saviours ignores and belies the role of the First World in creating through economic exploitation the circumstances of the distress suffered by refugees. As David Goldberg (1993: 174, cited in Razack, 1995: 49 fn 10) has argued, '[P]ower is here expressed, managed, and extended in and through representing racial Others to themselves and to the world.'

Razack goes on to demonstrate that the gender persecution discourse often employs the imperial frames of the West in the representation of women seeking asylum. She identifies authors who, for example, make central the 'problem' of Islamic states. The tendency to trace the problem to oppressive patriarchal cultures, which in this description stand apart from our apparently benevolent, less patriarchal culture is also evident in many commentaries on female genital mutilation. One effect (Razack, 1995: 56) in both these cases is a creation of 'imagined Exotic Other Females in need of their [Western feminist] benevolent protection', and hence a failure to 'engage Third World women as subjects'. Another effect is the obscuring of Western hegemony, specifically 'the West's implication in the contemporary patterns of global economic exploitation'. What remains undertheorized in this account (Razack, 1995: 54) is 'how many of these wrongs work in concert with other systems of oppression, systems that benefit some women at the expense of others'.

Because of these concerns, Razack asks feminists to reconsider the usefulness of a 'violence against women' narrative, and hence of a gender or man—woman frame, *in cases where it obscures the operation of power between First and Third Worlds*. For example (Razack, 1995: 52), when a man—woman frame is applied to an examination of IMF loans, 'gender inequality replaces First World/Third World relations in this approach, if not by design then by impact. It is not the conditions of the loans themselves, but how they affect men and women differently that becomes the focus', or the problem. Within a man—woman framework, says Razack (1995: 59), 'it is not possible to discuss the ravages of colonialism and neocolonialism on the economies of the South'. 'Violence against women', like the category 'women' itself, can be employed either for or against feminist goals. Its use has to be examined for its effects in each case (Bacchi, 1996). With Inderpal Grewal and Caren Kaplan (1994: 17), Razack would claim that '[I]f feminist political practices do not acknowledge transnational cultural flows, feminist movements will fail to understand the material conditions that structure women's lives in diverse locations.'

Razack (1995: 71) provides pointers for useful reframings of the issue. For one, she suggests locating the problem for women seeking asylum on the grounds of gender persecution in the state rather than in the culture. At a more general level, she recommends the reframing put forward by the feminist lawyer Roberta Clarke, who suggests that 'feminists reframe the issue moving from women as victims (violence against women) to men as aggressors (violence by men)', *while* holding states responsible 'for the many ways in which they support the production of violent men' (see the discussion above concerning the need to bring together an analysis of male batterers *and* the social relations which produce violence against women). This kind of reframing means that a bill which enables women to obtain protection orders will not be seen as a 'panacea, but as one element of a multi-pronged strategy in which the goal would be to change social structures that propel men to be violent and condone their excesses'. Clearly, Clarke's reframing is useful for both the refugee context and for the 'problem' of 'violence against women' generally, since it shifts the focus from the pathology of the woman as victim to 'the patterns of the violence of the man', and to 'the state's failure to implement measures against him or for her'.

Conclusion

Razack makes an important disclaimer in her critique of gender persecution discourse. She (1995: 48) explains that

> in recognizing the limits of how gender persecution is utilized in law, I do not suggest that we abandon it. Instead, I want to explore ways in which we might talk about women and the violence they experience, in their communities, about the interlocking systems of oppression, and specifically about the way in which there is First World complicity in both the sexual and racial persecution of Third World women.

Her goal is to find ways to speak about violence against women 'without invoking an imperial relation' (1995: 71).

The argument in this book is that close attention to problem representations in policy proposals, including those put forward by feminists, provides insights into the problematic effects of some framings. This prepares us to do several things: to contest policy proposals we oppose by exposing the assumptions which lie behind them, and to examine our own discursive frames to see what they buy into. If, in our desire to assist some women to gain asylum, we produce the problem in ways that have a range of undesirable effects – culturally 'othering' the women concerned, refusing to recognize

the role of Western economic practices in the creation of the problem
– then we need to examine and reassess the problem representations
which lodge in our proposals. If, in our desire to remove some
women from danger in their homes, we provide support for a legal
framing which denies their agency and strengthens legal sanctions
against targeted populations, including whites and Blacks living in
poverty, then we need to rethink the shape of our proposals for
change and where they lead. The goal, as Razack describes it, is to
find less destructive and more useful problem representations, representations which recognize the complex interactions of Western
imperialism and local patriarchies, representations which recognize
the complex needs of refugee and other women.

10

SEXUAL HARASSMENT: WHAT IS SEXUAL ABOUT IT?

I have selected sexual harassment as the last chapter in the book for several reasons. It is among the most recent challenges posed by feminists to the sexual status quo and, arguably, it stands as '*the* success story of twentieth-century feminism [original emphasis]' (Gallop, 1997: 27). We have here a classic case of the 'creation' of a 'social problem', using Murray Edelman's formulation (1988: 13), where behaviours which existed formerly emerge as a named 'social problem' and the target of selected interventions. As Julia Wood (1994: 18) describes: '[W]hile sexual harassment has always occurred, until recently it was not named and, thus, had no *social* existence [original emphasis].' Sexual harassment appears also to be the quintessential challenge to the public/private dichotomy, reframing personal experiences of sexual hostility as public crimes.

At the same time a number of feminists are expressing concern about the way in which the 'problem' is being framed. Wendy Pollack (1990: 48) claims, for example, that '[W]omen have named sexual harassment, but have lost control of the content of its definition.' Other authors (Bingham, 1994; Brant and Too, 1994; Wise and Stanley, 1987) suggest that it is time to 'rethink sexual harassment'. The collection edited by Shereen Bingham (1994: 1) calls for a reconceptualizing of sexual harassment as 'discursive practice' on the grounds that '[M]en continue to harass women sexually with alarming frequency, and the typical solutions (e.g. saying "no" or filing a complaint) have not proven very helpful.' A What's the Problem? approach can be seen as useful here, focusing as it does on the discursive construction of policy problems. The argument throughout has been that, in order to assess policy proposals, we need to uncover the problem representations they contain and to examine these for their effects. In this chapter, we will apply the approach to the 'discovery' of 'sexual harassment'. In the process we will reflect upon the nature and effects of feminist interventions.

It might be pointed out that there are, in most pieces of legislation dealing with sexual harassment and in most employer policies which derive from this legislation, explicit detailed definitions of the phenomenon, and hence there is no need to dig any further or to try to 'read off' problem representations from policy proposals – we have been told what the problem is! To an extent this is so and we will spend a good deal of this chapter analysing standard definitions and investigating their implications. At the same time it is important to ask why sexual harassment is represented, in contrast to many other issues, as *requiring* precise definition. This very characterization, I will be arguing, provides important insights into what the problem is represented to be.

Sexual Harassment as Sex Discrimination

More than any of the other issues examined in this book, it is clear that feminists played a prominent role in the naming of sexual harassment. Catharine MacKinnon (1979: 27–8 in Pollack, 1990: 41 fn 16) traces the origins of the term to the Working Women United Institute, the Alliance Against Sexual Coercion, and Carroll Brodsky's *The Harassed Worker* (1976). The term had sufficient currency in 1975 for the *New York Times* to assume that its readers would be familiar with it (Nemy, 1975: 38). A 1980 *Newsweek* article (Press, 1980: 81, cited in Tong, 1986: 165 fn 1) described sexual harassment as 'the boss's dirty little fringe benefit' which has been 'dragged out of the closet'. In 1980 the Melbourne Working Women's Centre initiated a campaign to incorporate the issue of sexual harassment into the ACTU Working Women's Charter, a campaign which was successful the following year (Bryson, 1994: 10). Sue Wise and Liz Stanley (1987: 28) trace the appearance of the term in England to 1981.

Wise and Stanley (1987: 48) assert that feminists who coined the phrase had in mind, in so doing, drawing attention to a particular form of intrusive male behaviour. That is, their emphasis was upon a *particular* expression of a more general phenomenon, the denigration and humiliation of women. Beyond this, they wished to draw attention to this *particular expression* of objectionable behaviour because of the way in which it was commonly excused as natural, as boys being boys. And finally, they wished to name the phenomenon to emphasize that women collectively experienced this behaviour. Hence it was not a personal interaction between a man and a woman, but the imposition of male prerogative on women because they are women.

As we saw in the last chapter, putting a public face to behaviour previously considered private is not an unproblematic project. This is because the channels available for use shape in part the way in which the problem is conceptualized. In particular, we saw how constructing violence against women in their homes as assault tended to reduce the problem to individual interactions and to make it difficult to address the systemic character of the problem. Pointing out, as Margaret Thornton (1991a: 458) does, that criminal law 'divorces the wrong from its social setting', does not mean to suggest that we should not use criminal law; rather it alerts us to the limitations of employing this channel for redress. The legal channels available to women who experienced sexual harassment before the phenomenon was named included either criminal law or civil torts, including battery, assault and the intentional infliction of mental or emotional disturbance (Tong, 1986: 154). The standard of proof required in criminal justice cases made this an unpromising route to follow. Attempts to use tort law face a number of difficulties, which Rosemary Tong (1986: 157) summarizes: a woman has to show that she had not consented to her harasser's 'sexual advances', that she is not a 'hypersensitive individual', and 'that she has indeed suffered harm as a result of her harasser's sexual misconduct'. Moreover, like criminal law, tort law leaves the matter as one between individuals, 'treating as individualized something that is a group or social injury' (MacKinnon, 1979: 172). Social context is considered irrelevant (Thornton, 1991a: 458). Because of these limitations, antidiscrimination law seems to promise more. To quote Tong (1986: 157):

> [B]ecause antidiscrimination law is sensitive to these power dynamics [between women and men], it can accomplish more for sexually harassed women than tort law. Whereas tort law views sexual harassment as an outrage to an individual woman's sensibilities and to a society's purported values, antidiscrimination law casts the same act either as one of *economic* coercion, in which the material survival of women in general is threatened, or as one of *intellectual* coercion, in which the spiritual survival of women in general is similarly jeopardized [original emphasis].

However, in Chapter 5, I noted that antidiscrimination law itself is limited in what it can achieve because it is complaint-based and because of the unequal power relations between complainants and respondents. Even in cases where the target of a complaint is a co-worker, sex discrimination complaints address the employer who is held liable for workplace conditions. Women who wish to press a charge of sexual harassment have to face the possibility of job loss, despite the protections against victimization.[1] And then of course there are the costs involved in a legal battle. Moreover, despite the fact that the legislation specifically addresses a systemic harm called 'sex discrimination', even in cases decided in favour of the complainant we are left with an *individual* employer who is told to toe the line. The way in which deep institutional structures create the circumstances within which this behaviour is allowed cannot be captured in legislation of this kind (Olsen, 1983: 1497, 1552).

This is not to say that having sexual harassment recognized as sex discrimination is not a major victory. The first cases in which this claim was considered and *rejected* make this clear. In *Corne* v. *Bausch*

& Lomb, Inc. (390 F. Supp. 161 [1975], U. S. Dist. Ct., D. Arizona, in Tong, 1986: 158), the court dismissed the complaint of two female clerical workers who 'sued for a violation of their civil rights based on sex discrimination', on the grounds that sexual harassment is a 'personal proclivity, peculiarity, or mannerism', which employers cannot be expected to extirpate in their employees. In *Miller* v. *Bank of America* (418 F. Supp. 233 [1976], U. S. Dist. Ct., N. D. California, in Tong, 1986: 158), the court dismissed the complaint of a female bank worker who was fired when she refused to be 'sexually cooperative' with her male supervisor because '[T]he attraction of males to females and females to males is a natural sex phenomenon and it is probable that this attraction plays at least a subtle part in most personnel decisions. Such being the case, it would seem wise for the courts to refrain from delving into these matters.' Moving sexual harassment from diagnoses like these which represent the problem to be either personal or natural behaviour to a recognition of sexual harassment as discrimination is a significant accomplishment. None the less, it is important to attend to the silences – to what remains unproblematized – accompanying the terms of reference within which it is framed. Sue Wise and Liz Stanley (1987: 201) make this very point:

> [I]n relation to sexual harassment, we need to examine which of men's behaviours are excluded from the definition as well as those which are included. We must ensure for ourselves that the pattern we are told is the pattern is *in fact* 'the pattern as we experience it' [original emphasis].

Sexual Harassment as Workplace Discrimination

With the exception of education,[2] sexual harassment is seen almost unilaterally as an employment problem, a problem faced by *working* women. This is true in Europe (see Hoskyns, 1996: 16) as well as in Canada, Australia and the United States. Here we need to recall that the numbers of women in the workforce were increasing dramatically in the post-1970s period and that, as we have seen throughout the book, to a large extent women's inequality was represented to be a matter of lack of access to the labour force. Drawing sexual harassment into work-related employment discrimination capitalized on this connection. Catharine MacKinnon (1979: 7) is explicit on this point:

> [L]egally, women are not arguably entitled, for example, to a marriage free of sexual harassment any more than to one free of rape, nor are women legally guaranteed the freedom to walk down the street or into a court of law without sexual innuendo. In employment, the government promises more.

While recognizing the strategic usefulness of tying sexual harassment to the equal employment opportunity agenda, it is important to remember the other points made in MacKinnon's comment – that such an emphasis on employment leaves street harassment and harassment at home untouched (Morgan, 1995: 98).[3]

The link with employment has other effects on understandings of what constitutes harassment. In Australia early policy development in the area specified that there could be a finding of sexual harassment only when the complainant could demonstrate a work detriment, for example, the loss of a job or a promotion. The classic case of quid pro quo harassment, in which women are instructed 'Sleep with me or you will be sacked' (Thornton, 1990: 47), captures this sense of work detriment. Along these lines the US Equal Employment Opportunity Commission Guidelines, first promulgated in 1980 (Pollack, 1990: 47), specified that '[U]nwelcome sexual advances, requests for sexual favors, and other verbal or physical conduct of a sexual nature constitute sexual harassment' when 'submission to such conduct is made explicitly or implicitly a term or condition of an individual's employment'. Significantly, employers could be held liable for harassment perpetrated by their workers (Tong, 1986: 161).

The EEOC Guidelines recognized both quid pro quo and hostile environment harassment; however, it took some time for the courts to pay heed to the latter. It was only in 1986 in the case of *Meritor Sav. Bank, FSB* v. *Mechele Vinson* (477 U. S. 57, 73, cited in Pollack, 1990: 53) that the US Supreme Court enlarged the legal definition of sexual harassment to 'include hostile or intimidating environments in addition to quid pro quo' (Wood, 1994: 29 fn 1). In Australia, feminists also fought for and won the elimination of references to work detriment and the recognition of illegal sexual harassment on the sole grounds that the behaviour 'offended, humiliated, or intimidated' the complainant (Sex Discrimination Commissioner, 1996: 16). This expansion of the understanding of sexual harassment is significant. The previous emphasis on work detriment played to the notion that, in order for a man to harass a woman, he had to hold some sort of hierarchical authority over her. Looking to an employer's responsibility to create an environment in which an employee could expect to work unharassed made it possible to draw attention to harassment by co-workers. This in turn allows attention to be directed to the social power men exert over women, by the fact of their being men.

The interpretations of 'hostile environment', however, continue to reflect some disturbing tendencies which we have noted in other legal recognitions of gender-based harms. For one, it seems that the degree of harm has to be so severe and so pervasive that the complainant needs to display signs of illness (see Riger, 1993: 216; Tong, 1986: 149). There is now recognition of a sexual harassment syndrome, reminiscent of the battered woman syndrome (see Chapter 9). A woman, however, who remains resilient and who continues to challenge her harassers is less likely to be able to convince the court that she faced a hostile environment. She can claim recognition only if she presents as pathological. John Lunny (1997: 34–5) offers an alternative framing. He points out that sexual harassment is covered by occupational health and safety legislation which carries an obligation for employers to guarantee workers 'a quiet enjoyment of employment'. This framing usefully relieves the woman employee of the need to prove that her conditions of employment were unbearable, but it still leaves uncertain what needs to be done to establish 'quiet enjoyment of employment'. This issue will be pursued later in the chapter.

Sexual Harassment as Unwelcome Advances

The *Meritor* decision (see above) provided a description of sexual harassment which has since become conventional wisdom. It stated that

> the fact that sex-related conduct was 'voluntary', in the sense that the complainant was not forced to participate against her will, is not a defence to a sexual harassment suit brought under Title VII. The gravamen of any sexual harassment claim is that the alleged sexual advances were 'unwelcome'. (*Meritor*, 488 U. S. at 68, cited in Pollack, 1990: 55)

Most common definitions of sexual harassment stress this very point, that the defining characteristic of the behaviour is that it is unwelcome, and generally feminists have approved of such a definition which seems to place the power to identify harassing behaviour in the hands of the woman. However, distinguishing sexual harassment as *unwelcome* discrimination places it in a category separate from other discrimination in ways which seriously undermine attempts to deal with it. The implication in this construction is that what we are talking about are ambiguous behaviours which need to be identified as unwelcome. No such qualification characterizes claims of race discrimination, which are deemed to be by their nature unwelcome. As I go on to discuss below, sexual harassment is singled out in this way because sexual harassment is confused both in public and legal discourse with sexual attraction and flirtation. It is this confusion which makes it necessary for women to spell out that they did not wish *this particular display* of attraction or flirtation. All the debate about just how men are supposed to know when to be flirtatious or not follows from this characterization. For example, the emphasis on the 'unwelcome' nature of the behaviour leads to the easy assumption that the respondent needed to be informed that the behaviour was indeed unwelcome; hence, first offences may be excused, unless they are egregious.

Drucilla Cornell (1995: 190) shares my concerns about the focus on 'unwelcome' behaviour, and suggests using instead the words 'unilaterally imposed'. Her goal here (1995: 200) is to shift the focus from 'whether the woman correctly perceived what happened' to 'whether the behaviour undermined the equal provision of the social bases of self-respect'. This change in language usefully refocuses on the perpetrators, making it possible to claim as sex-based harassment 'unilaterally imposed' insults and slurs along lines similar to those in racial vilification.[4] As mentioned above, there is never a need in racial vilification cases to prove that the slurs were 'unwelcome'.

The emphasis on specificity in definitions of sexual harassment likewise follows from a presumption that in such matters (that is, sexual matters) there are many grey areas and hence we need to be as precise as possible about what is unacceptable. The emphasis on precision meanwhile helps to create the issue in the public mind as a *sexual* issue where, as we all 'know', ambiguity abounds. Men, we are told, frequently get the 'wrong signals', in effect excusing their behaviour while creating women responsible for their own harassment.

In an attempt to short-circuit this kind of reasoning, feminists have developed the concept of the reasonable woman. Generally policy proposals specify that the behaviour complained of has to be offensive or humiliating by some commonly recognized standard, that of the reasonable person. Feminists have been quick to alert jurists to the fact that, as in law generally (see Naffine, 1990), the reasonable person is taken to mean the reasonable *man*, leaving women's needs and perceptions unaddressed. In *Rabidue* v. *Osceola Refining Company* (1986 in Wood, 1994: 24) a 'reasonable woman' standard was invoked for the first time. Judge Damon Keith 'held that the conditions of women's and men's lives differ and may inform legitimately dissimilar interpretations of behavior, specifically what is intimidating and offensive'. At one level this recognition of the subjectivity hidden in the supposedly objective standard of the reasonable person, and appeals to women's experiences as the basis of a new standard, indicate a significant victory. As MacKinnon (1987: 105, cited in Wood, 1994: 24) states, 'the legal claim for sexual harassment marks the first time in history . . . that women have defined women's injuries in law'. At the same time, as with the characterizing of sexual harassment as 'unwelcome behaviour', there are some troubling aspects to the invocation of a 'reasonable woman' standard. Just what is a 'reasonable woman' and how does a woman qualify as meeting this standard? What kinds of behaviours would act as counter-indicators of her reasonableness? Would white and Black women measure up equally? Would a lesbian qualify as a 'reasonable woman'? Even more pointedly, why in both 'unwelcome behaviour' and 'reasonableness' does the focus of enquiry shift from the perpetrator and his behaviour to the one making the complaint? Why do women yet again become the focus of scrutiny? In part, this is due to the nature of the complaint process but, I would suggest, in greater part it is due to the creation of sexual harassment as *sexual* harassment.

Sexual Harassment as *Sexual* Harassment

Above I noted that, when feminists put a label to sexual harassment, their intention was to draw attention to a sub-category of offensive male behaviour which was commonly accepted as natural and personal. But in the process of its naming the problem representation changed. Wise and Stanley (1987: 48, 53) put it this way: sexual harassment is commonly characterized as men using power to get sex, usually from women, whereas the point feminists were trying to make was that men often use sex to 'do power' or 'accomplish power' over women. Feminists frequently make the point that sexual harassment, like rape, is about power not sex, but this needs some clarification. Clearly the behaviour targeted here often (but not always) uses *sex* to exercise power and this needs to remain part of the analysis. Elizabeth Grauerholz (1994: 43 fn1) notes, for example, that

> [A]lthough there is nothing sexually pleasurable for victims of sexual harassment, for harassers, there may indeed be an element of sexual titil- lation. In fact, the coercive element of these acts may make the sexual element more stimulating. Such a response is not unusual in a culture such as ours that routinely eroticizes sexual violence in popular culture, especially in pornography.

In addition, we need to recognize that the woman sexually harassed experiences the harassment in particular ways because the channel for harassment is often sexual innuendo or sexual behaviours (refer to the discussion of the lived effects of discourse in Chaper 2). However, what needs to be clarified is that sexual harassment has nothing to do with sexual *attraction*.

Even in discussions of sexual harassment which recognize a power dimension to the interaction, it is commonly assumed that the man was at some level 'attracted to' the woman. The common description of sexual harassment as an 'unwelcome sexual *advance*', both in legislation (Sex Discrimination Commissioner, 1996: 16) and in feminist analyses (Cornell, 1995: 171; Tong, 1986: 157) carries this impression. This characterization of the behaviour creates the grounds for all the confusion about the boundary between flirtation and harassment. We are asked, How can a man know when his 'legitimate' attraction to a woman will be rebuffed? Beyond this, there is an assumption that men are natural sexual aggressors. In quid pro quo harassment, for example, the argument is that the man uses bribery or extortion to get what he 'wants', which is 'sexual satisfaction' from the woman. Australia's Sex Discrimination Act (Sex Discrimination Commissioner, 1996: 16) defines sexual harassment using the somewhat quaint and heavily gender-laden language of 'an unwelcome request for *sexual favours* [emphasis added]'. I say gender-laden because the language captures the conventional notion that men *seek* sexual 'favours' and women *bestow* them. The framing seems to assume and even to accept that men are in some sense 'driven' by instincts which make them resort to what can only be described as antisocial conduct. The male sexual instinct operates here as the unnamed villain, its existence presumed rather than queried.

On the other side there is a presumption that women passively await men's sexual advances, either accepting or rejecting them. This can be seen in a definition of hostile environment as that which would 'offend, humiliate or intimidate' a reasonable person. Jenny Morgan (1995: 92) notes how the term 'offend' plays to a notion of *moral* offence, linking us back to the realm of personal feelings and sensitivities. The term is also used in an attempt to distinguish 'legitimate' sexual 'advances' from harassing ones. This becomes a problem because of shifting sexual mores. For example, it is not uncommon for women to be told that, in our more sexually liberated times, the kinds of behaviours they object to are common place and generally accepted. Women who complain of harassment then appear as wowsers, puritanical spoilsports protecting the dated moral standards of a by-gone era. In a well-known Australian case, Justice Einfeld awarded no damages to the women he found to be victims of sexual harassment on these very grounds, that much of what was complained of was 'mild if ridiculous *advances* or conduct [emphasis added]', and could be considered within the bounds of the normal life experiences of most women (Bacchi and Jose, 1994b: 264). As Margaret Thornton (1990: 50) puts it, Einfeld 'invented a "reasonable woman" who should have been able to dismiss both physical and verbal overtures in view of her experience of the world'. Since then Einfield, whose judgment 'attracted widespread disapprobation' (Thornton, 1990: 51), has recanted and accepted a different 'reasonable woman' standard which reflects something other than his impression of what a reasonable woman would expect and accept. But just what is this new reasonable woman standard? Within a general understanding of sexual harassment as *sexual* harassment, it is difficult to consider reasonableness without reflecting upon 'sensitivity'. While in some cases 'sensitivities' will be respected and will be rewarded with damages, the terms of analysis remain wide open to abuse. The kind of interrogation which rape victims face about previous sexual behaviour and dress could easily be invoked as contradicting the complainant's self-presentation as 'offended'. The same kinds of questions directed at victims of domestic violence (or survivors of male violence, to use more appropriate language; see Kirkwood, 1993: 154) – Why didn't she leave if she was offended? Why didn't she act sooner? (see Mahoney, 1992) – could be used to undermine the genuineness of a complaint of 'offence'. The options then are to present as beaten by the behaviour, as sick, *or* as a liar. And once again, the woman remains the focus of scrutiny. As Wendy Pollack (1990: 83) states, '[E]mphasis on the woman's perspective as a standard can too easily be used to treat sexual harassment as an isolated, personal and trivial experience.' Drucilla Cornell (1995: 170) makes a similar point when she argues that feminists who talk about the reasonable woman standard have 'bought into a tort scheme'.

It is interesting just how many feminists feel impelled to insist that sexual harassment depends upon the perceptions of the one harassed. Wise and Stanley (1987: 44), for example, state unequivocally that 'most "sexual harassment" is a matter of perception on the part of the recipient.' We are told that 'a reasonable woman and a reasonable man are likely to differ in their judgments of what is offensive' (Riger, 1993: 217). Wendy Pollack (1990: 68 fn 129) agrees that men and women are 'vulnerable in different ways' and are 'offended by different behaviors'. Feminists do this, I would suggest, primarily because sexual harassment has come to mean *sexual* harassment and hence the whole discussion has shifted to debates about moral standards and 'reasonable' offence. In these debates it has appeared necessary, understandably so, to do everything possible to strengthen *women's* claims to make judgements on these issues. However, if what we are talking about is harassment which uses sex to control women, none of these debates is necessary. Instead of buying into the emphasis on subjective standards, which opens the floodgates to discussions about misrepresentation by the woman or about the man being misunderstood, we need to challenge the impression that sexual harassment is about breakdown in communication.

The focus on 'different perspectives' recreates some very old stereotypes about men misperceiving women's intentions and plays into the popular representation that indeed men and women inhabit different worlds (see Gray, 1993). Paradoxically, at the same time, we produce a gender-neutral understanding of the problem. The production of sexual harassment as gender-neutral is paradoxical because of the way in which our notion of sexual harassment fits into dominant constructions of male and female sexuality, with men driven by sex to demand certain things of women. We would not then expect women to *sexually* harass men. But the women who are portrayed as capable of doing this are, not coincidentally, the new liberated working women in well-paid positions, such as the lead character, Meredith (played by Demi Moore), in the 1994 Barry Levinson film *Disclosure* (Walker, 1998: 213). The women who can harass then are unwomanly women, 'like-men' women. Jane Gallop (1997) also objects to the gender-neutral characterization of sexual harassment which allowed her to be accused of sexual harassment.[5] Moreover, invoking a 'reasonable woman' standard means that, unless a woman perceives the behaviour as 'offensive', no offence has occurred. Jan Lucas (1991: 64) provides a useful corrective to the tendency to make sexual harassment depend upon whether the recipient is able to identify it or not. She insists: '[S]exual harassment, like racism, is a structural feature of social relations which exists regardless of whether the sufferers or aggressors are aware of it or not.' An emphasis on 'different perceptions', in my view, simply excuses intolerable behaviour.

Sexual Harassment as Sexual *Harassment*[6]

The case that I am making here is that all the debates and discussions about what is *really* sexual harassment and what is *mere* innocent 'flirtation' build upon a misrepresentation of what is going on, which is overtly hostile treatment of women. The reasons for that hostility are undoubtedly complex. There is evidence to suggest that one reason is a desire to mark women as 'ill fitting' in certain environments. For example, women are more likely to be harassed when they attempt to enter nontraditional work sites (Bryson, 1994: 26), confirming a link between harassment and the desire to exclude women (see also Kelly, 1988: 104). Further counterfactual information for this interpretation comes from a study in the Netherlands which reveals a link between low risk of sexual harassment and workplaces characterized by 'relatively small inequality between the sexes with respect to numbers and hierarchical position' (Rubenstein, 1988: 146, cited in Bryson, 1994: 23).

In 1993 Lois Bryson (1994: 28) conducted an enquiry into sexual harassment in the Australian Defence Forces and listed the following as the types of behaviour about which women complained. I quote these examples *in toto* because of their centrality to my argument:

- Displaying pornographic posters involving a woman and, when the two women on the site objected, putting up more posters depicting sexually explicit acts including bestiality and sodomy.
- Verbal abuse of two women because they complained about the display of hard-core pornographic posters. Men on site told one woman that she was paid a man's wage in a man's workforce and had no right to complain.
- Ransacking a woman's quarters and putting items of her underwear on display.
- Smearing excrement on the toilet facilities installed for a woman.
- Putting dog droppings in the desk drawer of a woman supervisor.
- Continually commenting on women's bodies and giving 'scores' to the size of their breasts etc. in such a way that the comments were overheard by the women themselves as well as by those to whom the comments were purportedly directed.
- A rape within the living quarters.
- A rape by a co-worker who later bragged to his work mates that he 'got her on the way home'.
- A sexual assault of a woman by pushing her down, lying on top of her and reaching inside her clothes to touch her while calling out to a mate to take a photograph.
- A woman being told 'This is a man's place, so just shut up and bend over that table there.'
- Two men following a woman, making comments about her size and making noises like pigs behind her in the queue at the canteen.

It would be difficult, in any one's terms, to characterize these behaviours as having anything to do with sexual *attraction*. Clearly they are harassing behaviours and they target women. Some are frightening; some we might call disgusting. But they are *not* mis-interpreted flirtation. Why then are we considering them as indications of *sexual* harassment? As Wise and Stanley (1987: 94) state, 'sexual harassment can be described as "sexual" only in the sense that one sex, male, does it to another sex, female.' Now some may argue that my examples are extreme and that there is a danger here that using such examples will divert attention from all the daily intrusions of male offensive behaviour on women and their space (see Wise and Stanley, 1987: 109). But I am suggesting that refocusing on the nature of the interaction and its basis in hostility to women, rather than on sexual attraction, is crucial. I use these more extreme examples only to illustrate what is really going on. Another example is that of lesbian baiting (see Bryson, 1994: 10; Wise and Stanley, 1987: 88). Lesbians are often tormented by men because they choose not to be with men sexually. One could hardly claim that what is at issue here is a misunderstanding of sexual flirtation. Rather, the harassment is meant to control and threaten women who refuse to conform to these men's impressions of what a woman should be. Again, Liz Kelly's (1988) notion of a continuum of sexual violence is useful here (see Chapter 9).

There has been much discussion of what might be gained and what might be lost by expanding the notion of sexual harassment to something called sex-based harassment or gender harassment. Some feminists fear that a broadening of the concept might make it unworkable; we might lose what we have won. I am reminded here of the debates among feminists about the potential gains and possible losses involved in replacing the category 'rape' with the category 'sexual assault' (see Allison and Wrightsman, 1993; Heath and Naffine, 1994; Matthews, 1994). My feeling at this time is that we should retain the category 'sexual harassment' because we still need to denaturalize a particular category of male harassing behaviours and because those behaviours carry a sexual character which impacts on the women who experience it (see discussion above). At the same time, I would suggest the importance of emphasizing that the basis of the interaction is male hostility to women, not misinterpreted flirtation. Reframing the problem as woman-hating behaviour has important implications for the kinds of 'responses' deemed necessary.

Employer Liability and Sexual Harassment

The linkage between sexual harassment and *sexual* harassment explains in part the alacrity with which employers have taken it up. Managers in *The Workforce 2000* survey, conducted by the Business Council of Australia (in Bryson, 1994: 7), ranked having a sexual harassment policy as the most important Equal Employment Opportunity strategy to have in place. Margaret Thornton (1991a: 465) points out that the desire to create workplaces free from sexual distractions means that sexual harassment fits readily into managerialist goals of effectiveness and efficiency. Della Pollock (1994: 118) spells out the connection: '[D]iscourses of prevention focus on harassment as a workplace issue in part, it seems, because harassment marks the apparent incompatibility of sexual and capitalist pursuits. In the name of progress, harassment must be stamped out because sexuality must be contained.' The fact that employers have introduced measures to curtail sexual harassment on the grounds that it is *sexual* harassment seems to sit oddly beside my claim that this very construction *limits* the impact of efforts to address sexual harassment. To understand the point of my argument, we need to look more closely at specific policy proposals. In the following section we will see that current sexual harassment regulations produce the problem as deviant sexuality, and that this results in restricted interventions and weak regulations. Seeing the problem as woman-hating behaviour, which I recommend, produces a very different agenda.

We have seen that sexual harassment has achieved recognition as sex discrimination and that this recognition has been accompanied by acceptance of employer liability for conditions in the workplace. Now we need to consider just what employers are expected to do to meet these obligations, since the founding premise of a What's the Problem? approach is the need to examine precise proposals to tease out problem representations. Although recent guidelines insist that organizations create environments free of sexual harassment, this is given little content and generally it is considered adequate for organizations to institute grievance procedures and to distribute leaflets describing the illegal nature of sexual harassment. In the United States, Title IX requires universities to adopt and publish grievance procedures 'providing for prompt and equitable resolution of student complaints of sexual harassment' (Tong, 1986: 161).

Grievance procedures vary but they generally involve the creation of a committee to investigate sexual harassment complaints. As with antidiscrimination law, once a grievance procedure is in place it becomes the responsibility of the one who is harassed to use it: 'it becomes their failure, rather than the institutions if they do not' (Brant and Too, 1994: 12). A related limitation of the grievance procedure approach is that such mechanisms suggest implicitly that the problem we are dealing with is one of individual aberration. Diane Purkiss (1994: 189) shows how this tone was established in one of the first texts to draw attention to the problem of male staff/female student sexual harassment, *The Lecherous Professor* (Dziech and Weiner, 1984). As Purkiss explains, this title suggests 'the separability and opposition between the professor and his lechery'. The 'lecherous' professor becomes the 'odd man out'. Such a construction also opens up the possibility of a defence along the lines that the professor (generally) is 'a pillar of the profession' and hence cannot 'be equated with that which is deviant from it'.

Writing about the problem of sexual exploitation in the caring professions, William White (1993) identifies a number of what he calls 'reductionist models of explanation . . . which tend to define the problem of sexual exploitation in ways that narrow our view of etiology, and restrict our vision of prevention and intervention strategies'. Two of these, the Perpetrator Morality Model and the Clinical Model, have clear similarities with the tendency to see sexual harassment as deviant behaviour. The first sees the problem as 'emerging from the evil of the perpetrating professional helper'. Such an approach 'allows the organisations to believe that they have addressed the problem of harassment or exploitation solely by extruding an identified sexual predator'. The Clinical Model sees the problem as psychopathology, either chronic or transient emotional disturbance. In this case the organization is again seen to be doing all that is required by taking steps to deal with the emotional disorder of the perpetrator, through counselling for example. Jenna Mead (1995: 169) talks about the way in which some explanations of sexual harassment are similarly reductionist. She is particularly concerned, as is Jenny Morgan (1995; see also Bacchi and Jose, 1994a), with the tendency to see the problem as *sexual* deviance. Here the problem is pathologized in a way that reduces the possibility that the deeper problems of sexual inequality, of sexism, of gender will be identified and dealt with. Seeing sexual harassment as *sexual* deviance also tends to focus attention on egregious sexual harassment, bypassing wider forms of sexual harassment such as persistent sexual comments and innuendo.[7]

We also need to consider how sexual harassment grievance procedures constitute those who use them. The *sexualizing* of sexual harassment means that women who use the procedures or who encourage their use become, in one interpretation, 'puritans', 'trembling creatures innocent of desire' (Garner, 1995: 210). In this interpretation, such rules and guidelines contribute to a disempowering paternalist construction of women as needing protection from men predators. This perspective can be seen as part of the recent characterization of some feminist approaches as encouraging a sense of victimhood in women (see, for example, Gallop, 1997; Garner, 1995: 168). There is no doubt, however, that it takes great courage to press a sexual harassment charge, especially in cases where the harasser holds institutional power over the one harassed. Hence, there is no clear logic linking sexual harassment procedures to a protectionist interpretation. The problem is that, due to power differentials and other disincentives, few charges will be pressed, leaving the paternalist understanding of sexual harassment dominant, and suggesting simultaneously that the 'problem' has been exaggerated – that is, that little harassment is taking place.

One way to undermine the charge of paternalism would, counter-intuitively, involve creating the conditions to facilitate the making of charges – hence showing women *actively contesting* men's presumed sexual prerogative (in contrast to being *passively protected*). But we are caught in a circularity here since in a sense complaint-based procedures constitute the accuser as aggressor and the accused as victim, innocent until proved guilty. The appearance of larger numbers of women accusers could serve then to cement the view that it is *men* who are under attack. The discourse of the mendacious woman (see

Naffine, 1992: 746–7) creates an opening here to suggest that men are under attack 'without cause'. Instead of images of strong women challenging men's behaviour, use of sexual harassment procedures becomes trivialized as part of a 'culture of complaint' (Mitchell, 1995).

Women are caught in a damned if you do, damned if you don't situation. If grievance procedures go underutilized, they are considered protectionist and/or unnecessary; if they are used, they become part of a 'culture of complaint'. It is important to consider what in the nature of these procedures produces these effects. I am highlighting how grievance procedures locate the 'problem' in individual aberration, leaving the impression that the 'problem' is containable and that organizations have indeed taken care of the 'problem' by setting up such procedures. White adds the Anomie Model to his discussion of reductionist explanations of harassment and exploitation. In this case the problem is considered 'the absence of a clear body of ethical standards defining appropriate and inappropriate conduct in worker–client relationships'. The result is often the proliferation of codes and 'awareness' training sessions. In all these examples, as White (1993: 82) sums up, we have a response in which '[A]n appendage is added – a policy, a person, a training seminar – none of which is intended, or likely by itself, to alter the nature of the organisational culture.' My hesitation earlier about the usefulness of employing occupational health and safety legislation hinges on this very point – what would employers be required to do to produce 'quiet enjoyment of employment'? Would their obligations stop at instituting grievance procedures? This would depend upon the understanding of the nature of the problem!

Conclusion: Sexual Harassment as Woman-Hating Harassment

Rosemary Pringle (1988) makes the important point that, in the construction of sexual harassment as *sexual* distraction from work obligations, sexual harassment rules recreate a form of the public/ private dichotomy, keeping sex where it belongs, at home. In contrast, identifying the problem as woman-hating harassment has none of these effects. Rather the analysis would focus upon the anti-woman content of the harassment and the way it is associated with attempts either to drive women out of particular organizations or to emphasize their lack of fit within those organizations. The examples from Bryson's (1994) study illustrate pointedly this characterization of the problem (see above). Here we are provided with a starting place for rethinking the relationship between organizational climate and sexual harassment, suggesting that sexual harassment is a product of a particular climate – one in which women hold little institutional influence – not the deviant behaviour of deviant individuals.

None of this is meant to exonerate the behaviour of individual harassers (see Bacchi and Jose, 1994a). Rather, it is meant to draw attention to the limitations of existing organizational policy and to hint at the need for a new agenda. If indeed the problem is not deviant individuals but organizational climate, what kinds of changes would be likely to make a difference? An understanding of the problem as woman-hating would necessitate policies addressed to two areas, examining existing institutional characteristics to detect the extent to which they are premised on a male norm, and seeing what can be done to increase women's presence as a necessary step to altering that norm. As can be anticipated, tackling the second question will necessitate thinking about what kind of a problem women's absence or underrepresentation might be and designing policies accordingly. Here I direct readers back to Chapter 5.

Lois Bryson (1994: 34) makes useful recommendations about the kinds of changes that might empower women within the armed forces and which would challenge the male-centred content of routines. She recommends including in recruitment policies a criterion 'which focuses on capacity to work harmoniously with people with a wide range of existing characteristics'. Note how this proposal by its nature identifies as the problem not a few deviant individuals, but job requirements. The proposal attempts to go beyond individualizing premises in the suggestion that we need to rethink the kinds of characteristics employees in general should have. The focus is shifted *from* the women harassed *to* all those holding jobs in an organization. Bryson also insists upon the need for more women to be present and for women to be encouraged to form women's action groups and committees, again recognizing the systemic character of the harassment currently facing female recruits.

For universities, I (1998) recommend among other changes, firm commitments to increase women's representation throughout university structures, a willingness to review curriculum for content on women, better child-care facilities, an examination of the effects of pedagogic practices on women (see Purkiss, 1994), and a reviewing of the nature of staff–student relationships (see note 4, this Chapter). I see these initiatives as better indications of a willingness to do something about sexual harassment than instituting grievance procedures, however necessary these may be. Lest it need repeating, nothing in this analysis is meant to suggest the wish to eliminate such procedures; nor does it in any way imply criticism of women who have fought long and hard to obtain and sustain them. Rather, the intention is to draw attention to how women's best efforts at change are being 'managed'. The analysis I offer here, which recommends policy addressed to organizational climate, produces the problem of sexual harassment as a desire to exclude women from particular occupational sites. The analysis can be extended to encompass street harassment as a desire to control women's movements more generally. In both cases, men's assumed prerogative to police women's behaviours needs to be problematized.

Notes

1 In Australia, the Human Rights and Equal Opportunity Commission reported in 1991 that one-third of those making complaints on the ground of sexual harassment had been dismissed for objecting and 10 per cent had resigned (Bryson, 1994: 12).

2 Title IX in the United States and antidiscrimination legislation in Australia extend the boundaries of compliance to educational institutions and the teaching relationships within them.

3 Queensland's 1991 antidiscrimination legislation includes as unlawful street harassment (see Morgan, 1995: 99). Britain's Criminal Justice and Public Order Act 1994 (section 154) makes intentional street harassment a criminal offence; the Protection from Harassment Act 1997 removes the need to prove intent. I would like to thank Jeanne Gregory for drawing this legislation to my attention.

4 While I find Cornell's stance on the problems with the notion of 'unwelcome' useful, I am less happy with other aspects of her reworked definition of sexual harassment. Specifically she (1995: 171) objects to 'unilaterally imposed sexual *advances* [emphasis added]', a framing of sexual harassment I am attempting to challenge. I take Cornell's point that her intent, in shifting 'the focus back on sex [in the sense of biological sex] and away from gender' is 'to provide standing for forms of sexuate being other than those that are based only on gender comparison', an obvious example being gays and lesbians. I would contend in contrast that we are dealing here with several different kinds of problems – anti-woman harassment and anti-gay and lesbian harassment – and that more would be accomplished by naming these for what they are rather than attempting to capture these behaviours within the terms of sexual harassment as it has come to be understood.

5 While I agree with Gallup's objections to the gender-neutral standard, I disagree with her position on staff–student sexual relations (see Bacchi, 1992b, 1994). While Gallop clearly approves and encourages staff–student sexual relations, I consider the behaviour professionally unethical. But I do agree that her particular case should not have been characterized as sexual harassment. This would have been clear if we had a notion of sexual harassment as woman-hating harassment, which is what women have been trying to curtail all along.

6 I would like to thank my Honours student Bronwyn Donaghey for drawing to my attention the significance of the shift in emphasis from *sexual* harassment to sexual *harassment*.

7 I would like to thank Carol Johnson for this point.

THE POLITICS OF POLICY STUDIES

This book develops a new way to think about and to approach policy analysis. The approach, called What's the Problem (represented to be)?, is contrasted with conventional approaches to policy in Part One of the book. In Part Two, the emphasis is upon how to apply the approach. To this end I consider a range of topics commonly considered central to resolving the problem of women's inequality. This larger 'problem' is also subjected to critical scrutiny.

The primary challenge I offer to conventional policy approaches is the suggestion that 'problems' do not exist out there, in the social world, waiting to be addressed and 'solved', but that 'problems' are created by the policy community. By this I mean that any policy proposal necessarily contains a diagnosis of the problem to be addressed. The policy proposal by its very nature identifies what is of concern and what needs to change. I call this a problem representation and suggest, as a first step in policy analysis, teasing out the problem representations which necessarily lodge in policy proposals. The argument, put briefly, is that it is impossible to assess policy proposals without doing this since, if in your view the 'problem' is misdiagnosed, you are unlikely to find the proposal helpful.

The book uses a social constructionist approach to policy problems. That is, it suggests that, although there are a range of objectionable conditions which need addressing, any attempt to deal with these conditions necessarily imposes a shape upon them. There is no way to access directly those objectionable conditions; hence we need to direct our attention to competing representations of those conditions. A focus upon representations requires a focus upon discourse. Stuart Hall's (1992: 291) definition of discourse makes this connection explicit: 'a group of statements which provide a language for talking about – i.e. a way of representing – a particular type of knowledge about a topic'. A What's the Problem? approach calls for attention to the discursive construction of problems within policy proposals and policy debate generally. Through this means, it assists in identifying the frames used to construe social 'problems'. A simple way to characterize a What's the Problem? approach is to say that it directs attention to problematizations rather than to problems, which are held to be inaccessible outside of the ways they are problematized.

In contrast to many social constructionist analyses, I insist that it is both possible and necessary to compare and assess competing representations of social problems. The criteria I elaborate for assessment focus on the *implications* of competing representations. By implications I mean the effects which appear to accompany or follow from particular representations. Three general categories of effects are identified: the ways in which subjects and subjectivities are constituted in discourse; the effects which follow from the limits imposed on what can be said; and the 'lived effects' of discourse (see Chapter 2). I highlight in particular how policies addressing domestic violence, sexual harassment and women's inequality recreate existent power relations by constituting their targets as either disadvantaged, sick or lacking in desired attitudes, while ignoring the power of those in positions of influence to designate the nature of 'disadvantage' and of 'desirable' attributes.

Chapters 1 and 2 focus directly on conventional policy literature, and some more recent developments in the field. In these chapters I elaborate the claim that we need to see approaches to understanding policy as themselves political. I show that technical rationalists like Herbert Simon (1961) and Eugene Bardach (1981) put their faith in central administration and technocracy, while political rationalists like Charles Lindblom (1980) and Aaron Wildavsky (1979) are pluralists and incrementalists. In different ways both groups imply that policy analysts can stand back from the policy process and offer species of advice to those in government. The kinds of advice offered include either insights into 'hard' empirical information and measurement (technical rationalists), or 'softer' information about political realities (political rationalism). By way of contrast, authors like Frank Fischer (1980, 1990), John Drysek (1990) and Giandomenico Majone (1989) recognize the analysts' necessarily normative involvement in advice-giving, but try to find ways to 'manage' the value dimension of policy analysis. In these accounts, the technical expert of the comprehensive rationalists and the conflict manager of the political rationalists is replaced by the analyst (or in the case of Drysek by the academic) as public critic.

A What's the Problem? approach sees policy analysis as necessarily involved in the discursive construction of policy problems. In this view, there is no outside to the process. Moreover, it contests any suggestion that governments and their advisers do their best to respond to 'problems' which they 'discover' or which are brought to their attention. This description of government activity, it is argued, misleads the public by suggesting that neutral arbiters are at work dealing with difficult situations and deciding, among other things, when to 'intervene' or when not to 'intervene'. Recognizing the role of the policy community in discursively contructing 'problems' (through policy proposals and political debate) produces a very different vision of the political process. For one, it confirms the incoherence of the intervention/non-intervention dichotomy (see Olsen, 1985). That is, we need to recognize the active role (and hence intervention) of governments in discursively constructing social problems as *not* requiring intervention. This indeed forms an important part of neoliberal rhetoric (see Watts, 1993/4: 116). Showing that governments, often through relationships with non-state actors, actively shape 'the background rules that affect people's domestic behaviour' and the legal rules which allow the 'free market' to function (Olsen, 1985: 836–7) subverts this rhetoric. Along related lines, governmentality scholars emphasize framings of problems which create political subjects as self-regulating, obviating the need for more intrusive 'interventions'. These challenges to the discovery/response model of policy making alter quite dramatically feminist debates about whether feminists should turn to the state or avoid 'inevitable' co-option. Recognizing the state's pervasive role in framing problems, and by implication nonproblems, highlights the impossibility of evacuating this discursive space. More will be said about this topic shortly.

Chapter 3 elaborates the social constructionist approach to social problems, clarifying where and how a What's the Problem? approach offers something new. In particular, I am critical of conventional social problems literature which seems to imply that there exists a number of discrete social problems which require separate analysis and assessment. I also recognize, with Roger Sibeon (1996), that this approach is dominant among American sociologists, illustrating that approaches to studying social problems are context-bound. Although the shape of Part Two, with separate chapters addressed to particular topics, appears to offer an analysis of discrete topics, the focus throughout is upon identifying common themes, illustrating a wider picture or pattern among more specific policy developments. One of the key features of this broader pattern is indeed the pervasiveness of the discovery/response model of interpretation which suggests that we are 'facing' discrete 'problems' which require discrete and simple 'solutions', for example, pay equity legislation or affirmative action legislation.

I describe Part Two of the book as a guide to method. By this I mean that I use the analyses in Part Two to illustrate the kinds of questions which need to be asked in a What's the Problem? approach. At the same time I impose an analysis. I would suggest that doing anything less would leave the impression that this is just another of those poststructuralist texts which leaves everything floating in the realm of representation. To counter this impression I offer my reading of 'women's inequality' and issues commonly tied to this 'problem'. I also borrow freely from other feminist writings on select topics to illustrate that a number of feminists have already been using the approach I recommend and to bolster my interpretation of particular policy developments. The material from other feminists is never offered in a purely summary fashion; rather it is introduced as part of my analysis.

It is possible but dangerous to pull together the major themes which emerge from Part Two, dangerous because of the need to simplify and hence to lose some of the nuance which accompanies more detailed study. None the less, it is a worthwhile exercise if only to illustrate that what this book is about is providing insights into the dilemmas of making change. I begin, in the Preamble to Part Two, by discussing the limitations of the dominant framing of 'women's inequality' as a labour market problem. That is, I think it important to recognize the extent to which the desire (on the part of governments and feminists) to get more women into paid labour has put its stamp upon the kinds of changes which have been encouraged and allowed. Specifically, measures addressing 'women' s inequality', when cast in this light, have been incorporationist and insufficiently critical of existing standards and institutions. In the period under investigation, the 1970s and 1980s, a number of Western democracies (the United States, Canada and Australia provide most of my examples) introduced equal pay and pay equity legislation, equal opportunity and affirmative action legislation, equity in education legislation, and some targeted support for child care. A What's the Problem? approach directs attention to the limitations of these legislative innovations. It asks what is problematized and what is left unproblematized in these initiatives. It asks how different groups of women and men are constituted within the discourses shaping these reforms and the debates around them. Put simply, it uncovers the assumption in policy approaches to date that all that women, and men for that matter, require to be free is some form of paid labour. In the process, it highlights the ways in which this normative vision ignores the exploitation of many working people, and the importance of people's nonworking lives.

Incorporationist policies are readily identifiable by their targets. In each case an incorporationist analysis focuses upon the outgroup and what they require to become ingroups. So, for equal pay, women are to be paid what men are paid. For equal opportunity to exist, women are to be allowed into men's occupations and boys' study areas. Like men, they will be 'freed' of child-care obligations to the extent that this is necessary for them to approximate men's lifestyles. If they have difficulty 'making the grade', it is because they lack something men have, either initiative or dedication, or because they hold the 'wrong' priorities, placing family ahead of work obligations. A What's the Problem? approach opens up an opportunity to question these priorities. It suggests that more attention needs to be focused upon the work and living conditions which women are encouraged to emulate. In the process it allows questions to be asked about who decides which job or study area is worth more, by what criteria, who decides that paid labour is definitive of personhood, who decides that what is desirable is 'freedom' from child care. The purpose thoughout is to put unasked questions onto the political agenda.

A What's the Problem? approach accepts nothing as given. Rather its purpose is to put the given into question. It accepts no delineation of existent social concerns. Rather, it probes the shape of those concerns and the implications of the shapes which are discovered. So, it asks why abortion is called a moral problem, why it is given this character and with what effects. Why is domestic violence called 'domestic'? What follows from this labelling? What needs to be altered in the implied characterization of the 'problem'? What is sexual harassment? What kind of a problem is it represented to be? What follows from this particular representation? In abortion policy we see how jurisdictional disputes between the state and the medical profession get played out over women's bodies. In responses to domestic violence we see how feminists' demands to have violence against women recognized as public crime have been co-opted by a law and order lobby. In sexual harassment grievance procedures the problem is created as the bad behaviour of a few deviant men and individual women are held responsible for identifying this behaviour.

Across the social problems surveyed, we observe the sheeting home of the responsibility for change to individuals. Equal opportunity is paradigmatic here where women are encouraged to develop the 'skills' to fit into existing workplace structures. While pay equity demands recognition of women's abilities, again individual women will be assessed by the degree to which they demonstrate characteristics deemed useful to the market. Child care will be offered as a 'choice', creating the possibility for some women to have access to 'men's' jobs. Education will prepare them for this role. In abortion, individual women will plead their case for sympathy. Battered women and sexually harassed women will be offered the same 'opportunity'. Meanwhile, the social processes which shape women's lives, which make abortion necessary, which leave them in homes to be battered, which create them as outcasts in particular work environments, go unaddressed.

I want to confront directly the charge that the kind of analysis offered here is impractical and utopian. It could be said that, while directing attention to the need for broad cultural and organizational change sounds good in principle, realistically we need to take what we can get and be thankful. Moreover, it may seem particularly inappropriate to highlight the limitations of initiatives, like affirmative action, at the very time when these are under attack (see Chapter

5). Does a What's the Problem? approach produce a counsel of despair, highlighting the inevitable limitations of working through the state's categories and hence through legal discourse? What are the practical implications of identifying dominant discursive frames which reduce social to individual problems, and which reveal the power of the market in dictating the conditions of our lives?

I suggested above that I do not consider it particularly useful to discuss feminist strategies in terms of an either/or approach to the state and to law: *either* work through it *or* do without it. This is because, as explained above, our lives are shaped inevitably by the ways in which policy problems are discursively constructed. My argument therefore is that feminists have little option but to engage with the state, and with extra-state institutions such as the law and the medical profession, in contesting constructions of problems which work to disempower women. What's the Problem? offers a tool to assist in identifying what needs to be contested, a task Eileen Fegan (1996: 84) describes as a necessary first step in engaging with the law.

The insights into the ways in which the problem of women's inequality is discursively constructed, moreover, allow us to see that, in the current attack on reforms such as affirmative action – and here we could add the attack on the welfare state generally – women are not facing some dramatic about-face in policy approach. Rather, the grounds for the swing to the right can be found in the very terms of analysis shaping many of the issues where feminists won concessions. I am thinking here of the disadvantage discourse which continues to shape discussions around equity, except now we are being told that women have indeed achieved equality and are no longer 'disadvantaged'. The new education discourse which describes the problem as 'girls beating boys' provides a poignant example of this (see Chapter 6). So too a construction of the problem of women's inequality as 'lack of access to paid labour', by leaving unaddressed the responsibilities of caring which women in the main shoulder, allows welfare cuts to be rationalized as simply the privatizing of care. In this usage, privatizing means getting women to do more caring. In another usage, the increasing tendency to privatize child care (Chapter 7) also fits the market-led model which framed child care services as primarily a means to facilitate women's workforce participation.

It is at this level that the book hopes to say something useful about feminists' strategies. It highlights the pervasiveness of discursive constructions which can work against the desire for structural change. Moreover, it shows how feminist interventions sometimes get absorbed because of the failure to challenge these discursive constructions. As a tool, What's the Problem? operates to uncover problematizations and their effects. It does not suggest that particular framings can be dispensed with but rather *that a sharp eye to their effects can provide a basis for interacting with them*. Carol Smart (1997: 115) comes to a similar conclusion. She recommends that feminists approach the state the way the women's health movement has approached medicine – challenging its framing paradigms all the while claiming better access to its services. A key point here is the need to recognize that feminist interventions will be shaped by context. Both political climate and specific cultural and institutional factors will affect the opportunity or lack of opportunity for discursive reframing. This means, as Jeanne Gregory says (personal correspondence, October 1998), that 'the work of identifying the best strategies to suit particular sets of circumstances can only be done by activists on the spot at the time'.

Elizabeth Kingdom's (1995: 7) insights into the difficulties involved in engaging with rights discourses are useful here. She makes the important point that 'there may be political contexts in which it is necessary to "play the game", to present campaigns in terms of right over body, to deploy the terms which the law recognizes'. At the same time she is well aware of the limitations of a rights discourse. Her practical advice (1995: 16) is that feminists 'consider in detail how various rights discourses are already operating, and what the chances are of supplementing or replacing anti-feminist rights discourse either with feminist rights discourse or with alternatives to rights discourse'. This tactic, which she describes as a 'conversion strategy', demands 'familiarity with exploitable shifts in rights discourse'. Because a What's the Problem? approach operates to unpack problem representations and, in the process, to identify discursive frames, it provides an ideal tool for the strategy Kingdom describes. It assists in providing the background knowledge needed to attempt discursive intervention/s.

Going further, I emphasize the need to apply a What's the Problem? approach to *feminists'* analyses of what needs to change. I recommend this because of the difficulties involved in recognizing the ways in which feminists' problematizations reflect deeply held cultural assumptions, given specific historical, economic and cultural locations. A greater sensitivity to the role professional affiliations play in shaping problematizations is also crucial, as we observed in the chapter on domestic violence for example (see Chapter 9). There we saw also the importance of broadening the feminist constituency, either directly or through affiliation, to guarantee that the voices of Black and poor women get heard. The goal here is to prevent the unthinking imposition of frames which enshrine the exploitation of these groups. The example of gender persecution as a grounds for asylum (see Chapter 9) illustrates the danger in allowing any feminist problem representation to stand unscrutinized while the feminist community is dominated by white, middle-class, Anglo-Saxon women. If one accepts my diagnosis that the kind of problem women's inequality has been represented to be is inadequate and shortsighted, feminists need to identify more precisely in what ways it needs to be expanded and how to design policies to capture the sorts of change which are desired. The implication of the analysis here is that this exercise is fraught with danger if feminists are unwilling to scrutinize the problem representations lodged within their analyses. The story of the way in which the *Butler* decision (1992) on pornography in Canada, which enshrined a 'harm against women' standard, has been used to harass gay and lesbian communities provides an object lesson here (see Cossman et al., 1997).

A What's the Problem? approach is a tool of analysis which can be applied to any policy area. It is designed to encourage a particular kind of thinking which is useful in any policy domain. I hope that this is clear in Part One, which generalizes the approach. Any policy proposal needs to be subjected to the kind of critical scrutiny encouraged by the approach. First, proposals need to be screened for problem representations and these then need to be analysed in terms of their effects, practical and discursive. As part of the first step it is useful to examine when and how a particular topic achieved social problem status. This is the point in time when problem representations are likely to be clearest and easiest to identify, because it is at this stage that policy approaches will be outlined and defended. As some social problems have a tendency to reappear in different historical periods, it is useful to identify contrasts and similarities in the shapes given to them at these times. The same is true for cultural variation in the shape and timing of social problem creation. Context is useful not only to identify the distinctive characteristics assigned social problems but also to uncover commonalities in social problem diagnosis.

This kind of analysis has been called genealogy (see Chapter 2). In their genealogy of dependency, Fraser and Gordon (1994: 332) insist that

[A] genealogy cannot tell us how to respond politically to today's discourse about welfare dependency. It does suggest, however, the limits of any response that presupposes rather than challenges the definition of the problem that is implicit in that expression.

Specifically, here, Fraser and Gordon mention as a goal recognizing the *problem implicit* in key policy terms and discourses such as 'welfare dependency'. This is precisely the task facilitated through the application of a What's the Problem? approach. In contrast to Fraser and Gordon, however, I believe that we have here a powerful tool of political analysis. Not only does the approach encourage the uncovering of barely disguised political agendas, it compels an analysis of the problem representations which lodge in all, including our own, proposals. This kind of critical analysis of presuppositions sharpens awareness of the extent to which our proposals have in-built limitations and biases, while suggesting a method for identifying framings of issues which move us closer to the goal of more egalitarian social relations. Marcia Westkott (1983: 212, cited in Bingham, 1994: 1) makes this point nicely: 'By clarifying that which we oppose, we set the groundwork for creating a vision of that for which we long.'

As this book is intended as a guide to the application of the method I call What's the Problem?, it is appropriate to summarize once again the stages in the process. What's the Problem? is intended to provide a tool for uncovering the frames that construct policy problems. Sometimes these are apparent in general public or political debate. Where more precision is required, students are directed to the specifics of policy *proposals*. The logic here is that these proposals will reveal what is represented to be the problem because what we propose to do will suggest what we believe needs to change. The task then is to open up the problem representations contained in policy proposals to critical analysis, teasing out the presuppositions which lodge there and speculating upon the implications of particular discursive constructions of the problem. Most importantly, there is a need to consider what goes unproblematized in particular discursive constructions. I also recommend applying this approach to feminist proposals for change. This could best be accomplished, I suggest, by encouraging critical exchange among feminists, and between groups of feminists and representatives of other outgroups. I invite and welcome contributions which assist in assessing the adequacy or inadequacy of the problem representations I offer in Part Two of the book. My goal, through focusing on what is represented to be the problem both in policy proposals and in feminist theorizing, is to produce more reflexive feminist analyses and to assist in the difficult task of designing context-sensitive proposals which minimize losses and maximize gains.

BIBLIOGRAPHY

Abella, Rosalie (1984) *Report of the Commission on Equality in Employment.* Ottawa: Supply and Services Canada.

ACOSS (Australian Council of Social Services) (1988) *Child Care: A Background Paper.* Paper No. 16. Sydney: ACOSS.

Ackelsberg, Martha (1992) 'Feminist Analyses of Public Policy', *Comparative Politics,* 24: 477–93.

Acker, Joan (1989) *Doing Comparable Worth: Gender, Class and Pay Equity.* Philadelphia: Temple University Press.

Acker, Joan (1991) 'Pay Equity in Sweden and Other Nordic Countries' in Judy Fudge and Patricia McDermott (eds) *Just Wages: A Feminist Assessment of Pay Equity.* Toronto: University of Toronto Press. pp. 247–53.

Acker, Sandra and Keith Oatley (1993) 'Gender Issues in Education for Science and Technology: Current Situation and Prospects for Change' in Suzanne de Castell (ed.) Special Issue of *Canadian Journal of Education: Against the Grain,* 18 (3): 254–72.

Agger, Ben (1993) 'Chapter 14: The Problem with Social Problems' in James A. Holstein and Gale Miller (eds) *Reconsidering Social Constructionism: Debates in Social Problems Theory.* New York: Aldine de Gruyter. pp. 281–300.

Albury, Rebecca (1993) 'Speech and Silence in Abortion Debates in Australian Parliaments', paper presented at the first National Conference of the Abortion Rights Network of Australia, South Brisbane, 20 November.

Allison, J. and Wrightsman, L. (1993) *Rape: The Misunderstood Crime.* Thousand Oaks, CA: Sage.

American Association of University Women (1987) *Pay Equity Action Guide.* Washington, DC: American Association of University Women.

Anstie, R., Gregory, R. G., Dowrick, S. and Pincus, J. J. (1988) *Government Spending on Work-Related Child Care: Some Economic Issues.* Centre for Economic Policy Research. Canberra: Department of Community Services and Health.

Armstrong, Pat (1996) 'The Feminization of the Labour Force: Harmonizing Down in a Global Economy' in Isabella Bakker (ed.) *Rethinking Restructuring: Gender and Change in Canada.* Toronto: University of Toronto Press. pp. 29–54.

Armstrong, Pat and Armstrong, Hugh (1988) 'Taking Women into Account: Redefining and Intensifying Employment in Canada' in Jane Jenson,

Elisabeth Hagen and Ceallaigh Reddy (eds) *Feminization of the Labour Force: Paradoxes and Promises*. Cambridge: Polity. pp. 65–84.

Armstrong, Pat and Armstrong, Hugh (1990) *Theorizing Women's Work*. Network Basics Series. Toronto: Garamond Press.

Armstrong, Pat and Armstrong, Hugh (1991) 'Limited Possibilities and Possible Limits for Pay Equity: Within and Beyond the Ontario Legislation' in Judy Fudge and Patricia McDermott (eds) *Just Wages: A Feminist Assessment of Pay Equity*. Toronto: University of Toronto Press. pp. 110–21.

Armstrong, Pat and Armstrong, Hugh (1992) 'Lessons from Pay Equity' in M. Patricia Connelly and Pat Armstrong (eds) *Feminism in Action*. Toronto: Canadian Scholars' Press. pp. 295–316.

Armstrong, Pat and Cornish, Mary (1997) 'Restructuring Pay Equity for a Restructured Work Force: Canadian Perspectives', *Gender, Work and Organization*, 4 (2): 67–85.

Arnot, M. (ed.) (1985) *Race and Gender: Equal Opportunities Policies in Education*. Oxford: Pergamon in association with the Open University.

Australia (1975) *Girls, Schools and Society: Report by a Study Group to the Schools Commission*. Committee on Social Change and the Education of Women Study Group. Woden, ACT: Schools Commission.

Bacchi, Carol (1980) 'The Nature–Nurture Debate in Australia, 1900–1914', *Historical Studies*, 19 (75): 199–212.

Bacchi, Carol (1986) 'The "Woman Question"' in Eric Richards (ed.) *The Flinders History of South Australia: Social History*. Adelaide: Wakefield Press. pp. 403–32.

Bacchi, Carol (1988) 'Feminism and the "Eroticization" of the Middle-class Woman: the Intersection of Class and Gender Attitudes', *Women's Studies International Forum*, 11 (1): 43–53.

Bacchi, Carol (1990) *Same Difference: Feminism and Sexual Difference*. Sydney: Allen & Unwin.

Bacchi, Carol (1992a) 'Affirmative Action – Is It un-American?' *International Journal of Moral and Social Studies*, 7 (1): 19–31.

Bacchi, Carol (1992b) 'Sex on Campus – Where Does "Consent" End and Harassment Begin?', *The Australian Universities' Review*, 35 (1): 31–6.

Bacchi, Carol (1993) 'The Brick Wall: Why So Few Women Become Senior Academics', *The Australian Universities' Review*, 36 (1): 36–41.

Bacchi, Carol (1994) '"Consent" or "Coercion"? Removing Conflict of Interest from Staff–Student Relations', *The Australian Universities' Review*, 37 (2): 55–61.

Bacchi, Carol Lee (1996) *The Politics of Affirmative Action: 'Women', Equality and Category Politics*. London: Sage.

Bacchi, Carol (1998) 'Changing the Sexual Harassment Agenda' in Miora

Gatens and Alison Mackinnon (eds) *Gender and Institutions: Welfare, Work and Citizenship*. Cambridge: Cambridge University Press. pp. 75–89.

Bacchi, Carol and Jose, Jim (1994a) 'Dealing with Sexual Harassment: Persuade, Discipline or Punish?', *Australian Journal of Law and Society*, 10: 1–14.

Bacchi, Carol and Jose, Jim (1994b) 'Historicising Sexual Harassment', *Women's History Review*, 3 (2): 263–70.

Bacchi, Carol, Thiele, Bev, Eveline, Joan and Currie, Jan (1992) *Shifting Ground: The Dialectics of Work/Care*. Report of an International Colloquium held at the Australian National University. Canberra: Australian National University.

Bachrach, Peter (1972 [1967]) *The Theory of Democratic Elitism: A Critique*, third edition. London: University of London Press.

Bachrach, Peter and Baratz, Morton S. (1963) 'Decisions and Nondecisions: An Analytical Framework', *American Political Science Review*, 57 (3): 632–42.

Backhouse, Peter (1996) 'Social Constructionism and its Relevance to Health Policy', *Annual Review of Health Social Sciences*, 6: 173–202.

Baker, Octave (1996) 'The Managing Diversity Movement: Origins, Status and Challenges' in Benjamin Bowser and Raymond Hunt (eds) *Impacts of Racism on White Americans*. Thousand Oaks, CA: Sage. pp. 139–56.

Bakhtin, M. (1968) *Rabelais and His World*. Cambridge, MA: MIT Press.

Bakker, Isabella (1991) 'Pay Equity and Economic Restructuring: The Polarization of Policy?' in Judy Fudge and Patricia McDermott (eds) *Just Wages: A Feminist Assessment of Pay Equity*. Toronto: University of Toronto Press. pp. 254–80.

Ball, Stephen J. (1990) *Politics and Policy Making in Education: Explorations in Policy Sociology*. New York: Routledge.

Bammer, Gabriele and Martin, Brian (1992) 'Repetition Strain Injury in Australia: Medical Knowledge, Social Movement, and De Facto Partisanship', *Social Problems*, 39 (3): 219–37.

Bannister, Don and Fransella, Fay (1977 [1971]) *Inquiring Man: The Theory of Personal Constructs*. Harmondsworth: Penguin.

Bardach, Eugene (1981) 'Problems of Problem Definition in Policy Analysis' in John Crecine (ed.) *Research in Public Policy Analysis and Management*, Volume I. Greenwich, CT: JAI Press. pp. 161–71.

Barrett, Michèle (1991) *The Politics of Truth: From Marx to Foucault*. Cambridge: Polity.

Barry, Andrew, Osborne, Thomas and Rose, Nikolas (eds) (1993) *Economy and Society*, 22 (3): 265–407. Special Issue: *Liberalism, Neo-Liberalism and Governmentality*.

Barthes, Roland (1967) *Elements of Semiology*. London: Jonathan Cape.

Bataille, Georges (1985) *Visions of Excess: Selected Writings, 1927–1939*. Translated by A. Stoekl. Minneapolis, MN: University of Minnesota Press.

Bauman, Zygmunt (1992) *Intimations of Postmodernism*. New York: Routledge.

Beilharz, Peter (1987) 'Reading Politics: Social Theory and Social Policy', *Australian and New Zealand Journal of Sociology*, 23 (3): 388–406.

Berger, Gilda (1986) *Women, Work and Wages*. New York: Franklin Watts.

Berger, Peter L. and Luckman, Thomas (1967) *The Social Construction of Reality: A Treatise in the Sociology of Knowledge*. New York: Doubleday/Anchor Books.

Berry, Mary Frances (1993) *The Politics of Parenthood: Child Care, Women's Rights and the Myth of the Good Mother*. New York: Viking.

Best, Joel (1989) *Images of Issues: Typifying Contemporary Social Problems*. New York: Aldine de Gruyter.

Bingham, Shereen G. (ed.) (1994) *Conceptualizing Sexual Harassment as Discursive Practice*. Westport, CT: Praeger.

Black, Donald (1989) *Sociological Justice*. New York: Oxford University Press.

Black, Maria and Coward, Rosalind (1990) 'Linguistic, Social and Sexual Relations: a Review of Dale Spender's *Man Made Language*' in Deborah Cameron (ed.) *The Feminist Critique of Language: A Reader*. New York: Routledge. pp. 111–33.

Blackburn, Jean (1982) 'Becoming Equally Human: Girls and the Secondary Curriculum', *Vise News*, 31: 16–22.

Blackburn, Jean (1984) 'Schooling and Injustice for Girls' in D. Broom (ed.) *Unfinished Business: Social Justice for Women in Australia*. Sydney: Allen & Unwin. pp. 3–18.

Blum, Linda (1991) *Between Feminism and Labor: The Significance of the Comparable Worth Movement*. Berkeley, CA: University of California Press.

Bordo, Susan (1993) *Unbearable Weight: Feminism, Western Culture, and the Body*. Berkeley, CA: University of California Press.

Bosso, Christopher J. (1994) 'The Contextual Bases of Problem Definition' in David A. Rochefort and Roger W. Cobb (eds) *The Politics of Problem Definition: Shaping the Policy Agenda*. Lawrence, KS: University Press of Kansas. pp. 182–203.

Boulet, Jac-André and Lavallée, Laval (1984) *The Changing Economic Status of Women*. A Study prepared for the Economic Council of Canada. Ottawa: Ministry of Supply and Services Canada.

Bové, Paul A. (1990) 'Discourse' in Frank Lentricchia and Thomas McLaughlin (eds) *Critical Terms for Literary Study*. Chicago: University of Chicago Press. pp. 50–65.

Brant, Clare and Too, Yun Lee (eds) (1994) *Rethinking Sexual Harassment*. London: Pluto Press.

Braverman, Harry (1974) *Labor and Monopoly Capital: The Degradation of Work in the Twentieth Century*. New York: Monthly Review Press.

Braybrooke, David and Lindblom, Charles E. (1963) *A Strategy of Decision:*

Policy Evaluation as a Social Process. Glencoe, IL: Free Press. London: Collier–Macmillan.

Breines, Wini and Gordon, Linda (1983) 'The New Scholarship on Family Violence', *Signs*, 8 (3): 490–531.

Brennan, Deborah (1992) 'The Dynamics of Child Care Provision in Australia, Britain and Sweden' in European Institute of Social Security, *Social Security: An International Conference at University of York, England, 27– 30 September, Volume 5: Adapting to Change: Gender Roles, Family Structures, Demography and Labour Markets.* York: Social Policy Research Unit, University of York. pp. 69–78.

Brennan, Deborah (1994) *The Politics of Australian Child Care: From Philanthropy to Feminism.* Cambridge: Cambridge University Press.

Brenner, Johanna (1987) 'Feminist Political Discourses: Radical versus Liberal Approaches to the Feminization of Poverty and Comparable Worth', *Gender and Society*, 1 (4): 447–65.

Brodie, Janine, Gavigan, Shelley A. M. and Jenson, Jane (1992) *The Politics of Abortion.* Toronto: Oxford University Press.

Brodribb, Somer (1992) *Nothing Mat(t)ers: A Feminist Critique of Postmodernism.* North Melbourne: Spinifex.

Brodsky, Carroll (1976) *The Harassed Worker.* Lexington, MA: Lexington Books.

Brookes, Barbara (1988) *Abortion in England, 1900–1967.* London: Croom Helm.

Bryan, Beverley, Dadzie, Stella and Scafe, Suzanne (1985) *The Heart of the Race: Black Women's Lives in Britain.* London: Virago.

Bryson, Lois (1994) *Dealing With a Changing Work Environment: The Issue of Sexual Harassment in the ADF.* A Report Prepared for the Assistant Chief of Defence Force Personnel, Headquarters, Australian Defence Force. Canberra: ADF.

Bumiller, Kristin (1988) *The Civil Rights Society: The Social Construction of Victims.* Baltimore, MD: Johns Hopkins University Press.

Burchell, Graham, Gordon, Colin and Miller, Peter (eds) (1991) *The Foucault Effect: Studies in Governmentability.* Chicago: University of Chicago Press.

Burt, Sandra (1988) 'Legislators, Women and Public Policy' in Sandra Burt, Lorraine Code and Lindsay Dorney (eds) *Changing Patterns: Women in Canada.* Toronto: McClelland and Stewart. pp. 129–56.

Burt, Sandra (1995) 'Chapter Thirteen: The Several Worlds of Policy Analysis: Traditional Approaches and Feminist Critiques' in Sandra Burt and Lorraine Code (eds) *Changing Methods: Feminists Transforming Practice.* Peterborough, Ontario: Broadview Press. pp. 357–78.

Burt, Sandra (1996) 'Global and National Imperatives and Women: Learning to Live Without the State', paper presented to the 6th International Interdisciplinary Congress of Women, Adelaide, 21–26 April.

Burton, Clare (1987) 'Merit and Gender: Organisations and the Mobilisation of Masculine Bias', *Australian Journal of Social Issues*, 22 (2): 424–35.

Burton, Clare (1988) *Redefining Merit*. Monograph No. 2, Affirmative Action Agency. Canberra: Australian Government Publishing Service.

Burton, Clare (1992) 'Comments on "Managing Diversity"'. Paper presented at National EEO Directions Conference, Perth. Unpublished paper.

Burton, Clare, with Hag, Raven and Thompson, Gay (1987) *Women's Worth: Pay Equity and Job Evaluation in Australia*. Canberra: Australian Government Publishing Service.

Butler, Elaine (1998) 'Persuasive Discourses: Learning and the Production of Working Subjects in a Post Industrial Era' in John Holford, Peter Jarvis and Colin Griffin (eds) *International Perspectives on Lifelong Learning*. London: Kogan Page. pp. 69–80.

Butler, Judith (1992) 'Contingent Foundations: Feminism and the Question of "Postmodernism"' in Judith Butler and Joan W. Scott (eds) *Feminists Theorize the Political*. New York: Routledge. pp. 3–21.

Butler, Judith (1996) 'An Affirmative View', *Representations*, 55: 74–89.

Byrne, Eileen (1992) *Women in Science and Technology: The Institutional Ecology Approach*. Volume I: Final Research Report. University of Queensland: Wista Policy Review Project.

Callinicos, Alex (1985) 'Postmodernism, Post-Structuralism, Post-Marxism?', *Theory, Culture & Society*, 2 (3): 85–101.

Cameron, Deborah (ed.) (1990) *The Feminist Critique of Language: A Reader*. New York: Routledge.

Canadian Law Reform Commission, Fetal Status Working Group (1986) *Options for Abortion Policy Reform: a Consultation Document*. Unpublished research paper, Protection of Life Unit, Law Reform Commission of Canada.

Cavanaugh, J. Michael (1997) '(In)corporating the Other? Managing the Politics of Workplace Difference' in Pushkala Prasad, Albert J. Mills, Michael Elmes, Anshuman Prasad (eds) *Managing the Organizational Melting Pot: Dilemmas of Workplace Diversity*. Thousand Oaks, CA: Sage. pp. 31–53.

Change (1977) 'La folie encerclée', October, pp. 32–3.

Chertos, Cynthia (1983) 'Hard Truths for Strategic Change: Dilemmas of Implementing Affirmative Action', *Women's Studies International Forum*, 6 (2): 231–41.

Chodorow, Nancy (1978) *The Reproduction of Mothering: Psychoanalysis and the Sociology of Gender*. Berkeley, CA: University of California Press.

Cleghorn, John E. (1992) 'Diversity: The Key to Quality', keynote address, 'Managing Diversity: The Quality Imperative' symposium, organized by the Alberta Multicultural Commission, 19–20 November.

Cobb, Roger and Elder, Charles (1983) *Participation in American Politics*, second edition. Baltimore, MD: Johns Hopkins University Press.

Codd, John A. (1988) 'The Construction and Deconstruction of Educational Policy Documents', *Journal of Education Policy*, 3 (3): 235–47.

Cole, D. (1984) 'Strategies of Difference: Litigating for Women's Rights in a Man's World', *Law and Inequality*, 33 (2): 33–96.

Collins, Larry (1982) 'The Politics of Abortion: Trends in Canadian Fertility Policy', *Atlantis*, 7 (2): 1–20.

Collins, Patricia Hill (1989) 'The Social Construction of Invisibility' in James A. Holstein and Gale Miller (eds) *Perspectives on Social Problems: A Research Annual*, Volume I. Greenwich, CT: JAI Press. pp. 77–94.

Commonwealth Schools Commission (1987) *The National Policy for the Education of Girls in Australian Schools*. Woden, ACT: Commonwealth Schools Commission.

Condit, Celeste Michelle (1990) *Decoding Abortion Rhetoric: Communicating Social Change*. Urbana, IL: University of Illinois Press.

Connell, R. W. (1987) *Gender & Power*. Sydney: Allen & Unwin.

Cornell, Drucilla (1995) *The Imaginary Domain: Abortion, Pornography and Sexual Harassment*. New York: Routledge.

Cossman, Brenda, Bell, Shannon, Gotell, Lise and Ross, Becki L. (1997) *Bad Attitude/s on Trial: Pornography, Feminism, and the Butler Decision*. Toronto: University of Toronto Press.

Crenshaw, Kimberle (1988) 'Race, Reform, and Retrenchment: Transformation and Legitimation in Antidiscrimination Law', *Harvard Law Review*, 101 (7): 1331–87.

Cuneo, Carl J. (1991) 'The State of Pay Equity: Mediating Gender and Class through Political Parties in Ontario' in Judy Fudge and Patricia McDermott (eds) *Just Wages: A Feminist Assessment of Pay Equity*. Toronto: University of Toronto Press. pp. 32–59.

Currie, Dawn (1988) 'Re-thinking What We Do and How We Do It: a Study of Reproductive Decisions', *The Canadian Review of Sociology and Anthropology*, 25 (2): 231–53.

Currie, Dawn (1990) 'Battered Women and the State: From the Failure of Theory to a Theory of Failure', *The Journal of Human Justice*, 1 (2): 77–96.

Currie, Dawn (1992) 'Abortion Law Reform in Canada: the Pendulum That Swings One Way' in Dawn Currie and Brian MacLean (eds) *Rethinking the Administration of Justice*. Toronto: Garamond. pp. 74–102.

Dagenais, Lucie France (1996) 'Description des approaches d'égalité entre les sexes education dans les provinces canadiennes', *Revue Canadienne de l'Education*, 21 (3): 241–56.

Dahlberg, Anita (1984) *Summary of the Research Report on the Equality Ombudsman*. Stockholm: Swedish Centre for Working Life.

Dalton, Tony, Draper, Mary, Weeks, Wendy and Wiseman, John (1996) *Making Social Policy in Australia: An Introduction*. Sydney: Allen & Unwin.

Danziger, Marie (1995) 'Policy Analysis Postmodernized: Some Political and Pedagogical Ramifications', *Policy Studies Journal*, 23 (3): 435–50.

Davies, Bronwyn (1989) *Frogs and Snails and Feminist Tales: Pre-school Children and Gender*. Sydney: Allen & Unwin.

Davies, Bronwyn (1994) *Poststructuralist Theory and Classroom Practice*. Geelong, Victoria: Deakin University.

Davies, Celia and Rosser, Jane (1986) 'Gendered Jobs in the Health Service: a Problem for Labour Process Analysis' in David Knights and Hugh Willmott (eds) *Gender and the Labour Process*. Aldershot, UK: Gower. pp. 94–116.

Dean, Mitchell (1992) 'A Genealogy of the Government of Poverty', *Economy and Society*, 21 (3): 215–51.

de Bruijin, Jeanne (1997) 'Comparable Worth and Equal Pay Policies in the European Union' in A. Geske Dijkstra and Janneke Plantega (eds) *Gender and Economics: A European Perspective*. New York: Routledge. pp. 153–62.

deHaven-Smith, Lance (1988) *Philosophical Critiques of Policy Analysis: Lindblom, Habermas, and the Great Society*. Gainesville, FL: University of Florida Press.

Delgado, Richard (1984) 'The Imperial Scholar', *University of Pennsylvania Law Review*, 132 (3): 561–78.

Derrida, Jacques (1983) 'The Time of a Thesis: Punctuations' in Alan Montefiore (ed.) *Philosophy in France Today*. Cambridge: Cambridge University Press.

Dery, David (1984) *Problem Definition in Policy Analysis*. Foreword by Aaron Wildavsky. Lawrence, KS: University Press of Kansas.

De Sève, Micheline (1996) 'Abortion in the Time of Perestroika', *Women: A Cultural Review*, 7 (3): 279–90.

Dimock, Marshall (1958) *A Philosophy of Administration*. New York: Harper.

Docksey, Christopher (1987) 'The European Community and the Promotion of Equality' in Christopher McCrudden (ed.) *Women, Employment and European Equality Law*. London: Eclipse Publications. pp. 1–22.

Drysek, John (1990) *Discursive Democracy: Politics, Policy and Political Science*. Cambridge: Cambridge University Press.

Dudley, Janice and Vidovich, Lesley (1995) *The Politics of Education: Commonwealth Schools Policy 1973–95*. Australian Education Review No. 36. Melbourne, Australia: The Australian Council for Educational Research.

du Gay, Paul (1997) 'Organizing Identity: Making Up People At Work' in Paul du Gay (ed.) *Production of Culture/Cultures of Production*. London: Sage. pp. 285–344.

Duncan, Simon (1996) 'Obstacles to a Successful Equal Opportunities Policy in the European Union', *The European Journal of Women's Studies*, 3 (4): 399–422.

Dunleavy, Patrick (1991) *Democracy, Bureaucracy and Public Choice: Economic Explanations in Political Science*. New York: Prentice-Hall.

Dutton, Mary Ann (1993) 'Understanding Women's Responses to Domestic Violence: A Redefinition of Battered Woman Syndrome', *Hofstra Law Review*, 21 (4): 1191–1242.

Dziech, Billie Wright and Weiner, Linda (1984) *The Lecherous Professor: Sexual Harassment on Campus*. Boston, MA: Beacon.

Economic Planning Advisory Commission (1996) *Future Child Care Provision in Australia*. Canberra: Australian Government Publishing Service.

Edelman, Murray (1977) *Political Language*. New York: Academic Press.

Edelman, Murray (1988) *Constructing the Political Spectacle*. Chicago: The University of Chicago Press.

Edwards, Derek (1991) 'Categories Are for Talking: On the Cognitive and Discursive Bases of Categorization', *Theory & Psychology*, 1 (4): 515–42.

Edwards, John (1987) *Positive Discrimination, Social Justice and Social Policy: Moral Scrutiny of a Policy Practice*. London: Tavistock.

Ehrenreich, Barbara (1989) *Fear of Falling: The Inner Life of the Middle Class*. New York: Pantheon Books.

Eisenstein, Zillah (1988) *The Female Body and the Law*. Berkeley, CA: University of California Press.

Equal Opportunity Commission (1982) *Towards Equality: A Casebook of Decisions on Sex Discrimination and Equal Pay 1976–1981*. Manchester: EOC.

European Commission (1994) *European Social Policy: A Way Forward for the Union*. Luxembourg: European Commission.

Evans, A. (1996) 'Perils of Ignoring Our Lost Boys', *Times Educational Supplement*, 28 June, p. 20.

Evans, Sara M. and Nelson, Barbara J. (1991) 'Translating Wage Gains into Social Change: International Lessons for Implementing Pay Equity in Minnesota' in Judy Fudge and Patricia McDermott (eds) *Just Wages: A Feminist Assessment of Pay Equity*. Toronto: University of Toronto Press. pp. 227–53.

Eveline, Joan (1994a) 'The Politics of Advantage: Managing "Work" and "Care" in Australia and Sweden'. PhD dissertation, Murdoch University, Perth, Western Australia.

Eveline, Joan (1994b) 'The Politics of Advantage', *Australian Feminist Studies*, Special Issue: *Women and Citizenship*, 19 (Autumn): 129–54.

Fegan, Eileen (1996) '"Fathers", Foetuses and Abortion Decision-Making: The Reproduction of Maternal Ideology in Canadian Judicial Discourse', *Social and Legal Studies*, 5 (1): 75–93.

Feinberg, Joel (ed.) (1984) *The Problem of Abortion*. First published 1973. Belmont, CA: Wadsworth.

Ferree, Myra Marx and Gamson, William A. (1996) 'The Gendering of

Abortion Discourse: Assessing Global Feminist Influence in the United States and Germany', paper presented at the International Interdisciplinary Congress on Women, Adelaide, April. Prepared for the book, *Social Movements in a Globalizing World*, edited by Dieter Rucht, Donatella della Porta and Hanspeter Kriesi (1999). New York: St Martin's Press.

Findlay, Sue (1991) 'Making Sense of Pay Equity: Issues for a Feminist Political Practice' in Judy Fudge and Patricia McDermott (eds) *Just Wages: A Feminist Assessment of Pay Equity*. Toronto: University of Toronto Press. pp. 81–101.

Fischer, Frank (1980) *Politics, Values and Public Policy: The Problem of Methodology*. Boulder, CO: Westview Press.

Fischer, Frank (1990) *Technocracy and the Politics of Expertise*. Newbury Park, CA: Sage.

Fischer, Frank and Forester, John (eds) (1987) *Confronting Values in Policy Analysis: The Politics of Criteria*. Volume 14. Sage Yearbooks in Politics and Public Policy. Newbury Park, CA: Sage.

Flax, Jane (1990) *Thinking Fragments: Psychoanalysis, Feminism and Postmodernism in the Contemporary West*. Berkeley, CA: University of California Press.

Foster, Victoria (1995) '"What About the Boys?" Presumptive Equality as the Basis for Policy Change in the Education of Girls and Boys', paper presented to the 1995 National Social Policy Conference, 'Social Policy and the Challenges of Social Change', 5–7 July, 1995, University of New South Wales. Published in Conference Proceedings, Volume One.

Foster, Victoria (1996) 'Space Invaders: Desire and Threat in the Schooling of Girls', *Discourse: Studies in the Cultural Politics of Education*, 17 (1): 43–63.

Foucault, Michel (1970) *The Order of Things: An Archeology of the Human Sciences*. Translated by Alan Sheridan. New York: Vintage Books.

Foucault, Michel (1975) *The Birth of the Clinic: an Archaeology of Medical Perception*. Translated by A. M. Sheridan. New York: Vintage.

Foucault, Michel (1977a) *Discipline and Punish*. New York: Pantheon.

Foucault, Michel (1977b) *The Archaelogy of Knowledge*. London: Tavistock.

Foucault, Michel (1978) 'Governmentality' in Graham Burchell, Colin Gordon, and Peter Miller (eds) (1991) *The Foucault Effect: Studies in Governmentality*. Hemel Hempstead: Harvester Wheatsheaf. pp. 87–104.

Foucault, Michel (1980) *Power/Knowledge: Selected Interviews and Other Writings 1972–1979*. New York: Pantheon.

Foucault, Michel (1981 [1970]) 'The Order of Discourse' in Robert Young (ed.) *Untying the Text: A Poststructuralist Reader*. London: Routledge and Kegan Paul. pp. 48–78.

Foucault, Michel (1981 [1976]) *The History of Sexuality*. Volume I. London: Penguin.

Foucault, Michel (1984) 'The Concern for Truth' in L. D. Kritzman (ed.)

Politics, Philosophy, Culture: Interviews and Other Writings 1977–1984. New York: Routledge. pp. 255–67.

Foucault, Michel (1991) 'Governmentality' in Graham Burchell, Colin Gordon and Peter Miller (eds) *The Foucault Effect: Studies in Governmentality.* Hemel Hempstead: Harvester Wheatsheaf. pp. 87–194.

Francis, L. P. (1993) 'In Defense of Affirmative Action' in S. M. Cahn (ed.) *Affirmative Action and the University: A Philosophical Inquiry.* Philadelphia, PA: Temple University Press. pp. 9–40.

Frank, Manfred (1992) 'On Foucault's Concept of Discourse' in Timothy J. Armstrong (trans.) *Michel Foucault Philosopher.* New York: Routledge. pp. 99–116.

Fraser, Nancy (1989) *Unruly Practices: Power, Discourse and Gender in Contemporary Social Theory.* Minneapolis, MN: University of Minnesota Press.

Fraser, Nancy (1994) 'After the Family Wage: Gender Equity and the Welfare State', *Political Theory,* 22 (4): 591–618.

Fraser, Nancy (1995) 'Politics, Culture, and the Public Sphere: Toward a Postmodern Conception' in Linda Nicholson and Steven Seidman (eds) *Social Postmodernism: Beyond Identity Politics.* Cambridge: Cambridge University Press.

Fraser, Nancy and Gordon, Linda (1994) 'A Genealogy of Dependency: Tracing a Keyword of the U.S. Welfare State', *Signs,* 19 (2): 309–36.

Friedan, Betty (1965 [1963]) *The Feminine Mystique.* Harmondsworth: Penguin.

Friendly, Martha (1994) *Child Care Policy in Canada: Putting the Pieces Together.* Don Mills, Ontario: Addison–Wesley.

Frye, Marilyn (1992) 'Getting it Right', *Signs,* 17 (4): 781–93.

Fudge, Judy and McDermott, Patricia (eds) (1991) *Just Wages: A Feminist Assessment of Pay Equity.* Toronto: University of Toronto Press.

Fulcher, Gillian (1989) *Disabling Policies? A Comparative Approach to Education Policy and Disability.* East Sussex: The Falmer Press.

Fuller, Richard C. and Myers, Richard R. (1971) 'The Conflict of Values' in Earl Rubington and Martin S. Weinberg (eds) *The Study of Social Problems: Five Perspectives.* New York: Oxford University Press. pp. 87–91.

Fuller, Richard C. and Myers, Richard R. (1971) 'The Stages of a Social Problem' in Earl Rubington and Martin S. Weinberg (eds) *The Study of Social Problems: Five Perspectives.* New York: Oxford University Press. pp. 92–4.

Gallop, Jane (1997) *Feminist Accused of Sexual Harassment.* Durham, NC: Duke University Press.

Game, Ann (1984) 'Affirmative Action: Liberal Rationality or Challenge to Patriarchy?', *Legal Service Bulletin* (Australia), 9 (6): 253–7.

Garner, Helen (1995) *The First Stone: Some Questions about Sex and Power.* Sydney: Picador.

Gaskell, Jane (1992) *Issues for Women in Canadian Education*. Working Paper No. 32. Ottawa: Economic Council of Canada.

Gaskell, Jane, McLaren, Arlene and Novogrodsky, Myra (eds) (1989) *Claiming an Education: Feminism and Canadian Schools*. Toronto: Our Schools/Our Selves.

Gelb, Joyce and Palley, Marion Lief (1987) *Women and Public Policies*, second edition. Princeton, NJ: Princeton University Press.

Gilbert, Pam (1996) *Talking About Gender: Terminology Used in the Education of Girls Policy Area and Implications for Policy Priorities and Programs*. A Women's Employment, Education and Training Advisory Group Project. Canberra: AGPS.

Gilligan, Carol (1982) *In a Different Voice: Psychological Theory and Women's Development*. Cambridge, MA: Harvard University Press.

Goldberg, David Theo (1993) *Racist Culture: Philosophy and the Politics of Meaning*. Oxford: Blackwell.

Gollancz, Victor (ed.) (1917) *The Making of Women: Oxford Essays in Feminism*. London: George Allen & Unwin.

Goodwin, Ness (1996) 'Governmentality in the Queensland Department of Education: Policies and the Management of Schools', *Discourse: Studies in the Cultural Politics of Education*, 17 (1): 65–74.

Gordon, Avery (1993) 'Twenty-Two Theses on Social Constructionism: A Feminist Response to Ibarra and Kitsuse's "Proposal for the Study of Social Problems"' in James A. Holstein and Gale Miller (eds) *Reconsidering Social Constructionism: Debates in Social Problems Theory*. New York: Aldine de Gruyter. pp. 301–26.

Gordon, Colin (1991) 'Governmental Rationality: an Introduction' in Graham Burchell, Colin Gordon and Peter Miller (eds) *The Foucault Effect: Studies in Governmentality*. With Two Lectures by and an Interview with Michel Foucault. Chicago: University of Chicago Press. pp. 1–52.

Gordon, Linda (1977) *Woman's Body, Woman's Right: a Social History of Birth Control in America*. New York: Penguin.

Gordon, Linda (1988) *Heroes of Their Own Lives: The Politics and History of Family Violence – Boston, 1880–1960*. New York: Viking.

Grauerholz, Elizabeth (1994) 'Gender Socialization and Communication: The Inscription of Sexual Harassment in Social Life' in Shereen Bingham (ed.) *Conceptualizing Sexual Harassment as Discursive Practice*. Westport, CT: Praeger. pp. 31–44.

Gray, John (1993) *Men are from Mars, Women are from Venus: a Practical Guide for Improving Communication and Getting What You Want in Your Relationships*. London: Thorsons.

Graycar, Regina (1995) 'The Gender of Judgments: An Introduction' in Margaret Thornton (ed.) *Public and Private: Feminist Legal Debates*. Melbourne: Oxford University Press. pp. 262–82.

Gregory, Jeanne (1987) *Sex, Race and the Law: Legislating for Equality*. London: Sage.

Gregory, R. G. and Duncan, R. C. (1981) 'Segmented Labor Market Theories and the Australian Experience of Equal Pay for Women', *Journal of Post-Keynesian Economics*, 3: 399–415.

Gregory, R. G. and Ho, V. (1985) *Equal Pay and Comparable Worth: What Can the United States Learn from the Australian Experience?* Discussion Paper No. 123. Canberra: Centre for Economic Policy Research.

Grewal, Inderpal and Kaplan, Caren (eds) (1994) *Scattered Hegemonies: Postmodernity and Transnational Feminist Practices*. Minneapolis, MN: University of Minnesota Press.

Gubrium, J. F. (1993) 'For a Cautious Naturalism' in James A. Holstein and Gale Miller (eds) *Reconsidering Social Constructionism: Debates in Social Problems Theory*. New York: Aldine de Gruyter. pp. 89–96.

Gusfield, Joseph R. (1989) 'Constructing the Ownership of Social Problems: Fun and Profit in the Welfare State', *Social Problems*, 36 (5): 431–41.

Habermas, Jürgen (1972) *Toward a Rational Society: Student Protest, Science and Politics*. Translated by Jeremy J. Shapiro. London: Heinemann Educational.

Hall, Stuart (1992) 'The Question of Cultural Identity' in S. Hall, D. Held and A. McGrew (eds) *Modernity and Its Futures*. Cambridge: Polity. pp. 277–326.

Hallock, Margaret (1993) 'Unions and the Gender Wage Gap' in Dorothy Sue Cobble (ed.) *Women and Unions – Forging a Partnership*. Ithaca, NY: ILR Press. pp. 27–42.

Hamilton, Roberta (1996) *Gendering the Vertical Mosaic: Feminist Perspectives on Canadian Society*. Toronto: Copp Clark Ltd.

Harding, Sandra (1990) 'Feminism, Science, and the Anti-Enlightenment Critique' in Linda Nicholson (ed.) *Feminism/Postmodernism*. New York: Routledge. pp. 83–106.

Hartmann, Heide, Roos, Patricia A. and Trieman, Donald J. (1985) 'An Agenda for Basic Research for Comparable Worth' in Heide Hartmann (ed.) *Comparable Worth: New Directions for Research*. Washington, DC: National Academy Press. pp. 3–33.

Harvard Law Review (1989) 'ReThinking *Weber*: The Business Response to Affirmative Action', 102 (3): 658–71.

Harvey, Edward B. and Blakely, John H. (1996) *Information Systems for Managing Workplace Diversity*. North York, Ontario: CCH Canadian Ltd.

Hawkesworth, Mary (1988) *Theoretical Issues in Policy Analysis*. New York: State University of New York Press.

Hawkesworth, Mary (1994) 'Policy Studies within a Feminist Frame', *Policy Sciences*, 27 (2–3): 97–118.

Heath, M. and Naffine, N. (1994) 'Men's Needs and Women's Desires:

Feminist Dilemmas About Rape Law "Reform"', *The Australian Feminist Law Journal*, 3: 30–52.

Heen, Mary (1984) 'A Review of Federal Court Decisions under Title VII of the Civil Rights Act of 1964' in Helen Remick (ed.) *Comparable Worth and Wage Discrimination: Technical Possibilities and Political Realities*. Philadelphia: Temple University Press. pp. 197–219.

Henderson, George (1994) *Cultural Diversity in the Workplace: Issues and Strategies*. Westport, CT: Quorum Books.

Hennessy, Rosemary (1993) *Material Feminism and the Politics of Discourse*. New York: Routledge.

Henriques, J., Hollway, W., Unwin, C., Venn, C. and Walkerdine, V. (eds) (1984) *Changing the Subject: Psychology, Social Regulation and Subjectivity*. London: Methuen.

Hepple, B. A. (1983) 'Judging Equal Rights', *Current Legal Problems*, 36: 71–90.

Herman, Didi (1994) *Rights of Passage: Struggles for Lesbian and Gay Legal Equality*. Toronto: University of Toronto Press.

Hinkson, John (1995) 'Governmentality: the Specific Intellectual and the Postmodern State', *Arena Journal*, 5: 153–84.

Hochschild, Arlie Russell (1983) *The Managed Heart: Commercialization of Human Feeling*. Berkeley, CA: University of California Press.

Holstein, James A. and Miller, Gale (eds) (1989) *Perspectives on Social Problems: A Research Annual*, Volume 1. Greenwich, CT: JAI Press.

Holstein, James A. and Miller, Gale (eds) (1993) *Reconsidering Social Constructionism: Debates in Social Problems Theory*. New York: Aldine de Gruyter.

Hoskyns, Catherine (1996) *Integrating Gender: Women, Law and Politics in the European Union*. London: Verso.

Howe, R. Brian (1991) 'The Evolution of Human Rights Policy in Ontario', *Canadian Journal of Political Science/Revue Canadienne de Science Politique*, 24 (4): 783–802.

Hutner, Frances C. (1986) *Equal Pay for Comparable Worth: The Working Woman's Issue of the Eighties*. New York: Praeger.

Ibarra Peter R. and Kitsuse, John I. (1993) 'Vernacular Constituents of Moral Discourse: An Interactionist Proposal for the Study of Social Problems' in James A. Holstein and Gale Miller (eds) *Reconsidering Social Constructionism: Debates in Social Problems Theory*. New York: Aldine de Gruyter. pp. 25–58.

Immigration and Refugee Board (1993) *Guidelines Issued By the Chairperson Pursuant to Section 65 (3) of the Immigration Act*. Ottawa: Immigration and Refugee Board.

Iyer, Nitya (1993) 'Categorical Denials: Equality Rights and the Shaping of Social Identity', *Queen's Law Journal*, 19: 179–207.

Jameson, Fredric (1972) The Prison-House of Language. Princeton, NJ: Princeton University Press.

Jenson, Jane (1986) 'Gender and Reproduction: Or, Babies and the State', Studies in Political Economy, 20: 9–46.

Jenson, Jane (1987) 'Changing Discourse, Changing Agendas: Political Rights and Reproductive Policies in France' in Mary Katzenstein and Carol McClung Mueller (eds) The Women's Movements of the United States and Western Europe. Philadelphia: Temple University Press. pp. 64–88.

Jenson, Jane (1988) 'The Limits of "and the" discourse: French Women as Marginal Workers' in Jane Jenson, Elizabeth Hagen and Ceallaigh Reddy (eds) Feminization of the Labour Force: Paradoxes and Promises. Cambridge: Polity Press. pp. 155–69.

Joffe, Carole (1995) Doctors of Conscience: The Struggle to Provide Abortion before and after Roe v. Wade. Boston, MA: Beacon Press.

John, Ian (1996) 'Different Discursive Constructions of the Relationship between Theory and Practice, and Approaches to Practice, in Psychology'. Available on request from Ian John, Psychology Department, University of Adelaide.

Johnston, P. (1984) 'Abused Wives: Their Perceptions of the Help Offered by Mental Health Professionals'. Unpublished Independent Enquiry Project, School of Social Work, Carleton University, Ottawa.

Jones, Alison (1993) 'Girls' School Achievement', keynote address to Education Review Office National Conference, Auckland, 14 December. Unpublished paper. Education Faculty, University of Auckland.

Julien, Lise (1987) Women's Issues in Education in Canada: A Survey of Policies and Practices at the Elementary and Secondary Levels. Prepared by the Secretariat of the Council of Ministers of Education, Canada. Toronto: Council of Ministers of Education.

Kellough, Gail (1996) Aborting Law: An Exploration of the Politics of Motherhood and Medicine. Toronto: University of Toronto Press.

Kelly, Liz (1988) Surviving Sexual Violence. Minneapolis, MN: University of Minnesota Press.

Kennedy, D. (1982) 'The Stages of the Decline of the Public/Private Distinction', University of Pennsylvania Review, 130: 1349–57.

Kenway, J. and Modra, H. (1989) 'Feminist pedagogy and emancipatory possibilities', Critical Pedagogy Networker, 2 (2&3): 1–17.

Kenway, Jane (1990) 'Non-traditional Pathways for Girls – Are There Alternatives?' Search, 21 (6): 181–4.

Kenway, Jane (1993) 'Learning from Girls: What Can Girls Teach Feminist Teachers?' in Lyn Yates (ed.) Feminism and Education. Special Issue of Melbourne Studies in Education. pp. 63–77.

Kingdom, Elizabeth (1991) What's Wrong with Rights? Problems for Feminist Politics of Law. Edinburgh: Edinburgh University Press.

Kingdom, Elizabeth (1995) 'Body Politics and Rights' in Jo Bridgeman and Susan Millns (eds) *Law and Body Politics: Regulating the Female Body*. Aldershot: Dartmouth. pp. 1–21.

Kingdom, John W. (1995) *Agendas, Alternatives and Public Policies*, second edition. New York: HarperCollins.

Kirkwood, Catherine (1993) *Leaving Abusive Partners: From the Scars of Survival to the Wisdom for Change*. London: Sage.

Kitsuse, John I. and Spector, Malcolm (1973) 'Toward a Sociology of Social Problems', *Social Problems*, 20: 407–19.

Kress, G. (1985) *Linguistic Processes in Sociocultural Practice*. Geelong: Deakin University Press.

Levitas, Ruth (1996) 'The Concept of Social Exclusion and the New Durkheimian Hegemony', *Critical Social Policy*, 16 (1), Issue 46: 5–20.

Lewis, Debra J. (1988) *Just Give Us the Money: a Discussion of Wage Discrimination and Pay Equity*. Vancouver: Women's Research Centre.

Lewis, Jane (1984) *Women in England 1870–1950: Sexual Divisions and Social Change*. Brighton: Wheatsheaf Books.

Lewis, Jane (ed.) (1993) *Women and Social Policies in Europe: Work, Family and the State*. Aldershot: Edward Elgar.

Lindblom, Charles E. (1980) *The Policy-making Process*, second edition. In Prentice-Hall Foundations of Modern Political Science Series. Englewood Cliffs, NJ: Prentice-Hall.

Littleton, Christine (1981) 'Toward a Redefinition of Sexual Equality', *Harvard Law Review*, 95: 487–508.

Loseke, Donileen R. (1993) 'Constructing Conditions, People, Morality, and Emotion: Expanding the Agenda of Constructionism' in Gale Miller and James A. Holstein (eds) *Constructionist Controversies: Issues in Social Problems Theory*. New York: Aldine de Gruyter. pp. 207–16.

Lucas, Jan (1991) 'Sexual Harassment, Current Models of Occupational Health and Safety and Women', *Australian Feminist Studies*, 12: 59–70.

Luke, Carmen and Gore, Jennifer (eds) (1992) *Feminisms and Critical Pedagogy*. New York: Routledge.

Lunny, John (1997) 'Sexual harassment and OHS: liability potential', *Complete Safety Australia*, September: 34–5.

Luthra, Rashmi (1995) 'The "Abortion Clause" in U. S. Foreign Population Policy: The Debate Viewed Through a Postcolonial Feminist Lens' in Angharad N. Valdivia (ed.) *Feminism, Multiculturalism, and the Media: Global Diversities*. London: Sage. pp. 197–216.

Lynch, Frederick (1989) *Invisible Victims: White Males and the Crisis of Affirmative Action*. New York: Greenwood Press.

Lyon, Christine M. (1995) 'Working Together – An Analysis of Collaborative Inter-Agency Responses to "The Problem of Domestic Violence"' in Jo

Bridgeman and Susan Millns (eds) *Law and Body Politics: Regulating the Female Body*. Dartmouth: Aldershot. pp. 201–12.

MacKinnon, Catharine (1979) *Sexual Harassment of Working Women: A Case of Sex Discrimination*. New Haven, CT: Yale University Press.

MacKinnon, Catharine (1983) 'The Male Ideology of Privacy: A Feminist Perspective on the right to Abortion', *Radical America*, 17 (4): 23–35.

MacKinnon, Catharine (1987) *Feminism Unmodified: Discourses on Life and Law*. Cambridge, MA: Harvard University Press.

Macklin, Audrey (1992) '*Symes v. MNR*: Where Sex Meets Class', *Canadian Journal of Women and the Law*, 5 (2): 498–517.

MacLeod, Linda (1980) *Wife Battering in Canada: The Vicious Circle*. Ottawa: Minister of Supply and Services, Canada.

MacLeod, Linda (1987) *Battered But Not Beaten: Preventing Wife Battering in Canada*. Ottawa: Canadian Advisory Council on the Status of Women.

Maclure, Maggie (1994) 'Review Essay: Language and Discourse: the embrace of uncertainty', *British Journal of Sociology of Education*, 15 (2): 283–300.

Maddox, Marion (1997) 'A Critique of the National Action Plan for the Education of Girls', unpublished paper. University of Adelaide, Politics Department.

Magid, Carolyn H. (1997) 'Does Comparable Worth Have Radical Potential?' in Patrice DiQuinzio and Iris Marion Young (eds) *Feminist Ethics and Social Policy*. Bloomington, IN: Indiana University Press. pp. 125–42.

Mahon, Rianne (1991) 'From Solidaristic Wages to Solidaristic Work: A Post-Fordist Historic Compromise for Sweden?' *Economic and Industrial Democracy: An International Journal*, 12 (3): 295–325.

Mahon, Rianne (1997) 'Child Care in Canada and Sweden: Policy and Politics', *Social Politics: International Studies in Gender, State and Society*, 4 (3): 382–418.

Mahoney, Martha R. (1991) 'Legal Images of Battered Women: Redefining the Issue of Separation', *Michigan Law Review*, 90 (1): 1–94.

Mahoney, Martha R. (1992) 'Exit: Power and the Idea of Leaving in Love, Work, and the Confirmation Hearings', *Southern California Law Review*, 65 (3): 1283–1319.

Majone, Giandomenico (1989) *Evidence, Argument and Persuasion in the Policy Process*. New Haven, CT: Yale University Press.

Manicom, Ann (1992) 'Review Essay: Feminist Pedagogy: Transformations, Standpoints and Politics', *Canadian Journal of Education*, 17 (3): 365–89.

Marcus, Sharon (1992) 'Fighting Bodies, Fighting Words: A Theory and Politics of Rape Prevention' in Judith Butler and Joan W. Scott (eds) *Feminists Theorize the Political*. New York: Routledge. pp. 385– 403.

Maroney, Heather J. (1992) '"Who has the Baby?" Nationalism, Pronatalism and the Construction of a "Demographic Crisis" in Quebec, 1960–1988' in M. Patricia Connelly and Pat Armstrong (eds) *Feminism in Action*. Toronto: Canadian Scholars' Press. pp. 237–65.

Martin, Jane Roland (1985) *Reclaiming a Conversation: the Ideal of the Educated Woman*. New Haven, CT: Yale University Press.

Martin, Jane Roland (1991) 'The Contradiction and Challenge of the Educated Woman', *Women's Studies Quarterly*, 19 (1&2): 6–27.

Matthews, N. (1994) *Confronting Rape: The Feminist Anti-Rape Movement and the State*. London: Routledge.

Mauss, Armand L. (1975) *Social Problems as Social Movements*. Philadelphia: J. B. Lippincott.

McCall, Michal (1993) 'Social Constructionism in Critical Feminist Theory and Research' in Gale Miller and James A. Holstein (eds) *Constructionist Controversies: Issues in Social Problems Theory*. New York: Aldine de Gruyter. pp. 181–92.

McCallum, Margaret E. (1989) 'Men, Women, and the Liberal Ideal: An Historian's Reflections on the Morgentaler Case', *Queen's Quarterly*, 96 (2): 298–313.

McCann, Michael (1994) *Rights at Work: Pay Equity Reform and the Politics of Legal Mobilization*. Chicago: Univeristy of Chicago Press.

McCrudden, Christopher (1986) 'Comparable Worth: A Common Dilemma', *The Yale Journal of International Law*, 11 (2): 396–436.

McCrudden, C., Smith, D. J. and Brown, C. (1991) 'Groups versus Individuals: the Ambiguity behind the Race Relations Act', *Policy Studies*, 12 (2): 26–35.

McDermott, Patricia (1991) 'Pay Equity Challenge to Collective Bargaining in Ontario' in Judy Fudge and Patricia McDermott (eds) *Just Wages: A Feminist Assessment of Pay Equity*. Toronto: University of Toronto Press. pp. 122–35.

McDermott, Patricia (1992) 'Employment Equity and Pay Equity: And Never the Twain Shall Meet?' *Canadian Woman Studies/Les Cahiers de la Femme*, 12: 24–7.

McHoul, Alec and Grace, Wendy (1993) *A Foucault Primer: Discourse, Power and the Subject*. Melbourne: Melbourne University Press.

McLaren, Angus (1978) 'Birth Control and Abortion in Canada, 1870–1920', *Canadian Historical Review*, 59 (3): 319–40.

McLeod, Julie (1993) 'Review Essay: Impossible Fictions? Utopian Visions and Feminist Educational Research' in Lyn Yates (ed.) *Feminism and Education. A Special Edition of Melbourne Studies in Education*. pp. 107–19.

Mead, Jenna (1995) 'Sexual Harassment and Feminism', *RePublica*, 2: 165–80.

Merton, Robert (1961) 'Social Problems and Sociological Theory' in Robert K. Merton and Robert A. Nisbet (eds) *Contemporary Social Problems*. New York: Harcourt, Brace & World, Inc. pp. 775–823.

Merton, Robert K. (1966 [1961]) 'Epilogue: Social Problems and Sociological

Theory' in Robert K. Merton and Robert Nisbet (eds) *Contemporary Social Problems*. New York: Harcourt Brace Jovanovitch. pp. 778-823.

Michalowski, Raymond J. (1993) '(De)Construction, Postmodernism, and Social Problems: Facts, Fiction, and Fantasies at the "End of History"' in James A. Holstein and Gale Miller (eds) *Reconsidering Social Constructionism: Debates in Social Problems Theory*. New York: Aldine de Gruyter. pp. 377–402.

Miller, Frederick (1994) 'Why We Choose to Address Oppression' in E. Cross, J. Katz, F. Miller and E. Seashore (eds) *The Promise of Diversity*. Irwin, NY: NTL Institute. pp. xxv–xxix.

Miller, Gale (1993) 'New Challenges to Social Constructionism: Alternative Perspectives on Social Problems Theory' in James A. Holstein and Gale Miller (eds) *Reconsidering Social Constructionism: Debates in Social Problems*. New York: Aldine de Gruyter. pp. 254–80.

Miller, Leslie (1993) 'Claims-Making from the Underside: Marginalization and Social Problems Analysis' in James A. Holstein and Gale Miller (eds) *Reconsidering Social Constructionism: Debates in Social Problems Theory*. New York: Aldine de Gruyter. pp. 349–68.

Mitchell, Susan (1995) 'The Culture of Complaint', *The Weekend Australian*, 15–16 April.

Mohanty, Chandra Talpade (1990) 'On Race and Voice: Challenges for Liberal Education in the 1990s', *Cultural Critique*, 14: 179–208.

Mohr, James (1978) *Abortion in America: The Origins and Evolution of National Policy, 1800–1900*. New York: Oxford University Press.

Morgan, Jenny (1995) 'Sexual Harassment and the Public/Private Dichotomy: Equality, Morality and Manners' in Margaret Thornton (ed.) *Public and Private: Feminist Legal Debates*. Melbourne: Oxford University Press. pp. 89–111.

Morgan, Patricia (1980) 'The State as Mediator: Alcohol Problem Management in the Postwar World', *Contemporary Drug Problems*, 9: 107–36.

Morris, Anne and Nott, Susan (1995) 'The Law's Engagement with Pregnancy' in Jo Bridgeman and Susan Millns (eds) *Law and Body Politics: Regulating the Female Body*. Dartmouth: Aldershot. pp. 53–78.

Morris, Cerise (1980) 'Determination and Thoroughness: The Movement for a Royal Commission on the Status of Women in Canada', *Atlantis*, 5 (2): 1–21.

Moss, Peter (1991) 'Day Care for Young Children in the United Kingdom' in Edward Melhuish and Peter Moss (eds) *Day Care for Young Children: International Perspectives*. London: Routledge. pp. 121–41.

Moss, Peter (1997) 'Early Childhood Services in Europe', *Policy Options*, January, February, pp. 27–30.

Moss, Peter and Penn, Helen (1996) *Transforming Nursery Education*. London: Paul Chapman Ltd.

Naffine, Ngaire (1990) *Law and the Sexes: Explorations in Feminist Jurisprudence*. Sydney: Allen & Unwin.

Naffine, Ngaire (1992) 'Windows on the Legal Mind: The Evocation of Rape in Legal Writings', *Melbourne University Law Review*, 18: 741–67.

National Commission on Education (1993) *Learning to Succeed*. Report of the Paul Hamlyn Foundation. London: Heinemann.

Nemy, E. (1975) 'Women Begin to Speak Out Against Sexual Harassment at Work', *New York Times*, 19 August, p. 38.

Ng, Roxana (1993) '"A Woman out of Control": Deconstructing Sexism and Racism in the University', *Canadian Journal of Education*, 18 (3): 188–97.

Nicholson, Linda and Seidman, Steven (eds) (1995) *Social Postmodernism: Beyond Identity Politics*. Cambridge: Cambridge University Press.

Nielsen, Ruth and Halvorsen, Marit (1992) 'Sex Discrimination Between the Nordic Model and European Community Law' in Niklas Bruun, Boel Flodgren, Marit Halvorsen, Håkan Hydén and Ruth Nielsen, *The Nordic Labour Relations Model: Labour Law and Trade Unions in the Nordic Countries – Today and Tomorrow*. Aldershot, Hants: Dartmouth Publishing Company. pp. 180–220.

Niland, C. and Champion, R. (1990) *Equal Employment Opportunity Programs for Immigrants: The Experience of Thirteen Organisations*. Commonwealth of Australia: Bureau of Immigration Research.

Nourse, Victoria F. (1996) 'Where Violence, Relationship, and Equality Meet: The Violence Against Women Act's Civil Rights Remedy', *Wisconsin Women's Law Journal*, 11 (1): 1–36.

OECD (1993) *Why Child Care Matters*. New York: OECD.

Okin, Susan Moller (1991) 'Gender, the Public and the Private' in David Held (ed.) *Political Theory Today*. Cambridge: Polity Press. pp. 67–90.

Olsen, Frances (1983) 'The Family and the Market: A Study of Ideology and Legal Reform', *Harvard Law Review*, 96 (7): 1497–1578.

Olsen, Frances (1985) 'The Myth of State Intervention in the Family', *University of Michigan Journal of Law Reform*, 18 (4): 835–64.

O'Malley, Pat (1992) 'Risk, Power and Crime Prevention', *Economy and Society*, 21 (3): 252–75.

Ontario (1978) *Sex-role Stereotyping and Women's Studies*. Toronto: Ministry of Education.

Ontario Status of Women Council (1974) *About Face: Towards a Positive Image of Women in Textbooks*. Toronto: Ontario Status of Women Council.

Orloff, Ann Shola (1993) 'Gender and the Social Rights of Citizenship: The Comparative Analysis of Gender Relations and Welfare States', *American Sociological Review*, 58 (June): 303–28.

'PA' News (1997) 'Nursery vouchers scheme goes nationwide', 1 April. <http://www.ge97.co.uk/news_archive/mar_31/story73550s.html>

Pal, Leslie A. (1992) *Public Policy Analysis, An Introduction*, second edition. Scarborough, Ontario: Nelson.

Pal, Leslie (1996) 'Missed Opportunities or Comparative Advantage? Canadian Contributions to the Study of Public Policy' in Laurent Dobuzinskis, Michael Howlett and David Laycock (eds) *Policy Studies in Canada: The State of the Art*. Toronto: University of Toronto Press. pp. 359–74.

Pateman, Carole (1981) 'The Concept of Equity' in P. N. Troy (ed.) *A Just Society? Essays on Equity in Australia*. Sydney: George Allen & Unwin. pp. 21–36.

Pateman, Carole (1983) 'Feminist Critiques of the Public/Private Dichotomy' in S. I. Genn and G. F. Gaus (eds) *Public and Private in Social Life*. London: Croom Helm. pp 281–303.

Paul, Ellen Frankel (1989) *Equity and Gender: The Comparable Worth Debate*. New Brunswick, NJ: Transaction Books.

Pfeiffer & Company (1993) *Training Catalogue*. San Diego, CA: Pfeiffer & Co.

Phillips, Anne and Taylor, Barbara (1986) 'Sex and Skill' in *Feminist Review* (ed.) *Waged Work: A Reader*. London: Virago. pp. 54–66.

Phillips, Susan (1996) 'Discourse, Identity, and Voice: Feminist Contributions to Policy Studies' in Laurent Dobuzinskis, Michael Howlett and David Laycock (eds) *Policy Studies in Canada: The State of the Art*. Toronto: University of Toronto Press. pp. 242–65.

Pierson, Ruth Roach (1995) 'Education and Training' in Ruth Roach Pierson and Marjorie Griffin (eds) *Canadian Women's Issues: Vol. II. Bold Visions*. Toronto: James Lorimer and Co. pp. 162–202.

Plaza, Monique (1980) 'Our Costs and Their Benefits', *m/f: a feminist journal*, 4: 28–39.

Plumwood, Val (1995) 'Feminism, Privacy and Radical Democracy', *Anarchist Studies*, 3: 97–120.

Pollack, Wendy (1990) 'Sexual Harassment: Women's Experience vs. Legal Definitions', *Harvard Women's Law Journal*, 13: 35–85.

Pollock, Della (1994) '(Un)Becoming "Voices": Representing Sexual Harassment in Performance' in Shereen G. Bingham (ed.) *Conceptualizing Sexual Harassment as Discursive Practice*. Westport, CT: Praeger. pp. 117–26.

Post, Robert (1996) 'Introduction: after *Bakke*', *Representations*, 55: 1–10.

Postman, Neil (1992) *Technopoly: The Surrender of Culture to Technology*. New York: Vintage Books.

Prentice, Susan (1988) 'The "Mainstreaming" of Daycare', *Resources for Feminist Research*, 17: 59–63.

Press, A. (1980) 'Abusing Sex at the Office', *Newsweek*, 10 March, p. 81.

Pringle, Rosemary (1988) *Secretaries Talk: Sexuality, Power & Work*. Sydney: Allen & Unwin.

Purkiss, Diane (1994) 'The Lecherous Professor Revisited: Plato, Pedagogy and the Scene of Harassment' in Clare Brant and Yun Lee Too (eds) *Rethinking Sexual Harassment*. London: Pluto Press. pp. 189–219.

Radin, Margaret (1991) 'Affirmative Action Rhetoric', *Social Philosophy & Policy*, 8 (2): 130–49.

Rainwater, Lee (ed.) (1974a) *Social Problems and Public Policy: Inequality and Justice*. Chicago: Aldine.

Rainwater, Lee (ed.) (1974b) *Social Problems and Public Policy: Deviance and Liberty*. Chicago: Aldine.

Razack, Sherene (1995) 'Domestic Violence as Gender Persecution: Policing the Borders of Nation, Race, and Gender', *Canadian Journal of Women and the Law*, 8: 45–88.

Reekie, Gail (1994) 'Reading the Problem Family: Post-Structuralism and the Analysis of Social Problems', *Drug and Alcohol Review*, 13: 457–65.

Rein, Martin and Schön, Donald (1977) 'Problem Setting in Policy Research' in Carol Weiss (ed.) *Using Research in Public Policy Making*. Lexington, MA: Lexington Books. pp. 235–51.

Remick, Helen (ed.) (1984) *Comparable Worth and Wage Discrimination: Technical Possibilities and Political Realities*. Philadelphia: Temple University Press.

Rhoads, Steven E. (1993) *Incomparable Worth: Pay Equity Meets the Market*. Cambridge: Cambridge University Press.

Rhode, Deborah L. (1993) 'Gender Equality and Employment Policy' in Sherri Matteo (ed.) *American Women in the Nineties: Today's Critical Issues*. Boston, MA: Northeastern University Press. pp. 253–73.

Rich, Adrienne (1976) *Of Woman Born: Motherhood as Experience and Institution*. New York: W. W. Norton.

Riger, Stephanie (1993) 'Gender Dilemmas in Sexual Harassment: Policies and Procedures' in Sherri Matteo (ed.) *American Women in the Nineties: Today's Critical Issues*. Boston, MA: Northeastern University Press. pp. 213–34.

Rochefort, David A. and Cobb, Roger W. (eds) (1994) *The Politics of Problem Definition: Shaping the Policy Agenda*. Lawrence, KS: University Press of Kansas.

Ronalds, Chris (1987) *Affirmative Action and Sex Discrimination: A Handbook on Legal Rights for Women*. Sydney: Pluto Press.

Rose, Nikolas (1993) 'Government, Authority and Expertise in Advanced Liberalism', *Economy and Society*, 22 (3): 283–99.

Rose, Nikolas and Miller, Peter (1992) 'Political power beyond the State: problematics of government', *British Journal of Sociology*, 43 (2): 173–205.

Rosenau, Pauline Marie (1992) *Post-Modernism and the Social Sciences: Insights, Inroads, and Intrusions*. Princeton, NJ: Princeton University Press.

Royal Commission on the Status of Women (1970) *Report*. Ottawa: Information Canada.

Rubenstein, Michael (1988) *The Dignity of Women at Work: A Report on the Problem of Sexual Harassment in the Member States of the European Community*. Brussels–Luxembourg: Office for Official Publications of the European Community.

Rubington, Earl and Weinberg, Martin S. (1971) *The Study of Social Problems: Five Perspectives*. New York: Oxford University Press.

Ryan, Edna (1987) 'Foreword' in Burton, Clare, with Hag, Raven and Thompson, Gay (1987) *Women's Worth: Pay Equity and Job Evaluation in Australia*. Canberra: Australian Government Publishing Service. pp. vii–viii.

Ryan, Edna and Conlon, Anne (1989) *Gentle Invaders: Australian Women at Work*. Ringwood, Victoria: Penguin.

Ryan, Lyndall, Ripper, Margie and Butterfield, Barbara (1994) *We Women Decide: Women's Experience of Seeking Abortion in Queensland, South Australia and Tasmania, 1985–1992*. Adelaide: Women's Studies Unit, Faculty of Social Sciences, Flinders University.

Sainsbury, Diane (ed.) (1994) *Gendering Welfare States*. London: Sage.

Sainsbury, Diane (1996) *Gender, Equality and Welfare States*. New York: Cambridge University Press.

Saunders, Peter (1994) 'Contextualizing Inequality', *Social Policy Research Centre Newsletter*, No. 53. Kensington: University of New South Wales.

Sawer, Marian (ed.) (1985) *Program for Change: Affirmative Action in Australia*. Sydney: Allen & Unwin.

Schambelan, Bo (1992) *Roe v. Wade: United States Supreme Court*. Annotated version. Philadelphia: Running Press.

Schechter, A. (1982) *Women and Male Violence: The Visions and Struggles of the Battered Women's Movement*. Boston, MA: South End Press.

Schneider, Anne and Ingram, Helen (1993) 'Social Construction of Target Populations: Implications for Politics and Policy', *American Political Science Review*, 87 (3): 334–47.

Schön, Donald A. (1979) 'Generative Metaphor: A Perspective on Problem-Setting in Social Policy' in Andrew Ortony (ed.) *Metaphor and Thought*. Cambridge: Cambridge University Press. pp. 254–83.

Schultze, Charles L., Fried, Edward R., Rivlin, Alice M. and Teeters, Nancy H. (1972) *Setting National Priorities: The 1973 Budget*. Washington: The Brookings Institute.

Scialabba, G. (1994) 'Only Words', *The Nation*, 31 January, pp. 135–7.

Sex Discrimination Commissioner (1996) *Sexual Harassment and Educational Institutions: A Guide to the Federal Sex Discrimination Act*. Sydney: Human Rights and Equal Opportunity Commission.

Shapiro, Michael J. (1988) *The Politics of Representation: Writing Practices in*

Biography, Photography, and Policy Analysis. Madison, WI: University of Wisconsin Press.

Shapiro, Michael J. (1992) *Reading the Postmodern Polity: Political Theory as Textual Practice*. Minneapolis, MN: University of Minnesota Press.

Shaver, Sheila (1993) *Women and the Australian Social Security System: From Difference Towards Equality*, Social Policy Research Centre, Discussion Paper No. 41. NSW: University of New South Wales.

Sheehy, Elizabeth (1996) 'Legalising Justice For All Women: Canadian Women's Struggles For Democratic Rape Law Reforms', *The Australian Feminist Law Journal*, 6: 87–114.

Sheldon, Sally (1995) 'The Law of Abortion and the Politics of Medicalisation' in Jo Bridgeman and Susan Millns (eds) *Law and Body Politics: Regulating the Female Body*. Dartmouth: Aldershot.

Sibeon, Roger (1996) *Contemporary Sociology and Policy Analysis: The New Sociology of Public Policy*. Wirral, Merseyside: Tudor.

Simon, Herbert A. (1961 [1945]) *Administrative Behavior: A Study of Decision-Making Processes in Administrative Organization*, second edition. New York: Macmillan.

Smart, Carol (1997) 'Feminist Interventions and State Policy' in Caroline Andrew and Sandra Rodgers (eds) *Women and the Canadian State: Les Femmes et l'État Canadien*. Montreal: McGill-Queen's University Press. pp. 110–15.

Sorenson, Elaine (1994) *Comparable Worth: Is it a Worthy Policy?* Princeton, NJ: Princeton University Press.

Spector, Malcolm and Kitsuse, John I. (1987 [1977]) *Constructing Social Problems*. Hawthorne, NY: Aldine de Gruyter.

Spender, Dale and Sarah, Elisabeth (eds) (1980) *Learning to Lose: Sexism and Education*. London: Women's Press.

Standing Committee on Health, Welfare and Social Affairs (1982) *Report on Violence in the Family: Wife Battering*. Chair: Marcel Roy. Hull, Quebec: Canadian Government Publishers.

Starr, Paul (1992) 'Civil Reconstruction: What to Do Without Affirmative Action', *The American Prospect*, pp. 7–14.

Stone, Deborah A. (1988) *Policy Paradox and Political Reason*. New York: HarperCollins.

Stringer, Joan K. and Richardson, J. J. (1980) 'Managing the Political Agenda: Problem Definition and Policy Making in Britain', *Parliamentary Affairs*, 33 (1): 23–39.

Sullivan, Thomas J. and Thompson, Kenrick S. (1994 [1988]) *Introduction to Social Problems*, third edition. New York: Macmillan.

Tanesini, Alessandra (1994) 'Whose Language?' in Kathleen Lennon and Margaret Whitford (eds) *Knowing the Difference: Feminist Perspectives in Epistemology*. New York: Routledge. pp. 203–16.

Tatalovich, Raymond (1996) *The Abortion Controversy in Canada and the United States*. Canadian-American Public Policy Association Occasional Paper Series, no. 25. Orono, ME: University of Maine.

Taub, Nadine (1985) 'Dealing With Employment Discrimination and Damaging Stereotypes: A Legal Perspective', *Journal of Social Issues*, 41 (4): 99–110.

Taylor, Bron (1991) *Affirmative Action at Work: Law, Politics, and Ethics*. Pittsburgh, PA: University of Pittsburgh Press.

Teghtsoonian, Katherine (1993) 'Neo-Conservative Ideology and Opposition to Federal Regulation of Child Care Services in the United States and Canada', *Canadian Journal of Political Science*, 26 (1): 97–121.

Teghtsoonian, Katherine (1995) 'Work and/or Motherhood: The Ideological Construction of Women's Options in Canadian Child Care Policy Debates', *Canadian Journal of Women and the Law*, 8 (2): 411–39.

Teghtsoonian, Katherine (1996) 'Promises, Promises: "Choices of Women" in Canadian and American Child Care Policy Debates', *Feminist Studies*, 22 (1): 119–46.

Theodoulou, Stella Z. and Cahn, Matthew A. (1995) *Public Policy – The Essential Readings*. Englewood Cliffs, NJ: Prentice-Hall.

Thomas, David A. and Ely, Robin J. (1996) 'Making Difference Matter: A New Paradigm for Managing Diversity', *Harvard Business Review*, 74 (5): 79–90.

Thomas Jr, R. Roosevelt (1990) 'From Affirmative Action to Affirming Diversity', *Harvard Business Review*, pp. 107–17.

Thomas Jr, R. Roosevelt (1991) *Beyond Race and Gender: Unleashing the Power of Your Total Work Force by Managing Diversity*. New York: American Management Association.

Thorne, Barrie (1993) *Gender Play: Girls and Boys in School*. Buckingham: Open University Press.

Thornton, Margaret (1990) 'In the Eyes of the Law' in Ed Davis and Valerie Pratt (eds) *Making the Link: Affirmative Action and Industrial Relations*. Sydney: Affirmative Action Agency & Labour-Management Studies Foundation, Macquarie University. pp. 47–54.

Thornton, Margaret (1991a) 'Feminism and the Contradictions of Law Reform', *International Journal of the Sociology of Law*, 19: 453–74.

Thornton, Margaret (1991b) 'The Public/Private Dichotomy: Gendered and Discriminatory', *Journal of Law and Society*, 18 (4): 448–63.

Thornton, Margaret (1995a) 'The Seductive Allure of EEO' in Norma Grieve and Ailsa Burns (eds) *Australian Women: Contemporary Feminist Thought*. Melbourne: Oxford University Press. pp. 215–24.

Thornton, Margaret (ed.) (1995b) *Public and Private: Feminist Legal Debates*. Melbourne: Oxford University Press.

Threadgold, Terry (1988) 'Language and Gender', *Australian Feminist Studies*, 6: 41–70.

Tinberger, Jan (1956) *Economic Policy: Principles and Design*. Amsterdam: North Holland Publishing Company.

Tom, Allison (1992/3) 'The Messy Work of Child Care: Addressing Feminists' Neglect of Child Care Workers', *Atlantis*, 18 (1&2): 70–81.

Tong, Rosemarie (1986) 'Sexual Harassment' in M. Pearsall (ed.) *Women and Values*. California: Wadsworth. pp. 148–65.

Torgerson, Douglas (1996) 'Power and Insight in Policy Discourse: Post-Positivism and Problem Definition' in Laurent Dobuzinskis, Michael Howlett and David Laycock (eds) *Policy Studies in Canada: The State of the Art*. Toronto: University of Toronto Press. pp. 266–98.

Troyer, Ronald J. (1993) 'Revised Social Constructionism: Traditional Social Science More Than a Postmodernist Analysis' in James A. Holstein and Gale Miller (eds) *Reconsidering Social Constructionism: Debates in Social Problems Theory*. New York: Aldine de Gruyter. pp. 117–28.

Tsolidis, Georgina (1993) 'Difference and Identity – A Feminist Debate Indicating Directions for the Development of Transformative Curriculum' in Lyn Yates (ed.) *Feminism and Education*. Special Edition of *Melbourne Studies in Education*. pp. 51–62.

Unger, Rhoda K. (1989) 'Sex, Gender, and Epistemology' in Mary Crawford and Margaret Gentry (eds) *Gender and Thought: Psychological Perspectives*. New York: Springer-Verlag. pp. 15–33.

Ungerson, Clare (ed.) (1990) *Gender and Caring: Work and Welfare in Britain and Scandinavia*. Hemel Hempstead: Harvester Wheatsheaf.

US Commission on Civil Rights (1982) *Under the Rule of Thumb: Battered Women and the Administration of Justice*. Washington: Government Printers.

US Committee on Ways and Means, and Committee on Economic and Educational Opportunities, Subcommittee of Human Resources and the Subcommittee on Early Childhood, Youth, and Families (1995) *Hearings: Child Care and Child Welfare*, 104th Congress, First Session, 3 February. Washington: US Government Printing Office.

US House of Representatives, Subcommittee on Human Resources of the Committee on Education and Labor (1988) *Child Care: Hearing*, 21 April. Washington: US Government Printing Office.

US Senate Committee on Labor and Human Resources, Subcommittee on Children, Family, Drugs, and Alcoholism (1988) *Hearings: Act for Better Child Care Services of 1987*, 100th Congress, 2nd session, 15 March and 28 June. Washington: US Government Printing Office.

Varga, Donna (1997) *Constructing the Child: A History of Canadian Day Care. An Our Schools/Our Selves Title*. Toronto: James Lorimer.

Very, Donald (1990) *An Economic Framework for the Evaluation of Child Care Policy*. Labor Market – Social Policy Occasional Papers No. 1. Paris: OECD.

Von Glaserfeld, Ernst (1995) *Radical Constructivism: A Way of Knowing and Learning.* London: The Falmer Press.

Walby, Sylvia (1992) 'Post-Post-Modernism?' in M. Barrett and A. Phillips (eds) *Destabilizing Theory: Contemporary Feminist Debates.* Cambridge: Polity Press. pp. 31–52.

Walker, Gillian A. (1990) *Family Violence and the Women's Movement: The Conceptual Politics of Struggle.* Toronto: University of Toronto Press.

Walker, John (ed.) (1998) *Halliwell's Film and Video Guide.* London: HarperCollins.

Walkerdine, V. (1990) *Schoolgirl Fictions.* London: Verso.

Walkerdine, V. (1992) 'Progressive Pedagogy and Political Struggle' in Carmen Luke and Jennifer Gore (eds) *Feminisms and Critical Pedagogy.* New York: Routledge. pp. 15–24.

Walkerdine, Valerie (1995) 'Subject to Change Without Notice: Psychology, Postmodernity and the Popular' in Steve Pile and Nigel Thrift (eds) *Mapping the Subject.* London: Routledge. pp. 309–31.

Wallace, Margaret (1985) 'The Legal Approach to Sex Discrimination' in M. Sawer (ed.) *Program for Change.* Sydney: Allen & Unwin. pp. 16–32.

Warren, Carol A. B. (1993) 'The 1960s State as Social Problem: An Analysis of Radical Right and New Left Claims-Making Rhetorics' in James A. Holstein and Gale Miller (eds) *Reconsidering Social Constructionism: Debates in Social Problems Theory.* New York: Aldine de Gruyter. pp. 59–85.

Warskett, Rosemary (1990) 'Wage Solidarity and Equal Value: Or Gender and Class in the Structuring of Work Place Hierarchies', *Studies in Political Economy*, 32: 55–83.

Warskett, Rosemary (1993) 'Can a Disappearing Pie be Shared Equally? Unions, Women and Wage "Fairness"' in Linda Briskin and Patricia McDermott (eds) *Women Challenging Unions: Feminism, Democracy, and Militancy.* Toronto: University of Toronto Press. pp. 249–62.

Watts, Rob (1993/4) 'Government and Modernity: An Essay in Thinking Governmentality', *Arena Journal*, 2: 103–57.

Weedon, Chris (1987) *Feminist Practice and Poststructuralist Theory.* Oxford: Blackwell.

Weeks, Wendy (1996) 'Women Citizens' Struggle for Citizenship' in John Wilson, Jane Thomson, and Anthony McMahon (eds) *The Australian Welfare State: Key Documents and Themes.* South Melbourne: Macmillan Education Australia. pp. 70–85.

Weeks, Wendy and Kate Gilmore (1996) 'How Violence Against Women Became an Issue on the National Policy Agenda' in Tony Dalton, Mary Draper, Wendy Weeks and John Wiseman, *Making Social Policy in Australia: An Introduction.* Sydney: Allen & Unwin. pp. 141–53.

Weiler, K. (1988) *Women Teaching for Change: Gender, Class and Power.* South Hadley, MA: Bergin & Garvery.

Weiner, Gabby (1994) *Feminisms and Education: an Introduction.* Buckingham: Open University Press.

Weiner, Gaby and Arnot, Madeleine (1987) 'Teachers and gender politics' in M. Arnot & G. Weiner (eds) *Gender and the Politics of Schooling.* London: Hutchinson and Open University. pp. 354–373.

Weiner, Gaby with Arnot, Madeleine and David, Miriam (1998) 'Who Benefits from Schooling? Equality Issues in Britain' in Alison Mackinnon, Inga Elgqvist–Saltzman and Alison Prentice (eds) *Education into the 21st Century: Dangerous Terrain for Women?* London: Falmer Press. pp. 94–106.

Westkott, Marcia (1983) 'Women's Studies as a Strategy for Change: Between Criticism and Vision' in G. Bowles and R. D. Klein (eds) *Theories of Women's Studies.* London: Routledge and Kegan Paul.

White, William (1993) 'A Systems Perspective on Sexual Exploitation of Clients by Professional Helpers', *Dulwich Centre Newsletter*, Nos. 3&4: 77–87.

Wiebrens, Casper (1988) 'The Netherlands' in Alfred J. Kahn and Sheila B. Kamerman (eds) *Child Support: From Debt Collection to Social Policy.* Newbury Park, CA: Sage.

Wildavsky, Aaron (1979) *The Art and Craft of Policy Analysis.* London: Macmillan.

Wilenski, Peter (1977) *Directions for Change: Review of New South Wales Government Administration.* Sydney: P. West.

Williams, Patricia (1991) *The Alchemy of Race and Rights.* Cambridge, MA: Harvard University Press.

Williams, Toni (1990) 'Re-forming "Women's" Truth: A Critique of the Report of the Royal Commission on the Status of Women in Canada', *Ottawa Law Review*, 22 (3): 725–59.

Williams, Wendy (1981) 'Firing the Woman to Protect the Fetus: The Reconciliation of Fetal Protection with Employment Opportunity Goals under Title VII', *Georgetown Law Review*, 69 (1): 641–704.

Wilson, William Julius (1987) *The Truly Disadvantaged: the Inner City, the Underclass, and Public Policy.* Chicago, IL: University of Chicago Press.

Wise, Sue and Stanley, Liz (1987) *Georgie Porgie: Sexual Harassment in Everyday Life.* London: Pandora.

Wood, Julia T. (1994) 'Saying It Makes It So: The Discursive Construction of Sexual Harassment' in Shereen G. Bingham (ed.) *Conceptualizing Sexual Harassment as Discursive Practice.* Westport, CT: Praeger. pp. 17–30.

Woolgar, Steve and Pawluch, Dorothy (1985) 'Ontological Gerrymandering', *Social Problems*, 32 (3): 214–27.

Yates, Lyn (1992) 'A tale of sound and fury – Signifying What? Feminism and Curriculum Policy in Australia' in Marjorie O'Loughlin and Victoria Foster (eds) *Through Girls' Eyes: Australian Research, Policy and Curriculum in the*

1990s. Forum of Education Monograph. Sydney: Sydney Faculty of Education, University of Sydney. pp. 93–117.

Yates, Lyn (1993a) *The Education of Girls: Policy, Research and the Question of Gender*. Australian Education Review No. 35. Victoria: The Australian Council of Educational Research.

Yates, Lyn (1993b) 'Feminism and Education: Writing in the 90s' in Lyn Yates, *Feminism and Education*. A Special Issue of *Melbourne Studies in Education*, pp. 1–9.

Yates, Lyn (1993c) 'The Theory–Practice Relationship in Schooling, Academia and Feminist Theory' in Jill Blackmore and Jane Kenway (eds) *Gender Matters in Educational Administration and Policy: A Feminist Introduction*. London: The Falmer Press. pp. 181–94.

Yates, Lyn (1994) 'Review Essay: Feminist Pedagogy Meets Critical Pedagogy Meets Poststructuralism', *British Journal of Sociology of Education*, 15 (3): 429–37.

Yeatman, Anna (1990) *Bureaucrats, Technocrats, Femocrats*. Sydney: Allen & Unwin.

INDEX

abortion
  early history, 148–51
  feminist perspectives, 159–63
  a medical problem?, 152–9
  period of reform, 151–2
Affirmative Action (Equal
    Employment Opportunity for
    Women) Act, (Australia, 1986),
    99, 101–2
ageing population, 135
antidiscrimination legislation, 93–6,
    98–103
  proving indirect discrimination,
    96–7
  and sexual harassment, 182–4
Armstrong, P. and Armstrong, H., 79,
    82, 84
Australia
  abortion, 149–50
  antidiscrimination legislation, 97,
    99, 101–2, 189
  child care, 131, 133, 134, 135, 136,
    138, 139, 141–2
  domestic violence, 173
  education, 115, 116, 117, 122, 124,
    125, 126
  pay equity, 76, 83
  sexual harassment, 182, 185, 189,
    191–2, 193, 196–7

Bacchi, C., 8, 45, 89, 94, 95, 97, 98, 99,
    104, 105, 110, 121, 124, 125, 130,
    131, 136, 137, 141, 145, 146, 149,
    151, 160, 164, 176
  and Jose, J., 189, 197
Bachrach, P., 26, 27, 32
Bardach, E., 23–4, 25
battered woman syndrome,
    169–72
birth control, 148–9
Black feminists, 118, 121, 124
boys' underachievement in
    education, 125–8

Braybrooke, D. and Lindblom, C., 25,
    30
Britain
  abortion, 149, 150, 151
  antidiscrimination legislation, 97,
    98, 99
  child care, 137, 139, 144
  education, 125
  pay equity, 75, 97, 98
  sexual harassment, 198
Bryson, L., 191–2, 193, 196–7
bureaucracy, 19

Canada
  abortion, 149–50, 151–2, 155–8
  child care, 130–1, 132, 133, 135, 137,
    138, 139, 140
  domestic violence, 173–5, 177
  education, 115, 116, 118, 121, 125
  managing diversity, 104, 106
  pay equity, 79, 82, 83, 87, 90, 91, 99
care/work dichotomy, 132–3
  see also work, paid; work, unpaid
caring professions, sexual
    exploitation in, 194–5, 196
child care
  as early childhood development,
    142–7
  as welfare, 137–42
  and women's inequality, 130–7
Christenson v. Iowa, 78
Civil Rights Act (US), 78, 94, 96
claims-making, social problems as,
    55, 56, 57, 59, 60, 162–3
class, 107–9, 119, 140, 149, 151
Cobb, R. and Rochefort, D., 36–7,
    45–6
comprehensive (technical) rationalist
    model of policy making, 17–18,
    20, 22–4
  and political rationalist approach,
    24–5
  as technocrats, 26

Condit, C., 157, 158, 159
Constructing Social Problems (Spector and Kituse), 55
contextual constructionists, 56–8
Corne v. *Bausch & Lomb, Inc.*, 183–4
Cornell, D., 158, 160, 187, 189, 190
criminalization of abortion, 149–51, 156

Davies, B., 113, 114, 119–20, 126–7, 129
Dean, M., 148, 150
decision making, 19
'decision space', 17, 20–1
dependence, genealogy of, 138–9
Dery, D., 27–8, 29, 30, 50, 64
'deviance' *see* labelling
'differences', 95, 124
  see also managing diversity
disadvantage(d)
  boys, 125–8
  discourse, 100–1, 104–5
  truly, 107–9
discourse(s)
  child care, 146
  content, 44–5, 61–2
  definitions, 39, 40, 41, 199
  'disadvantage', 100–1, 104–5
  of exit, 170–1
  'gender' in education, 127–8
  'needs', 137, 161
  of oppression, 117, 119–22
  rights, 159–61, 205
  skills, 85–6, 89
  sources of, 43–4
  see also language; policy as discourse
discrimination
  affirmative action, 98–103
  different meanings of, 78–9
  direct, 93–6
  indirect, 96–8
  managing diversity, 103–7, 109–10
  structural, 80–1, 94–5, 96, 98, 103–4
  truly disadvantaged and Regent's decision, 107–9
  see also education, equal access
discursive interventions, 45
'discursive world', 54

divorced women, 135–6
  see also single mothers
Doe v. *Bolton*, 154–5
domestic violence
  battered woman syndrome, 169–72
  family violence, 166–9
  gender persecution, 177–80
  language of, 164–6, 172
  spousal assault, 172–7
Drysek, J., 33–5, 39
Dudley, J. and Vidovich, L., 17–19

Economic Council of Canada, 79
Edelman, M., 6, 42, 58, 95, 181
education
  aims of, 112–15
  boys' underachievement, 125–8
  equal access, 115–17
  girls', 121–5
  socialization, stereotypes and sex roles, 117–21
Employment Appeal Tribunal (Britain), 97
'enunciative position', 55, 57
Equal Opportunity and Elimination of Sexism (Australia, 1980), 117
equal pay *see* pay equity
Equal Pay Act (US, 1963), 77–8
European antidiscrimination law, 99, 100
European Commission, 107–8
European Union, child care, 132, 137, 141

families
  'breakdown' of, 167, 174–5
  child care subsidies for poor, 139–40
  responsibilities of, 79, 89
    public/private dichotomy, 133–5, 136
  see also domestic violence; single mothers; traditional domestic roles
feminism
  and governmentality, 47–8
  hostility towards, among girls, 123–4

perspectives on abortion, 159–63
perspectives on oppression, 117,
    119–20
and postmodernism, 43
poststructuralist education theory,
    114, 119–21
and social constructionism, 54–5,
    63–4
subjectivities, 114
see also What's the Problem?
    approach
feminization of poverty, 73, 87, 145
Fischer, F., 32–5
foetal rights, 157–8, 160, 161
Foster, V., 125, 126
Foucault, M., 2, 39, 40, 41, 42, 45, 47,
    55, 58, 60, 61, 149
France, equal pay initiative, 77
Fraser, N., 10, 161
    and Gordon, L., 137, 138, 206

Gaskell, J., 118, 119, 121–2
gender persecution, 177–80
genealogy, 40–1
    of abortion, 148–51
    of dependence, 138–9
    of equal pay for equal work, 75–80
    of social problems, 51–3
Germany, abortion policy, 161
Gilbert, P., 117, 122, 127–8
Girls, Schools and Society (Australia,
    1975), 115, 116
Gordon, L., 37, 147, 149, 150, 166–8,
    173
    and Fraser, N., 137, 138, 206
governmentality, 47–8, 53, 85, 105,
    114, 150, 165–6, 176
grievance procedures, 194, 195–6

Hawkesworth, M., 19, 32, 44, 63

Ibarra, P. and Kituse, J., 50, 54, 56, 57,
    59, 60, 61–2
incrementalism, 17, 18, 25
individualizing of social problems,
    58, 109
    see also public/private dichotomy
'interest groups', 102–3

job evaluation schemes, 81–4
Jose, J. and Bacchi, C., 189, 197

Kalanke v. *Freie Hansestadt Bremen*,
    100
Kellough, G., 151, 152, 155, 157, 158,
    161–2
Kituse, J. and Ibarra, P., 50, 54, 56, 57,
    59, 60, 61–2
Kituse, J. and Spector, M., 50, 54,
    55–6, 58–9, 162
labelling theory, 52–3, 58, 137, 138
language
    of choice, 139–40, 170–1
        rights and privacy, 159–62
    competing theories of, 38–9
    of domestic violence, 164–6, 172
    of morality, 155–6
    of 'problem definition', 37
    role of, in shaping policy *see* policy
        as discourse
    and social constructionism, 56–7
    see also discourse(s)
Lecherous Professor, The (Dziech and
    Weiner), 194
lesbians, 171, 192–3
Levitas, R., 107–8, 141, 147
Lindblom, C., 17, 18, 19–20, 25, 26,
    30
    and Braybrooke, D., 25, 30

MacKinnon, C., 159, 182, 183, 184–5,
    187
McLeod, J., 114, 120, 127
Majone, G., 34–5
managing diversity, 103–7, 109–10
Marschall v. *Land Nordrhein-Westfalen*,
    100, 101
maternity leave, 97
medical profession, 149, 150, 1⁻
    154–5, 156, 163
'men's jobs'
    women wor¹
        81, 1.
    and 'wome
menstrual tabc
Meritor Sav. Ban.
    Vinson, 185, .
Miller v. *Bank of A¹.*

National Policy for the Education of Girls in Australian Schools (1987), 122–3, 124
'needs discourses', 137, 161
nursery voucher scheme, 139, 140

Ontario Pay Equity Act (1987), 83, 90
oppression discourses, 117, 119–22

'participation research', 32–3
pay equity, 72–4
  affirmative action reforms, 80–1
  equal pay for equal work, 75–80
  equal pay for work of equal value, 80–5
  skill and work, 85–7
  and wage solidarity approaches, 87–9
  What's the Problem? approach, 89–91
policy as discourse, 39–48
  and contextual constructionism, 58
political rationalist models of policy making, 17, 18–19, 20, 21, 24–31
  and postpositivism, 32–5
Politics of Affirmative Action, The (Bacchi), 110, 136, 176
population, ageing, 135
population control, 149, 153–4, 158
positivism *see* comprehensive rationalist model of policy making
post-traumatic stress disorder, 170
postmodernism, 18–19, 64
  affirmative and sceptical, 38, 43, 61
  and feminism, 43
  and political rationalist models of policy making, 32–5
  poststructuralist theory of education, 119–22
  social problems and policy, 60–3
  see also discourse(s); language; subjectification versus socialization
postpositivism *see* postmodernism
poverty
  child care policy, 137–47
  feminization of, 73, 87, 145
power relations, 169, 171, 176

prejudice *see* stereotypes
privacy rights, 153, 159–62
Problem of Abortion, The (Feinberg), 157
problem definition, 20, 21, 27, 34, 36–7
'problem families', 134
problem identification, 20–1
problem representation, 21, 35–9
  antidiscrimination legislation, 94
  child care, 136, 139
  domestic violence, 164, 165–6, 175
  education, 114, 116
  equal pay, 74, 79–80, 82
  meaning of, 36
  nesting of, 112, 131
  sexual harassment, 181–2, 194
  see also What's the Problem? approach
problem setting, 26–7, 30, 34
problem solving models, 19–20
problematizations, 41, 47, 62–3
  see also problem representation; What's the Problem? approach
'pseudo problems', 28, 64
psychosocial model of family violence, 168–9
public choice models of policy making, 19, 22
public/private dichotomy
  abortion, 153–5, 159–62
  child care policy, 133–5, 140–2, 143, 145–6
  domestic violence, 172–7
  organizational culture and sexual harassment, 196–8
  see also discrimination, structural

Rabidue v. *Osceola Refining Company*, 187
Rainwater, L., 51–2, 67–8, 143
rational comprehensive model *see* comprehensive rationalist model of policy making
realist/anti-realist debate, 53–5
'reasonable woman' standard, 187–90, 191
refugees *see* gender persecution

Rein, M. and Schön, D., 25–6, 27, 30,
32, 39
relativism, charge of, 37–8
*Report on Violence in the Family: Wife
Battering* (Canada, 1982), 173–5
'reverse discrimination', 99
rights *see* discourse(s), rights; foetal
rights; privacy rights
Rochefort, D. and Cobb, R., 36–7,
45–6
Roe v. *Wade*, 152–3, 154, 155, 156, 157,
159
Royal Commission on the Status of
Women (1967, Canada), 115, 118

Schön, D., 29, 39–40
and Rein, M., 25–6, 27, 30, 32, 39
science and technology subjects,
115–16, 123, 125, 126
self-interest, 19, 22
self-interest/responsibility
dichotomy *see* public/private
dichotomy
sex discrimination *see* discrimination
Sex Discrimination Acts
Australia, 97, 99
Britain, 99
sex role theory
and domestic violence, 169
see also stereotypes, sex roles and
socialization
*Sex-role Stereotyping and Women's
Studies* (Canada, 1978), 118
sexual harassment, 181–2
and employer liability, 193–6
girls' experience of in schooling,
122–3
as sex discrimination, 182–4
as *sexual* harassment, 188–91
as sexual *harassment*, 191–3
as 'unwelcome advances', 186–8
as woman-hating harassment,
196–8
as workplace discrimination, 184–6
shelter movement, 165, 175
single mothers, 138–9, 140, 145, 147
see also divorced women
skill, image of, 88–9
see also discourse(s), skills

skill and work, 81, 85–7
Social Construction of Reality, The
(Berger and Luckman), 53
social constructionism, 53–7
'social exclusion', 107–8
Social Postmodernism (Nicholson and
Seidman), 43, 61
social problems
history of, 51–3
postmodernism and policy, 60–3
social construction of, 55–7
sociology of, 28, 50–1, 59
social problems theory
critique, 166
and What's the Problem?
approach, 57–60
socialization
stereotypes and sex roles, 117–21,
126–8
versus subjectification, 44, 119–20,
122, 126–7
Sorenson, E., 78, 84
Spector, M. and Kituse, J., 50, 54,
55–6, 58–9, 162
spousal assault, 172–7
Stanley, L. and Wise, S., 181, 182, 184,
188, 190, 192
stereotypes, 94–5, 100–1, 105
sex roles and socialization, 117–21,
126–8
Stone, D., 4, 5, 36
subjectification versus socialization,
44, 119–20, 122, 126–7
subjectivities, feminist, 114
Sullivan, T. and Thompson, K., 50,
51
Sweden
child care, 131, 132, 136, 139, 143,
146
domestic violence, 176
pay equity, 83, 88, 89, 97

teachers, role as socializers, 119, 122
technical rationalism *see*
comprehensive rationalist model
of policy making
technocracy, 26, 32, 34, 35, 48
Teghtsoonian, K., 132–3, 140, 145
Thompson, K. and Sullivan, T., 50, 51

Thornton, M., 182, 183, 185, 189, 193
Tong, R., 183–4, 185, 189
traditional domestic roles, 81, 85–6, 90, 97, 106–7
truly disadvantaged, 107–9

Under the Rule of Thumb: Battered Women and the Administration of Justice (US, 1982), 173, 174–5
United States
  abortion, 149, 150, 152–5, 156, 157, 159
  affirmative action debate, 103, 108
  antidiscrimination legislation, 78, 94, 96, 97, 98–9, 103, 108
  child care, 130, 131, 132, 135, 140, 142, 143, 144, 145, 147
  diversity management, 104, 106; see also managing diversity
  domestic violence, 165, 173, 174–5
  education, 117
  pay equity, 75, 77–8, 83
  sexual harassment, 182, 183–4, 185, 186, 194
universities, 108, 194, 197

value(s), 17, 18, 20, 21, 22–3, 26
  conflict, 30, 33
  identification, 32
  judgements, 34
Vancouver Women's Research Centre, 82
victims of discrimination, 95, 109
'victim blaming', 168
Vidovich, L. and Dudley, J., 17–19

wage solidarity approaches, 87–9
Walkerdine, V., 113, 114

Wards Cove, 97
What's the Problem? approach
  boys' underachievement in education, 125–8
  child care, 133, 134, 145–7
  and claims-making, 62–3
  and comprehensive rationalist approach, 24
  definitions, 1–13, 15–16, 48–9, 65–71, 199–207
  pay equity, 89–91
  policy as discourse, 41–2, 45–6
  and political rationalist approach, 27–8, 29, 31, 33
  and postmodernism, 64
  and social problems theory, 57–60
  see also problem representation; problematizations
White, W., 194–5, 196
Why Child Care Matters (OECD), 142, 143, 144
Wildavsky, A., 27, 28–9, 33
Wise, S.and Stanley, L., 181, 182, 184, 188, 190, 192
Women's Bureau (US), 75
work, paid
  child care policy, 130–7
    for poor women, 137–42
  and maternity leave, 97
  'women's jobs', 79, 81–2, 126
    and 'men's jobs', 84–5
work, unpaid, 81, 85–6, 90, 97, 106–7
'working conditions', 86–7
workplace discrimination, 95–6, 184–6, 193–6

Yates, L., 112–13, 114, 116, 121, 122, 124–5